MONROE COLLEGE LIBRARY

3 7340 01015536 1

DISCARDED

D0984427

DISCARDED

IDENTITY

12811353

LIBRARY

MONROE BUSINESS INSTITUTE

IDENTITY

Cultural Change and the Struggle for Self

434 MAIN STREET
NEW ROCHELLE, NY 10801

ROY F. BAUMEISTER

New York   Oxford
OXFORD UNIVERSITY PRESS
1986

155.2
B

3822

19.95

Oxford University Press

Oxford   New York   Toronto
Delhi   Bombay   Calcutta   Madras   Karachi
Petaling Jaya   Singapore   Hong Kong   Tokyo
Nairobi   Dar es Salaam   Cape Town
Melbourne   Auckland

and associated companies in
Beirut   Berlin   Ibadan   Nicosia

Copyright © 1986 by Oxford University Press, Inc.

Published by Oxford University Press, Inc.,
200 Madison Avenue, New York, New York 10016

Oxford is a registered trademark of Oxford University Press.

All rights reserved. No part of this publication may be
reproduced, stored in a retrieval system, or transmitted,
in any form or by any means, electronic, mechanical, photo-
copying, recording, or otherwise, without the prior per-
mission of Oxford University Press, Inc.

Library of Congress Cataloging-in-Publication Data

Baumeister, Roy F.
Identity : cultural change and the struggle for self.

Bibliography: p.
Includes index.
1. Identity (Psychology—History.   2. Self—History.
3. Civilization, Occidental—History.   4. Civilization,
Occidental—Psychological aspects.   I. Title.
BF69.B38 1986   155.2   85-25946

ISBN 0-19-503715-4

Printing (last digit):   9 8 7 6 5 4 3 2 1

Printed in the United States of America

To my mentors, with profound thanks:
Edward E. Jones
Douglas K. Detterman
Joel Cooper
John MacGregor

Preface

The nature of identity can be regarded as a philosophical question, yet in this book I will try to explore it not with philosophical methods but with the methods of social science. That means assembling a fair amount of empirical evidence and deciding which possible explanations fits the evidence best.

What sort of empirical evidence is available? My background is that of an experimental psychologist, but no series of laboratory experiments is likely to explain the nature of identity, although some important clues may emerge. My search for a method led me to an unusual step. I decided to use history as a quasi-experiment. By doing this I felt that I could ascertain when identity crises actually began occurring in our history. Presumably these occurrences would be the result of certain social changes just prior to that historical period. Once I understood those changes, I would know what had made identity problematic, and I would probably also gain insight into the nature of identity.

My approach is not radical in terms of the logic of inference from empirical evidence. In fact, it conforms to a time-honored procedure in psychology—approaching the study of something by studying the phenomena that accompany its loss. The same logic underlies Freud's efforts to understand the nature of the psyche by studying insane persons, the physiological psychology that learns about the function of some part of the brain by destroying it and seeing what functions deteriorate, and current efforts to learn about the nature of intelligence by studying the mentally retarded.

Yet the evidence I needed lay outside my field—in history, sociology, and literature—and two methods were available to me for this interdisciplinary work. One option was to do original research in all the relevant disciplines. The other was to rely on secondary sources when dealing with other fields—thus practicing only my own discipline and leaving the research in other areas to the scientists and scholars working there. The first approach entailed going back to historical records, reading the original diaries and letters and census books, reading through a reasonably large portion of Western literature, then analyzing sociological and political trends of the last several centuries. I might live long enough to complete such a task, but if I did there would be two serious flaws in the final product. First, I would be using methodologies and making judgments outside my field. Second, I would be generating the evidence for my own conclusions. It is not feasible to use anything like the double-blind controls of a good experiment in historical and literary criticism, just as drawing psychological conclusions directly from such evidence seems suspect.

I settled, therefore, on the second approach—that of relying on the work of historians, sociologists, and literary critics. That seems to be the preferable approach, as long as one makes a reasonable effort to read both sides of controversial issues, something sometimes harder to do than it sounds. It is not difficult to read a book in another field and evaluate how conclusive its arguments are. It is difficult, however, to know what the accepted truths and controversial positions are in another field. The greatest danger in the methodology I have used in the interdisciplinary sections of this book is not that the current generation of scholars will turn out to be egregiously mistaken about most things. Instead, the greatest danger is that I may have overlooked or underestimated the controversial nature of some of my sources. To avoid that possibility, I have gone to some lengths to describe both sides of several key controversies, such as those concerning the emergence of individuality and the possibility that adolescence was discovered or transformed during the Victorian period.

Each discipline has its own rules of inference about what conclusions may be drawn from what kinds and amounts of evidence. In this book I use historical evidence to draw psychological conclusions. By using the inference models and the concepts of psychology, I am drawing conclusions that the historian would not draw from the same evidence. But this is a psychology book and should be read and evaluated as such.

The use of literary criticism deserves a comment. I have used literature as one kind of historical evidence. My assumption is that the literature of an era reflects the basic problems and concerns of that era. Therefore, changes in literary themes from one era to the next can be taken as indicative of changes in the human condition. An alternative thesis, however, is that some changes may have been the result of changes in the audience for whom the works were written. This may be most plausible in considering past centuries when only certain segments of the population were literate. I have no solution to this issue, except to use literature in conjunction with other forms of evidence and to keep that reservation in mind.

This book, then, is based on what social science currently has to offer that seems relevant to identity. All the evidence is not yet in. But the question of identity is a recurrent one, and one that people will continue to explore.

Cleveland, Ohio   R. F. B.
October 1985

Acknowledgments

Many people have contributed to this book. The students in two of my seminars were very helpful in challenging some ideas and bringing up others. Here, I wish to acknowledge a few individuals to whom I am deeply indebted.

My largest debt is to Dianne Tice, who made valuable contributions to many parts of this book. Probably every chapter benefited from her efforts, although Chapters 5 and 9 particularly bear her stamp.

Susan Knell provided invaluable assistance by guiding me into the developmental literature covered in Chapter 8, and Jeremy Shapiro contributed substantially to Chapter 9. Barry Levy was particularly helpful in getting me started in the historical literature.

I owe thanks to Steve Berglas, who first encouraged me to write a book, and to Doug Detterman, who encouraged me to write it despite contrary advice because "the only reason to be a professor is to be able to work on whatever you want."

The physical preparation of the book was made possible by the sophisticated word-processing skills and painstaking efforts of Cathy Steffen and Michelle Bey, both of whom have my gratitude.

Lastly, I wish to thank the individuals who volunteered to read and critique the first complete draft of this book. Foremost among these are my colleagues Paget Gross and Brian Mullen, who wrote thorough and thought-provoking responses to each chapter. I was also greatly aided by the comments and criticisms made by Kathleen Placidi, Donna Baumeister, Gordon Hodgins, Mim Blair, and Cathy Rauch. Thanks to each of you.

Contents

IDENTITY

1

Introduction

The search for identity is a pervasive theme in our society. Characters in popular books and movies often comment about not knowing who they are. Serious novels portray individuals struggling to create, define, and fulfill themselves. Magazine articles describe the fine points and latest subtleties of selfhood. Social scientists use the term "identity" in a variety of ways to explain an assortment of phenomena. Nearly everyone is familiar with the popular vocabulary of the search for identity: "finding yourself," "identity crisis," "self-actualization," and so on.

Despite the familiarity of these popular terms, they lack precise definition. The differing usages of the term "identity" by social scientists reflect an imprecise understanding of identity even among researchers. And despite the proliferation of self-help advice on identity in magazines and books, as well as the abundance of fictional portrayals of searches for identity, most of us would probably find it hard to list the steps necessary to establish a sound identity.

In short, we seem to feel we have problems with identity even though we lack a clear idea of what identity actually is. This book is concerned with both the nature of identity and the problem it poses for the modern individual.

The modern desire for identity is different from some of the other modern appetites. Identity is not a recent invention, like television sets, that everyone suddenly began to want. People have always had identities. The modern difficulty with identity must be understood as resulting from a change in identity, or rather in the way identity is created and shaped. Unlike our ancestors, who seemed to know who they were without much trouble, we have somehow come to use uncertain or unreliable means for defining ourselves.

Several years ago a woman was found naked and unconscious in a ditch in Florida. Her health and consciousness were restored, but she had total amnesia. Nothing could be learned about who she was. She appeared on television, asking any viewer who recognized her to contact the local authorities. This woman literally did not know her identity. But most identity problems are nothing like this woman's problem.

An identity is a definition, an interpretation, of the self. Names and addresses are labels that provide some information about the self and therefore help to define identity. But they provide only a partial definition. An identity crisis is not resolved by checking one's wallet for one's name and address. People who have problems with identity are generally struggling with the more difficult aspects of defining the self, such as the establishing of long-term goals, major affiliations, and basic values.

Several modern trends and events can be understood within the context of identity problems. To illustrate this, I shall briefly review some features of modern life in terms of three major problems of identity: self-knowledge, personal potentiality and fulfillment, and the relation of the individual to society.

Self-knowledge

In the sixteenth century knowledge of self seemed nearly perfect and indisputable. One writer of that era, Michel de Montaigne, introduced his autobiography with the boast that no writer had ever known a topic better than Montaigne knew his because Montaigne was writing about himself (Auerbach, 1946; Weintraub, 1978). Today, self-knowledge enjoys no such confident certainty. Self-deception, unconscious motivations, selective perception and memory of events, and interpretive biases have all been recognized as major obstacles on the path to self-knowledge.

The twentieth century's quest for accurate self-knowledge has ranged from the scientific to the occult. Psychoanalysis was established early in this century as a means of increasing self-knowledge on an individual basis, and as a way of perhaps curing certain mental illnesses. Throughout this century, people have sought psychoanalysis, even those who do not define themselves as mentally ill.

At the more popular and less expensive end of the scale, astrology has been revived and transformed into a means of mass personality assessment. Newspapers print daily horoscopes, and "experts" offer detailed astrological assessments for small fees. Although the validity of astrologically based self-knowledge has not been established in scientific studies, most people can generally find something that seems valid in their horoscopes (cf. Meehl, 1956), and so astrology persists. Likewise, the consultation of "biorhythms" or the analyses of personal "auras" and other such practices appeal to the general appetite for fast, easy, and inexpensive ways to increase self-knowledge.

In the mid-1970s, a best-selling novel by Alex Haley, followed by a popular series on television, traced the novelist's lineage back several generations. The imagination of the American public was captured by *Roots*, and a major obsession was inspired. Many people were soon busily researching their genealogies. Why? The promise of vivid self-knowledge gained by library work seemed too attractive to pass up. The genealogical research was not always easy, of course, but the techniques were clear-cut, a matter of definite questions with definite answers. Finding one's roots seemed to offer what the quest for self-knowledge lacked the most, a well-defined method. Unfortunately, one's ancestry is no longer a vital part of one's identity. It now usually makes very little difference who your great-grandfather was. The "roots" obsession can be seen as a misguided attempt to gain self-knowledge by reviving an obsolete feature of identity. And since useful self-knowledge failed to emerge from the study of individual ancestries, this fad died an early death.

Even illegal drugs were briefly pressed into service in the quest for self-knowledge. Psychedelic drugs were alleged to promote insight into oneself (e.g., Cohen, 1967; Grof, 1975; Hofmann, 1983). They were used in psychotherapy, often with apparently successful results, which may lend some plausibility to claims about their power to produce insight. In the 1960s, the appeal of LSD was at first due to its reputation for stimulating profound self-knowledge (e.g., Klavetter & Mogar, 1967; Mogar, 1965). Later, LSD was increasingly used for fun and entertainment which, ironically, it was less effective than other drugs at providing. As a result, its use declined (see Baumeister & Placidi, 1983).

Thus, self-knowledge has been sought in everything from analysis of the stars to analysis of dreams, and from mind-altering chemicals to dusty genealogical charts. The range of methods we have tried testifies to the importance of the question and to our lack of reliable ways to find the answer.

Potentiality and Fulfillment

Another aspect of identity is the discovery and fulfillment of one's potentiality as a unique individual. In psychological theory the goal of such fulfillment is found in the popular concept of self-actualization (e.g., Maslow, 1968). But what is self-actualization? Everyone wants to be self-actualized, but few have a clear understanding of what it is.

Pop psychology books frequently promise fulfillment and self-actualization to their readers. What they claim to provide can include enhanced self-esteem, or more fun, or financial success. The techniques they offer are similarly diverse, ranging from positive thinking to self-hypnosis to new sex techniques. Because these books continue to sell, they must be appealing to some perennial need. As with diet books, however, the definitive way to achieve self-actualization is elusive, and so new books and articles continue to appear.

For the more energetic seeker of self-fulfillment, Oriental religions and meditations offer a wide range of techniques. Americans have long had periodic but brief interludes of fascination with Oriental ideas. However, the most recent interest in Orientalism may be more substantial and durable than its predecessors (e.g., Cox, 1977). Centers for Zen and Tibetan Buddhism now flourish here, turning away more people than they can accommodate. And transcendental meditation (TM) has become big business, to the point where mainstream America has begun to accept meditation as compatible with normality.

The quest for ways to fulfill one's potentiality infects the down-to-earth segments of society as well as its spiritual sophisticates. Even the Armed Forces seek to cash in on it. For several years, the main advertising theme in recruiting has been to portray military service as a means of self-actualization under the slogan, "Be all that you can be."

It is not just the techniques of fulfillment that have become a problem. Models of fulfillment held out to the average person have also changed. This is perhaps most apparent in the recent cultural history of woman's place in society. Our society spent about a century convincing women that their proper ideal of fulfillment lay in being housewives and mothers. Then, in the 1950s and 1960s, the housewife and mother suddenly became the symbol for the unfulfilled human being: exploited, stifled, and bored (cf. Margolis, 1984).

Relationship of Individual to Society

Identities exist only in societies, which define and organize them. Thus, the search for identity includes the question of what is the proper relationship of the individual to society as a whole.

This search for the proper relationship affects politics and legislation. The trend over the past century has been to have society, especially as embodied in the central government, take increasing responsibility for the individual. And many recent political controversies reveal our questioning of how government ought to treat its individual citizens. Is it the responsibility of the government to provide an adequate income or complete medical care for all elderly citizens? Should medical care be provided for everyone? How much help does the government owe to the poor, the unemployed, the mentally ill? And how much should federal laws restrict the freedoms of individual citizens to own guns and to pray, or not pray, in school? How much should the privacy of individual lives be shielded from official curiosity?

The search for the proper relationship of the individual to society is also evident at the individual level. One year *Newsweek* magazine reported that people were moving from large cities to small towns in order to find peace of mind and a sense of community. The very next year the same magazine reported that people were moving into renovated or "gentrified" sections of big cities because of the advantages of those communities.

Some people even go so far as to found their own communities, thus reviving the Utopian spirit of the nineteenth century. The hippie communes of the 1960s were the best known among these, but there have been others, such as feminist communes. The point of founding such a community is usually to try out a new version or vision of the way individuals should relate to each other and, thus, to society.

An extreme form of community behavior is found in cults. Their appeal resides partially in how they resolve the issue of the relationship of the individual to society. Cult members and ex-members frequently cite the sense of membership in a nurturant, supportive community as a prime reason for belonging to the cult (e.g., Cox, 1977). Religious cults do typically concern themselves with human potentiality and fulfillment, and often even suggest techniques for achieving fulfillment. They also exhibit their own Utopian way of life, of which Jonestown was a sad example.

Another segment of society objects to the way in which it is supposed to fit in but has no positive alternative scheme. Juvenile delinquency was interpreted by Erikson (1968) as the insistence on a

"negative identity"—the troublesome behavior of juvenile delin-
quents was displayed to mark them as people who *did not* follow the
expectations of society.

Society is pervaded by the search for solutions to problems of
identity. Has this always been the case? I do not think so. The
purpose of this book is to understand the modern dilemmas of
identity as well as the nature of identity. My methods for arriving at
that understanding are those of social science and deserve a brief
comment.

The first half of this book examines the historical changes and
developments that involve identity, the basic point being that finding an identity has become a problem in the course of social changes
in our history. Ascertaining when and how identity became a
problem is likely to tell much about the nature of the problem. It
may also tell a great deal about the nature of identity itself. When I
began this project, my plan was simply to discover at what historical point identity crises began to occur, and then to evaluate the
social changes occurring just prior to that particular time. It quickly
became apparent, though, that identity did not become problematic
all at once. Instead, there seems to have been a series of historical
stages by which it became problematic. Half of this book is devoted
to understanding those stages.

Using history as data for learning about identity presents problems, however. The evolution of modern society is, in a sense, only
one case history, comparable in many respects to a single clinical
case report. Without experimental control groups, this approach
lacks the precision and certainty of laboratory work.

The problem of generalization is a difficult one. I have focused on
American society and, to an extent, on its roots in Western European societies. If other cultures traverse the same stages at different
speeds, the sequence of stages is itself conceptually sound and
generally valid. The important question is whether that sequence
holds true for other cultures—that is, do they (or will they eventually) arrive at problems of individual identity for the same reasons
our culture has? If so, then these may be universal features of human

identity. If not, then this study is valuable only within the confines of our culture. The answer to the cross-cultural question must wait for other researchers and other books.

Generalization within our culture is also a problem. The farther back one goes in our history, the more exclusively the evidence is based on white, upper-class, Christian, educated males. This is not the fault of historians—it is a matter of who left behind the most records. Even when it comes to modern history, I have devoted very little of this book to ethnic minorities, lesbians, migrant laborers, Moslems, handicapped persons, and others who may differ in important ways from the culturally dominant set. In short, the historical picture I offer is a case history based on the most influential and highly visible part of the population. As a result, I have been cautious in generalizing about others. Again, it is up to other researchers and other books to make such comparisons and contrasts explicit.

The second half of this book is based on psychological evidence about identity and presents such related topics as brainwashing. It reviews research on how children acquire identities, on how the two main types of identity crises occur and are resolved, and on how identity can be forcibly destroyed or altered. The purpose is to shed light on what identity is and how identity can become vulnerable or problematic. Once again, though, it is necessary to be cautious about generalizing across cultural and subcultural boundaries. Some research samples were even restricted by gender, so one must be hesitant about generalizing between men and women. The studies of brainwashing of American prisoners in the Korean War, for example, were done exclusively on males because as a rule only men were sent into combat. It is not certain that women would respond to brainwashing techniques in the same way that men did.

Before proceeding to the history of identity, it is necessary to offer a system of concepts for talking about identity. Concepts are the tools of philosophers, so I begin by borrowing from their work. Chapter 2 is therefore devoted to the concepts necessary for a discussion of identity.

2

Basic Conceptual Issues

Psychologists are hardly the first thinkers to consider questions about the nature of the self and personal identity. Throughout the centuries, the philosophers were the first to delve into these issues. This chapter looks at the contributions of several major philosophers, and this review serves as a point of departure for a structural model of identity.

Descartes

René Descartes (1596–1650) is famous for asking himself, over and over, how he could be sure of each thing he knew. Nothing seemed certain. Finally, when he tried to doubt that he existed, the uncertainty ended: "I think, therefore I am" ("cogito, ergo sum"). Everything else could be doubted, but he was certain that he existed. In a sense, he was saying that self-knowledge was the most secure of all knowledge. That chair over there could be a hallucination, but I exist.

Generations of philosophers have picked over Descartes' argument and have come up with a variety of criticisms. The main point seems to be this: In actuality, we don't learn that we exist from observing that we think. As Kant pointed out, you already have to know that you exist in order to know that you are thinking. "I think, therefore I am" is thus misleading; it is not true that we exist *because* we think.

Descartes, after all, just pretended to doubt that he existed. Deep down he knew it all along. Schizophrenics, who really confront their own nonexistence, are neither comforted nor cured by "cogito ergo sum." Descartes' formula does not work.

Still, Descartes' thinking contains one point that is important for this discussion—the idea that knowledge of self is inferred from empirical evidence.

Hume

David Hume (1711–1776) confused and embarrassed the reigning British thinkers of his time by asking a lot of unanswerable questions about accepted ideas. He had no patience with notions like "The whole is more than the sum of its parts," for what more had been added? He pointed out that the fact that something has happened in the past is no logical guarantee that it will happen in the future—so what makes us believe the sun will rise tomorrow?

The self fared no better with Hume than did tomorrow's sunrise. He said he understood the self to be the mind and its contents. If the contents were changed it was no longer the same self. In fact, every time one saw or learned something new, the totality was changed, so the self thus became different. His famous question was "What then gives us so great a propension . . . to suppose ourselves possest of an invariable and uninterrupted existence thro' the whole course of our lives?" And he concluded that "the identity, which we ascribe to the mind of man, is only a fictitious one."

The implication of Hume's argument is that the self is not something one can directly know, perceive, imagine, visualize, grasp, or otherwise hold in any way. I can hold this spoon, see it, know just what it is like and what it is good for. But not the self. I cannot even form a clear idea of what the self is. I can focus on my spoon, blotting out the rest of the world, but I cannot do that with the self.

Kant

Immanuel Kant (1724–1804) struggled to resolve the paradoxes Hume had presented. The answers he found have been influential ever since and contain some valuable insights.

Kant agreed that the self could not perceive itself directly. The self is the perceiver, not the perceived. It cannot perceive itself any more than a camera can take a picture of itself. It can only see other objects, events, and circumstances. Given this, how is self-awareness possible?

The key to Kant's solution was that the self can perceive events, and perception is an event. The self could perceive its own acts of perceiving and thus gain indirect knowledge of self. True, the self cannot perceive itself directly, in isolation, but the self *can* catch itself in the act of doing something.

This is how one actually is aware of oneself. Imagine riding a bicycle without self-consciousness—you are attending only to the road, the traffic, etc. Then you become self-conscious; you become aware of yourself-riding-the-bicycle. You catch yourself in the act of riding. Thus, the self is not known in isolation or by itself. The self is always and only known in relation to the world. Self-awareness is a superimposed awareness.

Kant thought that the pure, real self actually existed although it could never be known directly to anyone. This "noumenal self" was supposedly behind the scenes, making the appearance of the phenomenal self possible. (The "phenomenal self" is the self as it appears in conscious experience, as opposed to any supposedly underlying or unconscious parts of the self.) Although recent thinkers have had serious doubts about the existence of noumenal selves, Kant's analysis of the phenomenal self is still valuable.

Kant emphasized what he called the synthetic unity of apperception. By this he meant that the unity of the self (the self that is gotten by this superimposed awareness) is made, not automatically given. The unity of the self is stitched together out of the series of momentary glimpses of self-awareness, which also explains why the self can become unraveled.

Kant thus offers these two points. First, it is easy not to know the self because the self cannot be known directly but can only be glimpsed in action (that is, can only be noticed in the process of doing something else). The "phenomenal self" is inferred or deduced from other perceptions or cognitions. Second, the unity of the self over time—crucial to any notion or model of identity—is not guaranteed or built in but is rather created somehow. The self is such an elusive thing because it is merely inferred from other experiences and is *somehow* stitched together across time.

Dilthey

Thus far, I have discussed experience in terms of momentary cognitions and perceptions, the sort of thing sometimes called "sense data." However, this is not the way we actually experience events. True, the self is inferred from experiences, but the important experiences are not momentary cognitions; they are units that last for hours, weeks, months, years. Experience is not instantaneous.

Wilhelm Dilthey (1833–1911) contributed an important and highly influential definition of experience. He maintained that an experience is any event or collection of events with a unity of meaning. For example, a love affair may be *an* experience because it has a unity of meaning even though it is comprised of events that are spread out over time and even though other events having nothing to do with the love affair occur between the specific events of the love affair. (If the love affair is unusually long-lasting and changes its meaning for the lovers, as when ardent lovers become married parents, then it may cease to be a single experience.)

The fact that the events comprising an experience are not temporally continuous or contiguous is an important clue to an understanding of how identity is stitched together across time. Thus, the lovers meet Wednesday evening. The next day, the man does his laundry and writes some letters while the woman attends a meeting and stops at the library. They meet again Thursday evening. The Wednesday and Thursday evening meetings are linked by being part of the same experience, even though the intervening events (laundry, library, etc.) were unrelated. If the experience spreads across time, and the self is derived (known) from experiences, then the self too can begin to have unity across time.

Dilthey's concept of experience helps to resolve Hume's paradox. Involvement in ongoing experiences provides a basis for being the same person across time. In the middle of an experience, one has possibilities for future events that are partly determined by past events. Continuity of identity is weakest when all one's involvements or ongoing experiences change abruptly. For example, if a man were to quit his job, divorce his wife, sell his house and possessions, move to a new state or country, permanently alienate his remaining relatives, and convert to a new religion, all in two months, it would not surprise anyone if he spoke of having a new identity.

Thus, an experience is a set of events spread out across time and united by a common meaning. If knowledge of self is derived from experiences, then it too can be spread out across time. Moreover, unity of meaning seems important in producing unity of identity. The sense of identity, in other words, is not just based on the physical self but depends on meaning. Because meaning occurs only within a contextual network of relationships, it seems safe to conclude that *identity is a linguistic construction*.

Analytical Approach

Analyses of the concept of identity generally focus on unity, especially in the sense of unity over time, or "continuity" (Broad, 1925; Erikson, 1968; Shoemaker, 1963). Unity during the present moment means that all your thoughts and wishes—all parts of you—are connected. Unity over time (continuity) means that today you are the same person as the person who existed last week. Continuity over time is a main criterion of identity.

A second criterion tends to be overlooked but is nonetheless important—differentiation. The purpose of an identification number or card or bracelet is to distinguish its owner from others who might be similar. A person having an identity crisis is not necessarily seeking continuity in his or her life; rather, that person may be seeking some mark of differentiation, something to set himself or herself off from others.

Differentiation tends to be neglected philosophically because somehow it is implied in the concept of continuity. Psychologically, however, continuity and differentiation are separate; they present different concerns and dilemmas to the individual trying to form an identity.

One analysis of the concept of identity based on the criterion of continuity is given by Sydney Shoemaker (1963). As Shoemaker puts it, the problem is more or less this: Yesterday someone broke the front window; how do I know whether I am that person? The obvious answer is that I remember—in other words, memory is responsible. But the obvious answer is wrong. Memory does not constitute identity; memory presupposes identity. Without identity, "I" could not remember that "I" broke the window yesterday, only that someone did. Memory gives no basis for deciding whether that someone was myself.

Although the continuity of the physical body is an important source of the sense of identity, Shoemaker concludes that this is not the only source. People have knowledge of identity that is not mediated by any cue. Knowledge of one's own identity is not purely physical self-knowledge. The body helps to define identity as a self that is continuous over time, but some "noncriterial" knowledge also contributes. Identity only starts with the physical body.

Phenomenological or Existential Approach

Shoemaker and others treated identity as an analytical problem. However, identity is popularly recognized as what is loosely called an "existential" problem. The relevance of existence (being) to identity deserves mention.

One approach to the understanding of Heidegger's (1927) highly influential discussion of being begins with the notion of possibility. You exist at this moment. Being always *is* at some particular place in the world; at this moment you probably exist in a chair, with a book in front of you. Various things are possible for you based on your present existence; for example, you may finish this chapter within the next half hour, or you may put it down to answer the telephone or cook a meal. Other things are not possible for you now, such as performing brain surgery (unless you happen to have both the requisite training and a patient), walking on the moon, or visiting the Great Wall of China. Your being determines ("projects") a set of possibilities and rules others out.

Identity is closely linked to possibility. Think of someone else much like yourself in general knowledge and physical makeup. Despite the general resemblance, you and that person have separate identities, and these identities have a great deal to do with what is possible for you (but not the other person) to do. Where you can go, whom you may kiss, what you may inherit, what obligations you have, and whom you must fear all depend on your identity. True, a stranger could conceivably kiss your spouse, but the meaning of that kiss—and his or her reaction to it—is likely to be quite different from a kiss between you and your spouse. In short, identity determines possibility.

Some possibilities become actualities; others do not. The jealous husband with gun in hand feels that he might shoot his wife and also feels that he might not. An hour later, one possibility has become actuality and the other has not. Both law school and medical school are possible for the college freshman, but the senior has usually made choices that rule out one or the other (or both!). Choice, either explicit or implicit, singles out one possibility from the set of possibilities and actualizes it.

Implications

These philosophical approaches to identity furnish us the following point of departure for a theory of identity, and a basic question suggests itself: How do we explain how the self can exist as *continuous* across time and as *distinct* from others? We must also explain how a person can *know* the self as both continuous and differentiated. Although part of the answer can be traced to awareness of the body, a full answer depends on the way people interpret their experiences, especially experiences that continue across time. In addition, identity must be understood in its context of possible events of *potentiality*.

Model of Identity

In the next few pages I outline the model of identity that will be used throughout this book. The model has several parts. First, there are two *defining criteria* of identity. Second, I suggest three functions of identity, which entail three *functional aspects* of identity. Third, there is an aggregation of *components* of identity, which are the basic units of self-definition. Finally, I delineate five basic types of *self-definition processes*. Identity components are acquired by the various self-definition processes, the components fulfill the defining criteria of identity, and normally each component has all three functional aspects of identity.

Defining criteria of identity. I have already suggested what are the two defining criteria of identity: continuity and differentiation. An effective identity is a well-defined identity, and it becomes well-defined if its parts adequately meet the defining criteria. In other words, something contributes to identity if it satisfies one or both of the defining criteria.

Continuity is a special case of unity, unity across time. Continuity entails being the same person today as yesterday or last year or next week. One's sense of identity is strengthened by things that require one to be the same person across time. An example of this is making promises. A promise links the self who made the commitment with the self who must fulfill the commitment at some later time.

Differentiation entails being different from others. One's identity must contain some elements that distinguish it from others. Some of these differentiate only quite broadly, by classifying someone in one of a few large categories. Gender is an example of this—lots of people have the same gender. Other things differentiate on a much more unique and individual basis, like one's name or Social Security number. It would seem that the more narrow differentiators are the more important ones because they differentiate one from everyone else, but this is misleading. True, being female only differentiates you from half the human race, but society makes considerable use of that distinction, so that broad category affects you in many ways. The point is, both broad and narrow differentiators are important for identity.

Functional aspects of identity. What good is it to have an identity? What are the functions of an identity? Three functions come to mind. First, a clear sense of one's identity helps one make choices. Questions like how to spend an afternoon or a year, whether to sleep with so-and-so, and what positions to apply for are easier to answer if one has an effective identity. Second, relationships to other persons are impossible without identity and difficult if one's identity is in transition or is poorly defined. Finally, a sense of identity furnishes one with a sense of strength and resilience, so that the impact of a specific misfortune or setback is diminished, and one's life can be oriented toward specific goals that include the fulfillment of certain potentialities. People seem to desire identity for the sake of one or more of these functions, and three *functional aspects* of identity may be inferred from these three functions.

The first functional aspect of identity is the individual's own structure of *values and priorities.* Self-definition involves aligning oneself with certain values that determine how people ought to behave and what they should strive for. It also involves finding personal goals that provide direction in one's own life. The structure of values and priorites enables the individual to make choices in a steady and purposive fashion.

A second functional aspect of identity is the *interpersonal aspect*, consisting of one's social roles and personal reputation. This is sometimes called the "social identity" or, to use Jung's term, the "persona." It combines interpersonal traits like friendliness and candor with role-defining designations such as policeman, mother, or team captain. Relationships with other persons are conducted on the basis of this functional aspect of identity.

The third functional aspect of identity is a sense of *individual potentiality.* To an extent, this aspect consists of having a realistic personal goal *and* sufficient self-esteem to believe one can reach that goal. Moreover, if progress toward the goal is obstructed or completely stopped, the person with a strong sense of potential is not destroyed but feels he or she has the potential to achieve alternative goals. Those who lack faith in their ability to accomplish anything worthwhile may describe their plights as identity crises.

The concept of fulfillment is closely linked to that of potentiality, for potentialities are what get fulfilled. Having an identity that contains a well-defined sense of potential is more than just having an idea of something one could do. It is having a belief that personal fulfillment can be achieved by doing that something. The potentiality aspect encompasses identity's actual and possible goals.

Identity components. Each identity contains an indefinite number of components. These are the units of self-definition. The unity of these units is a unity of meaning. Examples of identity components are being a dentist, a Christian, a genius, rich, an honest person, a loser, resourceful, the fattest person in Cincinnati, a parent, a virgin, strong, a former swimming champion. Any partial definition of the self is an identity component—any valid answer to "Who are you?"

The components constitute identity by fulfilling the two defining criteria of identity: They provide the individual with differentiation and continuity of self-definition. Thus, being a dentist differentiates one from people with other jobs. Being a dentist also provides continuity, insofar as one continues to be a dentist day after day, year after year.

Identity components also contain the three functional aspects of identity. Being a dentist may be linked to placing a high value on professional security and prosperity; it also entails priorities like keeping one's appointments and having good X-ray equipment. The interpersonal aspect of identity is clearly involved in being a dentist, for that identity component shapes one's relationships in ways large (one spends much of one's time caring for others), medium (one's reputation in the community is as a prosperous and respectable citizen), and small (the neighbors addresss one as "Doctor"). The third functional aspect of identity, sense of personal potentiality, is also tied to being a dentist. While in college and dental school one was already guided by the vision of oneself as a potential dentist. At forty-five, being a dentist may furnish one with a sense of the potential money one could earn—enough to withstand some bad investments, to own several impressive cars, or to afford to pay Princeton tuitions for three daughters simultaneously. One's potentiality is also constrained by being a dentist, for a practicing dentist is unlikely to come up with a major scientific discovery, become a television celebrity, achieve mystical enlightenment, or have a great deal of power.

Obviously, people vary both in what and how many identity components they have. Each person has some components that are quite important (I call them major identity components) and others that are minor or unimportant. Of course, the same component (e.g., being rich or being a Christian) can be major for one person and minor for another.

Self-definition processes. Self-definition is a matter of acquiring identity components. Identity components can be acquired in five different ways. These five self-definition processes are summarized in Table 1, where they are arranged according to how problematic they are. In other words, type I is the easiest self-definition process because it creates no problems for the user. Type V self-definition is a difficult and complex way of creating identity.

Type I self-definition refers to assigned components of self. Family lineage and gender are clear examples of this type. One does not have to do anything to become male or female; one is born that way and remains that way. Type I self-definition is thus passive, stable, and unproblematic, except for those rare individuals who desire sex-change operations. By "unproblematic" I do not mean there are no problems associated with the identity component. Clearly, for example, one may have problems because of being born a man that one would not have if one were a woman (or vice versa). But, in most cases, these problems have to do with the social consequences and expectations of being male or female, rather than being problems with how to become male or female. To put it another way, although the component itself may give rise to prob-

TABLE 1. *Self-definition Processes*

Type	Description	Problem	Example
I	Assigned component	None (stable, passive)	Family lineage, gender
II	Single transformation	Achievement: Single self-definition by one standard	Motherhood, knighthood
III	Hierarchy of criteria	Achievement: Frequent or continual redefinition of self by one standard	Wealth (among the middle class)
IV	Optional choice	Choice is available: Alternative options exist, but one option is dominant or clear guidelines exist	Religious or political affiliation (in pluralistic society)
V	Required choice	Person is required to find criteria for choosing among incompatible alternatives	Choice of mate or career (in modern society)

lems, the initial self-definition process for acquiring the component is not a problem.

Thus, a society that is based on and organized around type I self-definition is likely to be a society in which identity is clear-cut and unproblematic. If who you are is based mainly on what you're born as, you are not likely to have an identity crisis.

The second type of self-definition process encompasses identity components that are acquired in a single transformation. Motherhood is an excellent example: One well-defined event makes you a mother. In many societies, becoming an adult is a single-transformation process, such as when the teenage male endures a fixed and traditional rite of passage and thereafter is a man. Reaching the criteria for this transformation may be difficult. If so, this type of self-definition can be a problem. On the other hand, the criterion or criteria are usually well-defined, as is the procedure for reaching them, so in that sense type II self-definition is not very problematic. Moreover, once the criteria are reached and the identity component is acquired, it is stable and unproblematic. Once acquired, the status of motherhood persists. Again, when I say continuing to be a mother is unproblematic I do not mean it is easy; it may entail years of strenuous toil and emotional turmoil. But, again, these are not problems of self-definition. There is no question as to *whether* someone is a mother. Her exertions are not causing her to be a mother. Instead, it is because she is a mother that the exertions are demanded of her. The identity is fixed. In that sense, identity components acquired by type II self-definition processes are stable and unproblematic.

Both the second and third types of self-definition processes involve achievement as the means by which identity components are acquired. The difference between them is in the range of measurement. Type II processes involve just one transformation, and people are classified as either having achieved or not having achieved that transformation. Moreover, all the criteria—and often there is only one, such as in the case of motherhood—need only be fulfilled once, at one particular time, as a prerequisite for the transformation. Type III self-definition, on the other hand, is based on a hierarchy of criteria. In middle-class society, the possession of money is a good example. It is an important component of identity because in such a society your identity is determined in part by how much money you have. There is no set amount, however, that can be used to distinguish the wealthy from the poor. Someone with $80,000 is richer than someone with $70,000, who in turn is richer than someone with $50,000. There is no comparable set of distinctions regarding motherhood. Someone with four children is not less of a mother than someone with six. Moreover, becoming wealthy does not necessarily occur in a single transformation, which makes it also unlike motherhood.

Type III self-definition is problematic in that it is never clearly finished. Having $80,000 does not end the process of self-definition by wealth. One can always earn more. One can also lose some of one's money. The point is that such components are *always subject to redefinition*. One has to keep proving and defining oneself.

Type III self-definition makes comparison and competition possible in identity. Because there is a clearly defined standard with an established hierarchy, one can compare oneself with other persons having similar identities. Two men may both be rich, but one is probably richer. Comparing oneself to others introduces a new sort of problem, one that emphasizes the interpersonal aspect of identity.

Type III self-definition is typically not problematic, however, with regard to criteria and procedures. The standards and procedures for becoming rich are well-defined—one must accumulate a lot of money, usually either through diligent and thrifty business activity or through speculation and exploitation. Thus, type III self-definition is more problematic than types I or II because one has to work much more to climb the hierarchy of criteria. But it is less problematic than types IV and V because the criteria are fairly clear.

Some self-definition processes seem to be mixtures of types II and III. In our society, for example, education is a hierarchical process in that there is a hierarchy of grade levels and an almost unlimited number of courses one may take. On the other hand, there are several well-defined single-transformation points of transition, such as graduation from college. Once one has graduated from college, the identity component of "college graduate" is retained for life with no question.

The fourth and fifth types of self-definition processes refer to self-definition by acts of choice rather than achievement. Choice becomes necessary when there are not one but several sets of criteria for defining identity and when these sets are incompatible. There are several possible ways to be, and they are not clearly arranged along an unequivocal dimension. With wealth (type III), there is no question of the evaluative hierarchy: It is better to have $80,000 than $70,000. But there is no straightforward way to determine whether it is better to be a Protestant or a Catholic. Once you decide to become a Catholic, the criteria for self-definition are rather clear—baptism, communion, belief, and so forth. How to reach that decision is extremely unclear, however. From a Catholic standpoint, of course, it is preferable to be a Catholic, but from a Protestant standpoint it is the other way around. This sort of problem never comes up with type II and type III self-definition.

It is misleading to lump all forms of self-definition by choice into a single category. For this reason I distinguish two types. Type IV refers to optional choice; type V refers to required choice.

The example of religious faith illustrates the distinction. An adult encountering Christianity for the first time might experience difficulty in deciding between Protestantism and Catholicism. If determined to become a Christian, that person's choice would resemble type V processes—the need to make a choice. In most cases, however, such decisions are not made in a vacuum because people are generally born into a family that belongs to one of those sects. If they find a compelling reason, they may convert from one to the other, but otherwise they will remain in their faith. That is the model for type IV self-definition. Choice is available but not required. In other words, the person may make a choice, but he or she does not have to make one—things can just go on as they are.

Another way to conceptualize type IV self-definition processes is to say that they occur within the context of an overarching value system. The person has ample guidelines for living, and only if a compelling reason is found will he or she betray or forsake those guidelines. Thus, one is raised as a Catholic, and one can always use the Catholic rules and values to make life's choices. And that is what one will tend to do unless one discovers some compelling reason to convert to Protestantism or atheism or some other system.

Type V self-definition, in contrast to type IV, does not offer the individual a passive option. The individual is required to make a choice. Mate selection is a good illustration of this type of process, at least in circumstances under which remaining unmarried is not an acceptable option. In mate selection there are presumably a set of options—the various potential spouses. They are incompatible options because one cannot marry them all. Each potential spouse has advantages and disadvantages; for example, the most charming one may be the least reliable with regard to household chores. In short, a choice must be made, but there is no single and unimpeachable guideline for making that choice.

This fifth type of self-definition is quite problematic. The person must choose although there are no clear rules for choosing. This becomes an identity problem when the person believes that the answer lies *within*. The identity is expected to contain values or priorities or preferences—what I will call *metacriteria*—for making such choices. For example, there is no single, unequivocal way of establishing whether it is better to be a physician, a lawyer, or a scientist, but many intelligent college students have to find some way of choosing among these incompatible ambitions. Our society expects them to know what they want, which means they must look within themselves and find the way to make the "right" choice. A society that requires people to make such choices will probably end up by requiring selves to contain answers, or metacriteria that can be used to generate answers. And even so, there is no clear or reliable procedure for manufacturing metacriteria. Type V self-definition, therefore, is highly problematic.

Criteria and metacriteria. Some clarification is in order since I have already used "criteria" to refer to continuity and differentiation of identity. From this point, I use *defining criteria* to refer specifically to continuity and differentiation. Identity is defined by things that fulfill the two defining criteria—in other words, whatever differentiates one from others and makes one the same across time creates identity.

The term *criteria* is reserved for the qualifications that are the prerequisites for having a particular identity component. Thus, for example, to be a parent you have to meet the single criterion of having a child. Being a surgeon requires meeting several criteria involving education, training, and employment. Self-definition by type III processes involves locating oneself along a hierarchy of criteria.

Lastly, I use the term *metacriteria* for the factors individuals use to make choices relevant to identity. The "meta" seems appropriate because such criteria are superordinate; they determine a choice between different sets of criteria. Thus, for example, the college student's choice between being a physician or an attorney is in practice a choice between trying to satisfy the various criteria for becoming a physician (beginning with gaining admission to medical school) and trying to satisfy those for becoming a lawyer (starting with admission to law school). If circumstances dictate taking one option rather than another, there is no need to speak of metacriteria. However, if the individual is confronted with two or more viable, mutually exclusive options, and the individual is expected to search within for the right answer, the issue then becomes a matter of whether the identity contains a particular entity that can point definitively one way or the other. Such entities are the metacriteria. One theme of this book is that our modern difficulty with identity results from the societal requirement that identities contain a large number of these metacriteria.

The structural model of identity is summarized in Table 2.

TABLE 2. System of Concepts for Identity

Defining criteria

1. Continuity over time
2. Differentiation

Functional aspects

1. Interpersonal identity (roles and reputation)
2. Potentiality
3. Structure of values and priorities (including metacriteria)

Components

All units of self-definition
1. Major components
2. Minor components

Self-definition processes

Type   I.   Assigned
       II.   Single transformation
      III.   Identity measured on hierarchy of criteria
      IV.   Optional choice
       V.   Required choice

System: The set of major components of identity contains the three functional aspects; most major components each have all three functional aspects. Components constitute identity by fulfilling the defining criteria. Components are acquired by means of the self-definition processes.

Summary

Rene Descartes was first to argue that knowledge of self is obtained from empirical evidence—that is, from experience in the world. Later David Hume suggested that the self was not an entity that could be directly known or perceived, and his critique of self-knowledge raised the question of how you could know yourself to be the same person throughout your life. Immanuel Kant affirmed that the self could not be known directly or in isolation, but could only be known through its action and interaction with the world. He maintained that the continuity of identity was actively created by the mind. Wilhelm Dilthey, taking another approach, defined experience as any event or set of events having a unity of meaning. Thus, if the self is derived from experience, then involvement in ongoing experiences furnishes a basis for continuity of identity across time. In fact, the unity of identity is constructed linguistically, by virtue of connections that have linguistic meaning.

Today modern analytical approaches to the problem of identity emphasize the issue of continuity across time. They indicate that identity may start with the physical body but suggest that identity cannot fully be explained in physical terms. Modern phenomenological theory links personal identity to potential action—that is, to possible actions and events, not just the ones that actually occur.

The structural model of identity proposed here contains two defining *criteria*, three *functional aspects*, a variable number of *components*, and five types of *self-definition processes*. The defining criteria are continuity across time and differentiation from others. The functional aspects are the interpersonal self, the structure of values and priorities, and the sense of personal potentiality. The components are all the units of self-definition—the ways in which the person might answer the question "Who are you?" The self-definition processes are (I) passive assignment of component, (II) single-transformation, (III) measured or hierarchical identity, (IV) optional choice, and (V) required choice.

3

Medieval and Early Modern History of Identity

This chapter reviews the major developments in identity prior to 1800, focusing mainly on the culturally and politically dominant parts of Western Europe and America. Prior to 1800 identity was not generally problematic, but several trends prepared the way for it to become so.

Medieval Europe

The problems and crises that plague modern identity formation were largely unknown in medieval Europe. Society was much more rigidly structured and inflexible than it is today. As a result, the large institutional structures for the most part formed an individual's identity. In other words, the individual received his or her identity without much personal struggle. Society operated on the basis of lineage, gender, home, and social class—all of which were fixed by birth. This organization of life according to type I (passive assignment) self-definition processes made identity largely unproblematic. Marriage and age-related transitions introduced single-transformation processes into identity but, again, the individual's role was often passive. Marriage, for example, was often decided and arranged by one's parents. There were occasional exceptions, but the general trends and patterns were quite different from those of modern life.

To understand the medieval mentality we must set aside one pervasive modern value—the fundamental, overriding importance of the individual human being. Medieval attitudes lacked this modern emphasis on individuality. Individuality can be understood as a combination of (1) placing value on the unique characteristics and particular experiences of each person, and (2) believing that each person has a special unique potentiality or destiny that may or may not be fulfilled (Weintraub, 1978).

A main reason for the relative indifference to individuality was the firm medieval faith in Christianity, which regarded life on earth as imitative or derivative of the ultimate, otherworldly realities (Auerbach, 1946; Huizinga, 1924/1954). In fact, the particulars of individual human experience were not very important. What mattered was the broad cosmic drama of faith and salvation. The life of a particular person was only a good or poor approximation of the archetypal patterns of heavenly or biblical events. The individual self was significant only as an example of the general struggle between good and evil, virtue and vice, faith and heresy, honor and disgrace. Our modern, individualistic view holds that the value of the individual life resides in what is special or unique about it; the medieval view considered the value of the person's life to reside in how well that life approximated the common ideal of correct Christian life.

One illustration of the medieval indifference to individuality is the way in which biography was practiced. (Actually, what they wrote deserves to be called hagiography, not biography.) Life histories were not written about very many persons during the Middle Ages, and those that were written were primarily the lives of saints. Even these writings exhibited nothing of what we would call "individual" or "realistic" (Altick, 1965, pp. 6–7). The authors were largely indifferent to matters of accuracy, portrayed all saints more or less according to a common stereotype, and would even embellish the life of one saint with miracle stories borrowed from the lives of others (Altick, 1965). The individuality, personality, and psychology of the individual were neglected. The person who had become a saint was just a means for the biographer to edify and inspire virtue in the reader.

If biography was rare in the Middle Ages, autobiography was almost nonexistent. The lack of autobiographical writing is a sign that people did not place much emphasis or value on the unique properties in the individual's experience and character. In the few autobiographies that were produced, the individual was always described as an approximation of the collective Christian ideal (Weintraub, 1978). Thus, even exceptional individuals such as Abelard and Petrarch tried to make their lives and their personalities conform to the general ideals and patterns.

In the late Middle Ages people increasingly learned to think in individual terms and slowly solidified concepts of the single human life as an individual totality. Learning to conceptualize an individual life and to think in terms of individuals are prerequisites for placing value and emphasis on individuality. These trends paved the way for individuality to become an important part of Western culture.

Perhaps the most profound and powerful move toward individualistic thinking was the revision of popular Christian beliefs and practices. In particular, a new view of Christian eschatology emerged around the twelfth century, which placed a greater emphasis on individual salvation and judgment. Earlier conceptions of the second coming of Christ, which entailed the end of time and the resurrection of the dead, were generally glorious and nonthreatening. Eternal salvation was pretty much guaranteed if you were a baptized Christian (Ariès, 1981, pp. 97–98). Salvation, in other words, was *collective*—it depended on your membership in the Christian community rather than on your actions as an individual.

In the twelfth century, however, this seems to have changed. Portrayals of the second coming began to stress the Last Judgment, in which souls were weighed and judged individually. The later medievals expected the archangel to evaluate your soul based on what you did during your life. Damnation to hell became a serious possibility and was seriously feared. By Petrarch's time in the fourteenth century, popular belief had further enhanced the importance of individual judgment by advancing the date. Instead of waiting until the end of time to be saved or damned, you were now judged while still on your deathbed (Ariès, 1981).

This shift shows a new sense of the continuity and totality of each single person's life; it put the all-important issue of salvation in individualistic terms. In the late medieval view, all the events of a life added up to something, namely net moral and spiritual worth, and that had drastic and eternal consequences. True, the goal or purpose of a life were shared in common in that everyone tried to conform to the same ideal patterns of piety, virtue, and duty. But success and failure were evaluated by an *individual* judgment.

The shift of Christian practices toward a more individualized basis was also reflected in the spread of the practice of individual confession of sins (Morris, 1972). After all, the confession is unlike other church rituals. One participates as an individual and presents one's own unique experiences, even though once again the overriding goals and themes invoke the general, collective model of the ideal Christian life.

The late medieval view retained its primary allegiance to general principles and universal truths, not individual experiences. But evidence suggests that individualistic thinking increasingly colored the way people understood and applied those universals. Prior to the twelfth century, sermons focused exclusively on Scripture and on the permanent and universal truths of theology, but during the twelfth century preachers began to use personal anecdotes and insights to illuminate their general points (Morris, 1972). Petrarch's writings during the fourteenth century show a major advance in the use of introspection and self-discovery as a means of understanding the universal Christian ideal of human perfection (Weintraub, 1978). The use of the personal as a means for understanding the general was also evident outside religious matters. Troubadours, for example, began to use experiences from their own lives in their love songs (Morris, 1972).

Late medieval literature also showed a rudimentary interest in personal experience. Occasional portrayals of psychological conflicts of those caught between conflicting obligations reflect this (Hanning, 1977). Such portrayals were not common, nor were they consistently maintained even by the same author, nor would the psychological characterizations be judged convincing and competent by modern standards. Still, the fact that they appeared at all suggests an incipient interest in the experience of the individual.

An intriguing literary development of the twelfth century was that dramatic plots began to use devices that depended on different characters having different points of view on the action (Hanning, 1977), as when one character was ignorant of important circumstances known to other characters. The use of such devices is a further suggestion that the late medievals were increasingly able to think in individual terms.

At the same time, literary plots explored new usages of time, emphasizing the continuity of each life (Hanning, 1977). A further sign of this growing is found in the stabilization of naming practices; a male now kept the same name for his entire life, and a female changed her name only upon marriage (Withycombe, 1947). Prior to this some surnames were acquired during adulthood, such as names based on one's adult characteristics (e.g., "Frederick Red-Beard" or "Louis the Fat"). That system was replaced by the hereditary transmission of surnames. The child received the father's surname at birth and retained it throughout life, except in the case of female marriage (Withycombe, 1947). It is necessary to add one qualification. Having the same name all one's life does suggest a solid conception of the unity of the human life, but the use of hereditary surnames frames the individual identity in terms of family lineage. The person is thus not named as a unique individual but as a current "trustee" of family status, honor, and property (cf. Stone, 1977).

Transition to the Sixteenth Century

The most dramatic social changes at the end of the Middle Ages were the spread of religious dissent and a great increase in social mobility. It is difficult to assess the impact on human identity of the breakup of the Catholic monopoly on religious truth, and it would be wrong to suggest that the Protestant Reformation rapidly or clearly produced a new type of personality.

The Protestant and Anglican schisms did have profound psychological effects, however. I would suggest that they affected everyone, both Catholic and Protestant, by undermining part of the universal consensus about religious truth. The religious schisms expressed and greatly increased prevailing doubts about the Christian model for living one's life. The loss of consensus foments private doubts and the individual expression of doubts (cf. Asch, 1955). In the Middle Ages one tried to conform to the collective ideal of the model Christian life; that was the purpose of life. Once the consensus about that model was undermined, one could *decide* whether to live by the traditional model or by the new Protestant model (which soon split into several models) or some combination. A single, unquestioned guide for the living of one's life no longer existed.

The religious schism, as well as the resultant plurality of life models, created a setting in which one's identity had to rely on some inner metacriteria. This pattern recurs with various identity components in the centuries that follow. In this historical pattern something that was used as a cause or basis of identity becomes its consequence. For example, in medieval Europe Catholicism was the only option. Who you were followed in large part from your Catholic Christian faith, which was "given." This faith provided the basis for defining the self in terms of *how good* a Christian you were. The Protestant Reformation, however, confronted people with a choice between Catholicism and Protestantism. Your adherence to Catholicism or Protestantism was no longer automatic; it became instead a matter of choice, and you needed a new basis for making this choice. Your basic faith now had to be based on some criterion.

Of course, not everyone faced this choice. Europe soon settled into a status quo by which many people were born Catholics and remained Catholics, while others were born Protestants and remained so. Christian plurality became an instance of type IV self-definition processes; choice was available but not required.

Actually, the problems of Christian plurality probably began during the papal schism of the fourteenth century. Out of the complex power politics of that time arose a situation in which there were two popes, each of whom excommunicated all the followers of the other. Barbara Tuchman's (1978) account of this episode suggests that considerable uncertainty and loss of faith in the Church resulted from the dual papacy. Indeed, she records a popular saying of that time that no one had entered heaven during that entire period.

The Protestant and papal schisms can be dated precisely, but the other development which brought the Middle Ages to a close—increased social mobility—was a gradual process that took place over many centuries. We can identify in this process two themes: first, social mobility transformed a relatively fixed and stable basis for identity into a changeable and problematic one. Social rank now became unstable and contingent on circumstances other than birth. Gradually even the basic criteria of social rank, namely wealth and lineage, became problematic as they came into conflict with each other. Second, social mobility made public life stressful, both by undermining traditional norms for formal social interaction and by making self-definition dependent on the uncertain course of commercial business. This may have led eventually to a retreat from public life and a corresponding emphasis on privacy, home, and family (Sennett, 1974).

Early Modern Period

My discussion of the early modern period focuses on six themes. Keep in mind, however, that, as in all historical accounts, periods overlap. The divisions here are used for the purposes of conceptual unity.

In the early modern period we can identify six social trends: First, there emerged a new concept of an inner or hidden self, symbolized

by concern over sincerity and over discrepancies between appearances and underlying realities. Second, the idea of human individuality developed into a widespread belief and value. Third, the
incipient cultivation of privacy symbolized the separation of social
life and personal life. Fourth, attitudes toward death underwent a
basic change, suggesting a growing concern over individual fate.
Fifth, people began to have an increasing role in the selection of
their own spouses, thereby putting a major component of adult
identity on a basis of personal choice. And sixth, there emerged a
heightened awareness of individual development and potentiality,
symbolized by new attitudes toward children.

1. *The hidden self.* In the sixteenth century the concept of the
person came to include having a kind of internal space and self not
directly visible in social actions and roles (Trilling, 1971). People
began to regard the self as a hidden entity that might or might not
be reflected in outward acts. The belief in a real self that is hidden,
that is not directly or clearly shown in one's public behavior, can be
regarded as a first step toward making identity a problem. An
abstract, hidden self is harder to know and harder to define than is a
concrete, observable self.

Obviously, this idea did not appear out of a void. The contrast
between the visible phenomena and underlying or hidden realities is
an old one in Western thought, dating back at least to Plato.
Christianity made extensive use of that distinction, and medieval
Christian thought regarded events in this world as imitations of the
ultimate realities of God's divine plan and of scriptural truth. This
medieval "figural" view of earthly reality as deriving from theological reality began to die out in the sixteenth century (Auerbach,
1946), but the distinction between appearance and reality survived
and took on a new significance. Indeed, it is fair to describe the
sixteenth century as obsessed with contrasts between appearances
and underlying realities. The philosophy, politics, and literature of
that era—from Berkeley to Machiavelli to Shakespeare—show tire-
less concern and preoccupation with that issue.

Applied to human beings, the contrast between appearance and
reality came in the sixteenth century to mean that persons might

deliberately avoid revealing their true selves by their actions. The sixteenth century was "preoccupied to an extreme degree with dissimulation, feigning, and pretense" (Trilling, 1971, p. 13). This is evident in the advice of Machiavelli and in the disguises and mistaken identities of Shakespeare's characters. Indeed, the great rise in popularity of the theatre in England and France reflected the new interest in acting and playing roles (Trilling, 1971), although actors were not the culture heroes they are today.

The new sensitivity to human deceit made possible the emergence of a new type of dramatic character, the villain, the character whom the audience recognizes as wicked but that is not recognized as so by the other characters in the play (Trilling, 1971). The villain's character consists of an underlying evil self beneath a misleading appearance created by dissembling. This type of character flourished into the nineteenth century, after which it was generally abandoned (by serious literature, at least) as not sufficiently "true to life" (Trilling, 1971, p. 14).

A related and revealing development was the emergence of sincerity as an important virtue in sixteenth century society. The word sincerity first appeared in English early in the century, and at first it was used to describe the pure and uncontaminated condition of things (e.g., wine). Soon, however, it began to be applied to persons, with its modern meaning of honest self-presentation (Trilling, 1971). Shakespeare used the word in that sense, and the importance of sincerity is attested by various lines in his plays, the most famous being Polonius' advice to Laertes: "This above all: To thine own self be true, and . . . thou canst not then be false to any man" (*Hamlet*, act I, scene 3).

Sincerity is of course a kind of equivalence between the visible appearance of the person and the self underneath. Making sincerity an important virtue reflected the new concern with inferring the hidden self from its acts and appearances. Thus, in the sixteenth century the self came to be regarded as something hidden and uncertain. Of course, it was the selves of others and not one's own self that was regarded as difficult to know. Self-knowledge was not recognized as highly problematic until the influence of Puritanism.

Nonetheless, it seems fair to say that sixteenth century society recognized at least one of the three functional aspects of identity as problematic—the interpersonal aspect.

2. *Individuality.* A fascination with the unique or special characteristics of the individual increased dramatically in the sixteenth century (Auerbach, 1946; Morris, 1972; Trilling, 1971; Weintraub, 1978). That development is sufficient to induce some writers to propose that individuality actually emerged in the sixteenth century (e.g., it was then that "men became individuals"—Trilling, 1971, p. 24). A more conservative definition of individuality is proposed on the basis of two criteria by Weintraub (1978). Individuality means placing value on unique characteristics *and* believing that each person has a special destiny or potentiality. Weintraub recognizes that the first criterion was abundantly met during the sixteenth century, but the second was not satisfied until the end of the eighteenth century. Still, the general conclusion is that it was during the early modern period (1500 to 1800) that individuality became a major value and a basic belief in Western society.

One important sign of individuality in the sixteenth century was the explosion of autobiographical writing. The Middle Ages produced very few autobiographies, only about one per century by one estimate (Weintraub, 1978). Late medieval writing about the self (e.g., Petrarch) showed evidence of sustained introspection, the desire for some kind of self-fulfillment, and the need for autonomous self-reliance. But the individual was not valued for what was special or unique; instead, the goal and ideal were still the general image of "the correct Christian life" (Weintraub, 1978, p. 112).

In the sixteenth century writers did however begin to describe their particular characteristics and personal idiosyncracies as if intrinsically important (Auerbach, 1946; Trilling, 1971; Weintraub, 1978). Thus Cardano's autobiography, written shortly before his death in 1576, includes thorough discussions devoted to such topics as his stature and appearance, lists of his friends and enemies, personal dishonors, his dreams, his manner of dress, his gambling habits, his conversational style, his eating habits, his manner of walking, his guardian angels, odd coincidences he had experienced, his itches and body odors, and so forth (Weintraub, 1978, ch. 7). Such lengthy elaboration of personal idiosyncracies marks a substantial departure from the medieval attitude.

Like autobiography, biographical writing became more prevalent during the early modern period. Together, the two developments indicate that writing about human lives became a major focus, and that suggests a heightened interest and valuation of the individual. Whereas the medievals recorded only the legendary, even mythologized, lives of saints and heroes, the postmedieval world developed a biographical interest in the life stories of others, notably literary figures. This began during the sixteenth century and led to radical changes in biography during the seventeenth century. A new attitude emerged—biographies should be factually accurate and should portray the individual (Altick, 1965). Even in the eighteenth century, though, individuality did not mean personality. In biography, portraying the individual meant describing where he lived, whom he married, what he achieved, how he died, and the like. If a biographer did include any personal material, it was all lumped together into a miscellaneous final chapter, often with the biographer's apology for including such trivia (Altick, 1965), pp. 192–193). This changed abruptly in the nineteenth century, but not before then.

The emphasis on individuality increased partly by a change in patterns of family identification. People gradually ceased to feel that their identities and the courses of their lives were essentially or irrevocably determined by their family descent. This "loss of a sense of trusteeship to the lineage" (Stone, 1977, p. 409) helped put the definition of identity on an individual rather than a collective basis. A related development was the decline in the power and importance of kin, that is, all relatives except the immediate family. Loyalty to the state and to one's religious sect replaced loyalty to the extended family matrix (Stone, 1977). The direction of political evolution turned from the medieval organization of localities comprised of families and toward the modern organization of states comprised of individuals. A further sign of the movement toward individuality and institutionalized individualism was the decline of vendetta justice (Stone, 1977). In vendetta justice family members were interchangeable; the vendetta was satisfied by murdering the son or cousin of the offending person. Similarly, a treason or crime by one person might have led to the punishment of the entire family. By the end of the sixteenth century in England, however, vendetta justice was largely replaced with the more modern form of justice which punishes only the offender (Stone, 1977). Thus the prevailing concept and practice of justice switched from identity based on family and lineage to individual identity.

Two final comments about individuality should be made. First, the appearance of the concept of the hidden self is compatible with individualistic thinking. Seeing the individual as having an internal space implies a new view of people as self-contained units. This is associated with a new emphasis on individual awareness. Moreover, these new ideas of internal space and self-awareness are reflected in the evolution of language (Rosenthal, 1984; Whyte, 1960), for powerful thoughts require words to express them. The word "self" first was a reflexive pronoun and an adjective that meant both "own" (as in ownership) and "same." It became a noun late in the Middle Ages, but as such it had a bad connotation: "Oure own self we sal deny, And folow oure lord god al-myghty" (ca. 1400, as quoted by the *Oxford English Dictionary*). By the same token, the word "conscious" is derived from a Latin expression for "to know with," unlike its modern meaning, which refers to knowing by oneself alone. In the sixteenth and seventeenth centuries, these words took on their modern meanings. "Conscious" was first seen in English with its modern meaning in 1620, and the noun "consciousness" in 1678. The connotations of self abruptly changed from bad to good at the end of the Middle Ages, and it suddenly began to appear in numerous compound words. Thus, in 1549 the word "self-praise" appeared, and by the end of that century it had been joined by self-love, self-pride, and self-regard, among others. Self-knowledge, self-preservation, self-made, self-pity, self-interest, and self-confidence appeared in the first part of the seventeenth century. The compound "self-consciousness" appeared in 1690. In German the pattern and dates were approximately the same as in English, and in

French the pattern occurred slightly later. These linguistic developments attest to the rising importance of the individual self and its inner awareness.

Second, the shift toward conceiving of persons as essentially containing inner spaces also meant a shift away from equating the person with his or her social role. In the sixteenth century the person became an individual unity with a separate existence independent of place in society (Trilling, 1971). By the eighteenth century social and institutional roles were understood as something added to the person, not part of the essence of the person (MacIntyre, 1981, p. 56). Thus the early modern period accomplished the conceptual separation of the person from his or her position(s) in the social order.

3. *Privacy.* Today we tend to regard privacy as a fundamental human right and a universal human need. But the medievals apparently got along quite well with minimal privacy; it may not even have occurred to them to want privacy. "In fact, until the end of the seventeenth century, nobody was ever left alone," asserts Ariès (1962). Only in the eighteenth century did rooms begin to have specialized functions, such as being reserved as bedrooms for the house's inhabitants, with the result that guests confined their visits to parlors and dining rooms. Prior to that a visitor could simply walk through any room in the house; at bedtime, portable beds were set up in various rooms, and overnight guests would typically pass through others' bedrooms on the way to their own bedrooms (Ariès, 1962).

In England as well as France, architectural innovations to enhance privacy first appeared in the eighteenth century. In particular, houses began to have corridors. Each room then opened onto a corridor, so that each room could be reached without one's having to pass through several other rooms. Privacy was also enhanced in eighteenth century England by the gradual replacement of "live-in" servants with servants who did not sleep in the same house with their employers (Stone, 1977).

The desire for and cultivation of privacy reflect the attitude that some part of life does not belong to public society. Privacy is conceptually related to the valuation of individuality, and it symbolizes the hidden self. Both privacy and individuality emphasize and strengthen the single self by separating it from the broader network of society. The separation of public and private domains of life (cf. Sennett, 1974) laid the foundation for a view of the self as being in conflict with society, a view which became widely influential during the nineteenth century.

4. *Death.* The importance of death as a source of authentic individuality has been emphasized in this century by existential and phenomenological thinkers (e.g., Camus, 1942; Heidegger, 1927). Heidegger described three ways in which death is a means of individuation. First, death delineates you precisely; what dies is exactly you and nothing else. Second, in an important sense, death accepts no substitutes; it is the one thing you have to do yourself. Third, death marks the end of your "becoming," or the transformation of your potentialities into actualities. The theme of Camus' novel *The Stranger* is that a passionless, apathetic man living an empty life is awakened to authenticity only by the realization of his impending death. In addition, mystical disciplines (e.g., Castaneda, 1972; Blofeld, 1970) have emphasized the usefulness of an awareness of death to lead the individual to a better understanding of self.

If awareness of death is thus intimately linked to self-awareness and individuation, then the history of death can provide evidence about the historical evolution of self-awareness and individuality. The evidence appears to confirm the argument that individuality became important during the early modern period. During this time the narrow focus on death in the final hour was abandoned. Instead, clergymen and others urged people to be aware of death throughout their lives, and it became fashionable to surround oneself with pictures and objects that reminded one of the brevity of human life (Ariès, 1981). As an awareness of death was diffused throughout the life span, the individuating power of this awareness presumably became more effective. This reinforces what we have already observed as an increasing awareness of individuality.

Attitudes toward death during the early modern period also curiously parallel the emphasis on the contrast between appearances and reality. In early modern Europe there was for a century and a half widespread hysterical fear of being buried alive (Ariès, 1981). People were afraid of seeming to die but actually being alive. This fear was reflected not only in proliferation of stories about premature burials but also in the wills and testaments people left. Many people left detailed instructions for ensuring that they were completely dead before burial was to be permitted! These included leaving the putative corpse lying for several days with bells attached to it so that any movement would create a sound, and even cutting the foot with a razor to ascertain whether the body would cry out (Ariès, 1981).

Thus early modern attitudes about death symbolize both the increased concern with individual fate, as a theme to be reflected on throughout life, and the tension between appearances and their underling reality.

5. *Choice of mate.* According to the historian Lawrence Stone (1977), a basic change in family formation and organization occurred during the second half of the early modern period. The absolute power of the father declined and was replaced by the view that there should be positive emotional ties within the family. Possibly as a corollary, it became increasingly necessary to arrange marriages that held the promise of good companionate relationships, which entailed consulting the preferences of the person who was to be married.

The traditional system had decided marriages without necessarily paying any attention to personal preferences. Parents chose spouses for their children on the basis of "economic or social or political consolidation or aggrandizement of the family" (Stone, 1977, p. 182). In other words, one's marriage was determined by and for the family. This system was replaced during the early modern period by a system under which an individual chose his or her own spouse and parents had only veto power. The spread of the new system coincided with an increasing reliance on individual motives in mate selection. People chose spouses who seemed likely to be compatible companions and with whom they shared a friendly affection. (This is still quite different from the modern reliance on passionate "romantic" love as the primary basis for selecting mates. Stone asserts that even into the eighteenth century parents and children agreed that passionate and physical attractions were bad bases for marriage because they were unreliable and temporary mental disturbances.)

Marriage is a major component of identity. Indeed, in view of the limited rights and opportunities available to women in past centuries, the choice of husband was probably the most momentous decision in the formation of many a woman's adult identity. Thus a basic change in the way marriage was decided signifies a major shift in the construction of identity. In seventeenth and eighteenth century England such a change occurred (Stone, 1977) in the shift from an institutional to an individual criterion as decisive in mate selection. Spouses were chosen by personal preferences and expectations for happiness; they were not based on the financial and social interests of the extended family. That shift is symptomatic of a general trend—identity had been determined by the institutions into which one was born, but increasingly it became determined instead by personal acts of choice based on criteria that were supposed to exist inside the person.

6. *Childhood and growth.* If the late Middle Ages had an increased sense of the *continuity* of the single human life, the early modern period contributed an increased awareness of human growth and development. A new view of childhood emerged, and it was put into practice with a vengeance.

The "discovery of childhood" began in the thirteenth century but became widespread only in the sixteenth century according to Ariès (1962). Prior to that, he says, children were not considered a different kind of creature from adults. Ariès is not talking about infancy; an infant cannot be mistaken for an adult. But late childhood, which runs from age six or seven to puberty, is an age at which people can walk and talk and take care of themselves sufficiently. Given that medieval life required relatively little responsible or mature choice from people, there was no need to consider the eight-year-old as qualitatively different from the thirty-year-old. Beginning around the sixteenth century, however, that qualitative difference *was* accepted, and of course that distinction continues to be accepted today. For example, one feature that supposedly distinguishes children from adults is the alleged "innocence" of children, their supposed lack of knowledge about or interest in sexual matters. Ariès (1962) observes that today we consider it wrong and even perhaps harmful to discuss sex or display erotica in front of children, but the medieval mentality had no such concerns. Ariès' arguments have been influential, although some other scholars have disputed his evidence (e.g., Hunt, 1970).

Actually, *two* concepts about late childhood emerged during the sixteenth century (Ariès, 1962). The first regarded children as amusing and beautiful creatures upon whose antics parents (and others) doted fondly. This was soon supplanted by a second attitude, which regarded children as unformed persons who needed guidance, protection, and education in order to become good adults. This second attitude attributed to the child the potentiality to become either good or bad. It followed that adult efforts were necessary to ensure that the child would grow up to be good. In practice this meant that family and school discipline became strict to the point of harshness. Ariès' observations are based in France, but Stone cites similar developments in England. "There can be no doubt . . . that more children were being beaten in the sixteenth and early seventeenth centuries, over a longer age span, than ever before" (Stone, 1977, p. 117).

The important implication of these new attitudes toward childhood is the enhanced awareness of human development, change, and potentiality. That awareness opens the way for some identity problems; the more you think of yourself as changing during life, the harder it is to find aspects of self that remain constant and thus unify the self into an identity. I have listed continuity across time as one of the two defining criteria of identity. That criterion is hard to satisfy if the continuity is that of a process of change rather than that of a stable component.

Moreover, the recognition that a person has various potentialities for future development raises the issue of choice. Once the firm moral and religious bases for making choices are abandoned, identity problems can be concerned with issues of choice. Indeed, the whole functional aspect of individual potentiality became a gigantic problem of choice by the nineteenth century.

But that is getting ahead of the story, because the early modern period did not yet confront such identity problems. The developments of the sixteenth to eighteenth centuries simply fulfilled the necessary conditions for making such problems possible. All six themes I have used in discussing the early modern period contribute to the identity problems faced by individuals in the centuries that followed. Conceiving of an inner or hidden self paved the way for making self-knowledge problematic. The increased concern with human individuality made the issue of individual identity important; it focused attention on it, as did the increased concern with individual death and fate. The separation of social and personal spheres of life required a new complexity in the self, as did requiring the self to contain criteria for making choices (as in selecting a spouse) that defined adult identity. The end of the early modern period did not yet experience identity per se as a problem, but identity was much closer to becoming a problem than it had been three centuries earlier.

Puritanism

Puritanism was an important cultural development of the early modern period, and it had its effect on identity and self-definition. The Puritans were a Protestant sect who based their practices on the teachings of John Calvin. They came to national power in England for two decades in the middle of the seventeenth century. After that they were defeated, and many left the country. Most of those who left came to "New England" (America) where they established Puritan communities which flourished into the nineteenth century. Thus their dominance lasted longer in America than it had in England, and it is reasonable to assume that their effects on the national psyche were stronger and longer lasting in America.

Most historians seem to agree that one main legacy of Puritanism was a vast increase in self-consciousness, and Puritan beliefs provide a good basis for that increase. Calvin emphasized that some people ("the Elect") were predestined to enter heaven, but most would spend eternity in hell. (Puritans believed in hell quite literally.) Because God knows everything, God knows what will happen to you; your eternal fate is already sealed when you are born. Calvin added a corollary that he regarded as minor but that had major consequences—there were ways in which you could tell whether you were among the Elect. But Calvin also said not to spend time wondering whether you were one of the Elect. It is doubtful, however, that the average Puritan could resist wondering whether he or she was to receive eternal salvation or eternal damnation! As a result, Puritans kept a close watch over their thoughts and acts in order to detect any possible signs of impiety or faithlessness that might reveal their eternal fate (Weintraub, 1978).

A second reason for the Puritan enhancement of individual self-consciousness was the highly private nature of their religion. Catholics did not have to face their God alone; they had an elaborate system of priests, nuns, rituals, and saints to mediate with God. The Protestants generally downplayed that structure, and the Puritans especially sought to do away with it. The Puritan thus did face God alone, in the privacy of the individual mind. Thus religious life was greatly *individualized* by Protestant and especially Puritan theology. It is worth adding that these trends favoring privacy and individuality were consistent with major themes of the early modern period.

The Puritan self, then, can be described as having an important hidden part; the acts and thoughts of the self are merely clues about the permanent and unchanging nature of the hidden self. Moreover, the eternal condition of this hidden self was either very good or very bad. A lifetime of human behavior, however, rarely reveals an uninterrupted and coherent pattern of either impeccable virtue or unmitigated depravity. As the average Puritan tried to infer the absolute and eternal condition of his soul from the inconsistent, ambiguous data of his daily life, something became obvious—the temptation to leap to an unwarranted conclusion that one was among the Elect. Puritans thus began to recognize the pervasive possibility of self-deception.

Puritans felt a strong aversion to hypocrisy (Weintraub, 1978). To some extent, this can be seen as an extension of the general concern over insincerity and deceptive self-presentation (e.g., Trilling, 1971) that characterized the early modern period. With the Puritans, however, the concern was not over the deliberate, calculated deception of others but rather focused on the temptation to deceive oneself. You *wanted* to believe yourself predestined to heaven, but were your virtuous acts signs of inner goodness or merely attempts to bolster your pride by creating the appearance of virtue? Did you take pride (a sin) in your good deeds, which would imply hypocrisy rather than true virtue? Yet how could someone deny any feeling of satisfaction from doing good deeds, or any pleasure at the possible implication that he might be one of God's chosen few? And so forth. The endless inner struggles of the Puritans are preserved for us in the unprecedented number of diaries they wrote; these reveal the Puritans' confrontation with the possibility of self-deception.

Concern over self-deception is very different from a concern over the insincerity or deception of others. Once the possibility of self-deception is accepted, self-knowledge can never be certain. For example, when the sixteenth century writer Montaigne described himself at length, he justified the project partly on the basis of its epistemological superiority over other forms of knowledge. For Montaigne, self-knowledge was regarded as precise, comprehensive, and (given some effort) perfect, but no cultural heir of Puritanism could ever again regard self-knowledge so highly. Indeed, the problem of self-deception implied that self-knowledge was *less* reliable than some other forms of knowledge precisely because there was so much incentive to distort and deceive in drawing conclusions about oneself.

Thus far I have discussed an increase in self-consciousness and an increased recognition of self-deception as two Puritan legacies. Two additional features of Puritanism pertaining to child development are relevant to identity—the practice of "breaking the child's will" and the adolescent rebellion or "sins of youth." Both patterns existed before Puritanism, but they were especially prevalent among the Puritans. I shall describe them together because they are related.

Puritan child-rearing techniques were linked to their belief that most (or all) children were innately depraved and in need of stern discipline to be steered toward righteousness (Greven, 1977; I rely on his discussion of "evangelical" Protestants in America). Privately obsessed with their own sinfulness, the Puritans considered the natural self an enemy of virtue. Child-rearing therefore took the form of a program designed to break the child's will. Complete subjugation and obedience of children to parents was stressed. Because of this, Puritans favored an isolated nuclear family over a family having numerous relatives, guests, servants, and so forth. They feared that grandparents or others might indulge the children or otherwise interfere with parental discipline. Children grew up with stern consciences and a well-cultivated readiness to submit to authority (Greven, 1977).

During adolescence many of these young Puritans, especially perhaps the males, went through something of an adolescent rebellion. In this rebellious phase the young person would indulge various lusts and sinful appetites. Presumably this occurred in part because the adolescent gave up on himself as a hopeless sinner once the sexual desires of puberty compounded his already strong sense of badness. The "sins of youth" phase often ended with an abrupt religious experience in which the young person's religious and authoritarian personality reasserted itself. A central part of these religious conversion experiences was that of submission to society's authoritarian patterns and ideals. The young Puritan dutifully returned to the fold and the mold (Greven, 1977).

The significance of these two trends deserves comment. The first, the emphasis on breaking the child's will, goes along with the early modern pattern of strict and sometimes cruel child-rearing. As stated earlier, that broader pattern is indicative of increased sensitivity to human development and potentiality. The second trend, the sins of youth, is an important forerunner of the modern identity crises experienced by adolescents.

One last feature of the psychological legacy of Puritanism, or in this case, of Protestantism in general, deserves mention—the emphasis on work. Ever since Max Weber's classic turn-of-the-century work (*The Protestant Ethic and the Spirit of Capitalism*) it has been common to describe the "Protestant ethic" as a set of values that stresses the importance of hard work as a means (and indication) of spiritual improvement. Work was valued for its own sake and not for extrinsic rewards such as money. If there was an extrinsic motivation in work, it was Calvin's suggestion that success in one's work was another sign that one was among the Elect because God would tend to bless the efforts of his chosen few. Thus a little extra hard work might tip the balance and produce the results which would imply that God was on your side.

The early American concept of success may well have been primarily one of inner success—the triumph of self-discipline, reason, and diligence over one's carefree, lazy, or pleasure-seeking impulses (Lasch, 1978). Ben Franklin's pithy maxims (e.g., "God helps them that help themselves") are often quoted as indicative of the Puritan emphasis on the spiritual significance of work (e.g., Lasch, 1978; Weintraub, 1978). One important consequence of this newly spiritual attitude toward work was a heightened identification with one's career, or one's "calling" as it was then known. The notion that one had a "personal calling" to a particular kind of work meant that one's destiny was intimately connected to one's occupation. The particular job thus gained in importance as an identity component.

Eighteenth Century as Transition

In the next chapter I discuss the Romantic period, which contained sweeping changes in identity and ushered in the new view of the human self that dominated nineteenth century thought. Of course, the Romantic developments did not arise spontaneously. In this brief section I cover the eighteenth century developments that prepared the way for the nineteenth century's concept of human identity.

At the root of the eighteenth century trends was the decline of Christianity, a difficult topic to write about because it is so easily misunderstood. I do not mean that everyone stopped believing in Christianity; there are still many devout Christians today. Nor do I mean that the most influential group or the majority rejected Christian beliefs, because outright repudiation of faith was rare. The institutional Church came under criticism, but that had happened earlier. Perhaps the best way to express the decline of Christianity during the eighteenth century is to say that it lost its grip on the collective mentality and was demoted from a major to a minor role in the daily lives of most people.

It is easy to see that Christianity's position in the collective mind of Western culture has declined. One need only consider how many modern works of literature, music, or art are inspired by a positive attitude toward Christianity and then compare the number with the Renaissance. The decline of Christianity has been a long process, and critical steps in this decline were taken in the eighteenth century.

Certainly there was outspoken criticism of Christianity during the eighteenth century. The best-known critics were perhaps Voltaire in Europe and Paine in America. The intellectual community in general considered itself in "the age of reason" and felt free to use logic to question Christian creed and practices. The typical result was not a wholesale rejection of religion. Rather, as in Deism, the result was a belief that a Supreme Being had set up the universe to run according to natural laws and had then more or less ceased to meddle in it. Psychologically, this attitude meant that God existed but didn't matter very much. For the pursuit of knowledge, scientific observation and philosophical analysis were preferred to biblical exegesis. For practical affairs, hard work and shrewdness were more effective than prayer.

Thus although the core doctrines of Christianity survived the eighteenth century, many consequences and applications of the Christian world view did not. The demise of two Christian ideas during the eighteenth century was related to important trends involving identity—the Christian political philosophy and the Christian view of morality as the essential means for achieving fulfillment.

Politics and social rank. The medieval Christian believed the social hierarchy to be fixed and legitimate. St. Augustine had written that God assigned to each person a definite place in the community. No person should therefore wish to change his or her place in that society. Augustine compared society to a living organism, the point being that social mobility made no more sense than for a finger to wish to become an eye (as Augustine put it). Political historians generally agree that medieval social theory was wholly dominated by Augustine's views (e.g., Nisbet, 1973).

The rise of the middle class during the early modern period gradually eroded this stability. People's beliefs about the proper or ideal relationship of the individual to society also evolved, as indicated in the discussion of privacy. This gradual evolution was minor, however, compared with the major shocks that came late in the eighteenth century. To put those developments in proper perspective, it is necessary to appreciate the fact that revolution for the purpose of political reform was unknown in Western history prior to the eighteenth century (Nisbet, 1973; also see Burke, 1978).

It would be difficult to overestimate the importance of the appearance of political revolution. After centuries of accepting the social order as stable and legitimate, people began to use violent means to change it. Beneath this change in behavior lay a radically altered view of how person and state ought to be related. Citizens of the eighteenth century apparently came to believe contemporary philosophical arguments that insisted the state depended on the consent of the governed or on a social contract by which the state had obligations toward its citizens. The revolutionary manifesto of the American colonists (1776) considered it a "self-evident" truth that "all men are created equal." The colonists' assertion would have been inconceivable to the medieval mentality. The medievals considered it self-evident that men were created unequal. God made aristocrats, and God made serfs and peasants, and if you assumed that God had his reasons for what he had done, then it followed that the aristocrats were innately better people than the peasants. At issue was the legitimacy of the system of social rank, which had for centuries been perhaps the most important basis of identity. Once that system fell apart, a new basis for assigning identity would be needed.

The decline of Christianity was not the only reason that the system of identity based on social rank became problematic during the eighteenth century. Practical and economic trends also put it in jeopardy.

The rise of the middle class, which accelerated throughout the early modern period, gradually upset the stability of the social order. Social rank had traditionally been defined by a combination of wealth, power, lineage, title, and social connections, all of which were intercorrelated. The rise of the middle class disrupted those correlations and created ambiguity among the criteria of social rank. Some middle-class individuals became quite wealthy. At the same time, some aristocratic families (according to the criteria of lineage) became poor.

There is no mystery about how some merchants became rich, but how aristocrats became poor requires some explanation, which has been offered by Stone (1977). A major part of the problem was apparently due to the new practice of allowing young people to choose their spouses. In previous centuries parents had arranged marriages, and these arranged marriages were a main means used by aristocratic families to raise money. Indeed, they were *the* main means for raising money because the late medieval reforms had limited the aristocrats' power to impose endless taxes on those who lived on their estates (see Tuchman, 1978). If an aristocratic family had fallen on financial hard times, the parents were sure to arrange a marriage that brought wealth into the family. Now that parents could no longer enforce marriages based on financial advantage, there was really no reliable way of infusing new wealth into the family; going into trade (business) was still unacceptable for aristocrats. The best they could do was to arrange for their children to meet the children of wealthy families and hope that nature would create an attraction sufficient to lead to a bolstering of the family finances. This was greatly complicated, however, by the fact that much of the wealth was drifting into the hands of the bourgeoisie.

The bourgeoisie knew that, money or no, they ranked below the aristocrats. If they could marry into the aristocracy, however, they felt they would be joining "the quality." So they began to expend considerable effort on learning to pass for "gentlemen" and "ladies." One's only hope of marrying into the aristocracy depended on effective concealment of one's humble origins. Toward the end of the eighteenth century, England had an increasing number of boarding schools that trained young, middle-class girls to pass for upper-class young ladies (Stone, 1977, p. 231).

Thus, during the eighteenth century social rank, which had long been a major component of identity, began to break down. Two main criteria of social rank, wealth and lineage, began to conflict because of a new middle class, and intermarriage between the humbly born rich and the highly born poor created further ambiguity. The legitimacy of the system of social rank was also undermined as people abandoned the medieval Christian view that God intentionally ensured that aristocrats were better people. The newer Calvinist belief that divine favor would be helped by financial success also helped to undermine the older view that a noble birth was a sign of God's favor. This was especially true in America, where the influence of Puritanism helped to prevent the establishment of a monarchy after the Revolution. Thus both in practice and in principle, the age-old system of assigning identity based on social rank deteriorated to the point of crisis.

So far I have considered the first of the two developments related to the decline of Christianity—namely, the abandonment of the medieval Christian political philosophy. The second development concerns the Christian moral scheme. The deterioration of this is linked to two important themes in the history of identity. The first is individuality; the second is the concept of human potentiality.

Morality and potentiality. In the medieval conception of mankind, the individual's goal in life was the achievement of Christian salvation. This meant going to heaven after death. The means for achieving it were twofold: participation in religious ritual, and daily practice of faith and virtue. Over the course of time, prevailing views placed more and more weight on the latter. Individuals were thus provided with a concept of human potential that gave meaning and purpose to life; they were also provided with a reasonably clear-cut set of procedures for fulfilling that potential. When Christianity lost its grip on society, however, this aspect of human identity fell into conceptual chaos.

According to MacIntyre, the traditional view of morality had three elements. The first was "untutored human nature" (1981, p. 52), often understood as being no better (and sometimes much worse) than the natural state of lower animals. The second was the concept of human potential or perfection, "man-as-he-could-be-if-he realized-his-*telos*." The third was the rules and precepts of morality, which enabled the individual to pass from the first state to the second.

The decline of Christianity removed the second element from the system. This removal left morality with only the concept of ordinary, perhaps depraved, human nature plus a set of rules to follow. But why should anyone follow such rules? They had lost their functional purpose. MacIntyre analyzes the philosophical exertions of eighteenth century moral philosophers as attempts to answer the unanswerable question of why anyone should behave in a morally good fashion. Even Kant, widely recognized as the greatest moral philosopher of that century, eventually conceded that a moral system falls apart conceptually without a teleological context. But this was not just a problem for philosophical debate. By the late nineteenth century, society in general was concerned with the issue of whether morality could survive without religious context.

For identity, the important point was that the person ceased to be regarded in *functional* terms. The concept of what a person was ceased to be a functional concept. Instead, "man is thought of as an individual prior to and apart from all roles" (MacIntyre, 1981, p. 56). To understand this it is necessary to recall that the earlier medieval concept of virtue included fulfilling the tasks and duties of one's station in society. The way the medievals understood it, the person was equated with the social roles. According to the medieval view, *in order to fulfill one's potential, one had to do the tasks assigned by society to him or her.*

When that system broke down, however, the person ceased to be equated with the social role. The Christian concept of human potentiality lost its appeal and powerful influence. In the new (eighteenth century) view, persons could be permitted to choose their own forms of potential to try to fulfill, instead of just accepting, what society assigned to them. A person's potentiality thus became an unknown instead of a fixed and known quantity.

In the medieval view, a blacksmith's oldest son had a moral obligation to become a loyal, diligent, and pious blacksmith himself. To reject that duty would jeopardize his chances of going to heaven. In the eighteenth century view, the blacksmith's son did not have a moral obligation to become a blacksmith himself. If he felt such an obligation, it was probably due to family pressure and was not based on the will of God. If he did yield to it and become a blacksmith, that was still not a means toward salvation. Moreover, he remained perhaps a person first and a blacksmith second.

The basic understanding of the individual's relation to society thus changed. People gradually ceased to equate the individual with the individual's place in society, and they ceased to feel that the person was morally obligated to fulfill the role assigned by society. In addition, fulfilling the assigned role was no longer the main means of achieving one's potential.

The decline of Christianity thus removed the Christian context and basis for morality. Morality survived as a set of rules about right and wrong, but morality was no longer the means used for fulfilling one's potentiality. As the concept of human potentiality became problematic with the decline of Christianity, the potentiality aspect of identity became a problem both in terms of technique and goals. This problem is essential to an understanding of the developments of the early nineteenth century—the Romantic concerns with love, passion, and creativity. Moreover, the decline of Christian moral and political views erased the requirement that the individual be content with his lot in society. This strengthened the general movement toward greater individuality because the concept of the person was separated from the concept of his or her place in the social structure.

Summary

In medieval Europe the important components of identity were largely defined for the individual by social structure and institutions. The medieval mentality did not place much emphasis on the uniqueness and worth of each individual. Still, several trends prepared the way for the valuing of individuality. One set of trends included a revision of Christian attitudes and practices to emphasize individual judgment, individual participation in Church ritual, and the use of individual viewpoints to understand the Church's collective themes and truths. Alongside these trends, we can observe a growing literary interest in themes pertaining to the individual perspective and intrapersonal conflict.

The transition from the medieval to the early modern period included two developments important for identity. First, the Protestant Reformation split the ideological consensus among the dominant classes about the correct version of fundamental Christian truth. Instead of being a firm basis for identity, Christian belief became itself somewhat problematic—and became a problem of identity. Second, social mobility made it quite possible to change one's rank in society, at least to some extent. Thus, one major component of identity (social rank) came to depend on individual achievement rather than on passive assignment.

In many areas the early modern period (1500 to 1800) witnessed a dramatic rise in individualistic attitudes and values, preparing the way for the modern problem of identity. New concepts of the hidden or inner self revealed the difficulty of knowing the true selves of others, and this was a step toward understanding that self-knowledge could be problematic. An increased desire for privacy symbolized both the emphasis on individuality and the split between public and private life. Concern over individual fate was reflected in early modern attitudes toward death, in the revision of marriage customs that left choice of spouse up to the potential mates themselves, and in new biographical practices. Finally, a new understanding of human growth and development emerged and was reflected in new attitudes about childhood.

To these larger trends the Puritans contributed an enhanced self-consciousness and an enhanced awareness of individual self-deception. In addition, they gave work a spiritual significance.

With the transition to the Romantic period, we see a great decline in the power and influence of Christianity. Two important consequences of this decline were a serious revision of basic political beliefs and a deterioration of the Christian moral scheme. These two consequences raised several problems for individual identity, including the search for proper models.

4

Identity in Modern History

Since the 1800s, identity has become more problematic for people. And it was the Romantics who first recognized it as such. As people ceased to be content with the Christian version of the goal of life, they began to try out new models of human fulfillment.

Romantic Era

The Romantic era covered the final decade of the eighteenth century and the first half of the nineteenth. Although the claim can't be made that many individuals had personal identity crises during that period, ample evidence indicates that identity did become much more problematic. Two main themes follow rather directly from the two transitional themes emphasized at the end of the previous chapter. First, the eighteenth century's rejection of the Christian models for human potentiality and fulfillment led the Romantics into a passionate search for new, secular models for human fulfillment. Second, the eighteenth century's rejection of the legitimacy of the traditional, stable political and social order led to a troubled recognition of the pervasive conflict between the individual and society. These two themes are substantially interwined.

With the decline of total belief in Christianity, attention shifted from the next life to the present life. People were less willing to defer fulfillment until after death. As a result, the Romantic era sought new images of fulfillment and new techniques for achieving fulfillment in this life. The Romantics became less tolerant of nonfulfillment in life. Life's frustrations and miseries were blamed on current social conditions, and this attitude helped to produce a view of society as oppressive to the individual.

The Romantic era is well known for its experimentation with new ideas of human fulfillment. These focused on work, especially creative expression in art and literature, and subjective passion, especially love. In addition, a vague but important interest in the cultivation of one's inner qualities emerged.

The first of these, creative expression, became a vital model for human fulfillment, giving artists, and especially the Romantic poets, a prestige that far surpassed that of their predecessors. In England writers were worshipped as heroes. Treated as celebrities, poets spawned a new interest in biographical detail; in fact, people began collecting relics of the famous and visiting their birthplaces. More important, literary criticism began to shift its focus from the work to the writer; the works were analyzed with the goal of understanding the person behind them. Debates raged, for example, about what sort of person and personality Shakespeare had been (Altick, 1965). People were fascinated with the personal lives of writers because such people were presumed to live rich inner lives. This fascination is only understandable if one accepts the premise that inner lives held some new interest for the Romantics. This is consistent with my argument that the Romantics were hoping to find in inner life a new image of human potentiality and fulfillment.

The second focus, love, took on a new significance during the Romantic era. In fact, this new concept of love was so important at that time that we have continued to associate amorous passion with that era, as in the term "romantic love." In literature, and presumably in life too, the experience of passionate love came to be considered an essential part of a fulfilled life. The literary emphasis on love was becoming strong by the middle of the eighteenth century, when the novel first appeared. As Leslie Fiedler has noted, "the subject par excellence of the novel is love or, more precisely, seduction and marriage" (Fiedler, 1982, p. 25). Novels connected love to marriage, thus rejecting the adulterous models of courtly love from earlier centuries. The switch may have been the result of a new middle-class audience. Pious bourgeois morality was far less tolerant of adultery as the epitome of love than the decadent hedonism of medieval aristocracy had been.

The general implication is that the Christian model of human potentiality and fulfillment by salvation in heaven was losing its appeal; people wanted a replacement for it. Love was a compelling model for secular fulfillment, so people began to attach more importance to love. It is plausible that an additional reason for love's appeal was that traditional Christian ideology had also assigned a prominent place to love. People could feel that they were not rebelling against all traditional values by giving love the central importance in life.

Fiedler's (1982) analysis of the Romantics is quite consistent with the argument that secular love replaced heavenly salvation as a popular ideal of fulfillment. In fact, Fiedler speaks of the Romantic era's attitude toward love as "the Sentimental Love Religion" and portrays it explicitly as a competitor with the Christian religion. He speaks of Richardson's novel *Clarissa* as "the first sacred book of the bourgeoisie" (p. 65). He even characterizes a common theme of these novels as the achievement of salvation by means of marriage—the male protagonist may be depraved, but he can be redeemed by marriage to a virtuous and virginal woman.

American novels did deviate somewhat from the European pattern. The mentality of great American fiction of that time is that of the preadolescent male—the love of women was either a threat or an impossible ideal, never a realistic goal. Most American writers of the nineteenth century were interested in female characters whose virtue and piety were so formidable that to have a sexual encounter with one of them would have seemed "blasphemous." Certainly, female protagonists in American novels showed very few signs of lust themselves. The American distaste for sex in literature is dramatized by its exclusion. Fiedler maintains that Hawthorne's *The Scarlet Letter* was the only important nineteenth century American novel that had passionate love as a central theme. And he points out that its one great moment of sexual passion is over long before the book even begins (Fiedler, 1982).

The American writers' ambivalence toward love did not signify an indifference toward all emotion. American writers turned toward fear and horror to give emotional intensity to their books. Edgar Allan Poe is perhaps the best-known writer of what has been labeled the genre of "horror pornography." Other writers emphasized adventure in a more general sense. These range from James Fenimore Cooper's mythic Indian stories to Herman Melville's sea stories. This interest in adventure seemingly begs the existential question of fulfillment. The hero is concerned with survival and with accomplishing well-defined tasks; he therefore has little time to worry about personal fulfillment. The implicit message is that the courageous adventurer is not troubled by uncertainties as to who he is or what he is to live for. Literary treatments (however inaccurate) of seafaring or frontier life may have been appealing *because* they envisioned a life untroubled by problems of conceptualizing potentiality and fulfillment.

In addition to creativity and love as two Romantic attempts to assemble a secular model of human fulfillment, a third attempt, the cultivation of one's inner self or latent potentiality, became apparent. This, to some degree, encompasses the other two. The Romantic concept of personal destiny entailed personal fulfillment by means of discovering one's special talents (or other inner qualities) and then laboring to maximize and express them.

The Romantic ideas about personal destiny apply to the *potentiality* aspect of identity, whereas the early modern period had dealt with the *interpersonal* aspect. But the approaches are similar. The early modern period developed the belief in the hidden self, which meant that the intentions and motives of a person had to be discovered. The Romantics made personal potentiality something that also had to be discovered, but discovered in a different way. Poetry, for example, had previously been regarded as arising from divine inspiration, but the Romantics began to think of poetry as deriving from the buried treasures within the self of the poet.

More profoundly, the early modern period had come around to the belief that the interpersonal traits and habits of each person were unique. The Romantics extended this by believing that the potentiality of each person was also unique. This change elevates the status of individuality from a matter of idiosyncracy to a matter of destiny. To appreciate the change, it is useful to examine the different ideas of the eighteenth versus the nineteenth centuries about what human nature might be like if people were never exposed to harmful or stifling influences (Simmel, 1950). In the eighteenth century the basic assumption was that ideal development would reveal human nature to be a constant. In other words, everyone would turn out pretty much the same if permitted to grow up under optimal conditions. People would all be kind, generous, honest, true, loyal, friendly, and so forth. The nineteenth century, however, rejected the idea that everyone would be the same, espousing instead the belief that optimal conditions for development would produce unique individuals (Simmel, 1950).

The Romantic belief that each person's actual character *and* innate potentiality were both unique, and the placing of value on that uniqueness, constituted the full measure of individuality (Weintraub, 1978). These beliefs articulated secular ideals that helped to fill the gap created when society turned away from Christianity's model for living. But these idealistic values were accompanied by a rather pedestrian trend, the growing interest in personality. As individuality evolved from a fascination to a goal, people began to use personality as a means of achieving uniqueness, and the importance of personality escalated.

For exceptional individuals such as Goethe or Byron, the cultivation of individuality might well have consisted of fulfilling one's creative potentiality or artistic destiny. For the ordinary person without such talents, however, the cultivation of individuality presented a problem. The solution was to cultivate personality. Personality is something that one can shape and control, and the large variety of possible trait configurations makes it relatively easy to achieve a semblance of uniqueness. Thus, personality could be regarded as the untalented or lazy person's route to individuality.

Some evidence provides indirect support for the belief in personality as a short-cut to uniqueness. In the 1970s a national survey asked Americans "What are some of the ways in which you're different from other people?" The overwhelming majority of answers fell into the "personality" category, although the most common alternatives (references to social roles, physical attributes, moral and religious attributes, and miscellaneous virtues) are equally plausible sources of differentiation. The volume of personality responses was more than triple the volume of all other categories combined (Veroff, Douvan & Kulka, 1981). To be sure, caution is needed in generalizing from twentieth century psychological research to the minds of nineteenth-century persons. Still, these results do emphasize the effectiveness of personality as something that makes one different from others. The second largest category of responses, morality, is also apparently a viable basis for differentiation but is of course difficult to achieve. To be more moral than your neighbors requires considerable self-discipline and exertion, whereas a personality different from those of your neighbors is relatively easy to attain. Thus, as people began to want to be different from each other, the growth of personality as a major component of identity was probably inevitable.

Whether or not interest in personality increased as a direct result of the desire for individual uniqueness, the point is still that personality came to be taken more seriously as a vital and central feature of each person's identity. One sign of this development during the Romantic era was the rapid increase in the quantity of personal material included in biographies (Altick, 1965). Instead of just an inspirational, objective account of some famous person, biographers sought to give the reader an understanding of what the individual was like, much as a personal acquaintance might have known him or her. Another sign of the increasingly central role of personality was seen in clothing. Clothing began to be understood as an expression of the personality of the wearer, extending even to the inner traits of the hidden self (Sennett, 1974). It is especially noteworthy that people believed clothes expressed personality, because until the eighteenth century clothes had mainly expressed social rank (Sennett, 1974). The change in the meaning of garb lends support to the hypothesis that personality gradually replaced social rank as the most important component of identity.

Thus far, I have discussed the Romantic era's search for secular models of fulfillment. The desire for fulfillment in this life instead of in the life after death contributed to a dissatisfaction with the then present social conditions. The theme of the individual versus society dominated nineteenth century literature, and the political developments of that century also indicate a broad awareness of that conflict.

The early Romantic literary heroes were full of great passions, high ideals, and unfulfilled longings. They each expressed some version of human fulfillment on earth. Society, however, made it remote and unattainable. Thus, one theme of the American novelist Nathaniel Hawthorne has been summarized as follows: "The social conditions deny men the chance to be fully men and women the chance to be fully women" (Anderson, 1971, p. 85). Society, in the Romantic view, ought to have helped people reach fulfillment; instead, it thwarted them. The Romantics keenly felt the discrepancy between social ideals and society in practice. In Romantic writing the individual lives by society's values and rules but comes to grief as a result of doing so.

Yet instead of turning inward, rejecting society, or cultivating existential values, the Romantic protagonists struggled along and suffered within the existing social structure. Life meant life-in-society; there were no alternatives. When the struggle became too much, the Romantic hero usually just died, as in the celebrated suicide of Goethe's young Werther.

But the Romantic unwillingness to reject society did not signify a general attitude of submissiveness toward society. On the contrary, Romantic writing emphasized the assertion of the individual self against society as never before. One literary critic's list of "key concepts" of nineteenth century American fiction includes "self-reliance, non-conformity, the rejection of the past, the denial of the imperatives of society . . . radical individualism" (Pütz, 1979, p. 33). Another critic summarizes the Romantic shift in attitude by saying that the Romantic protagonist approached life by asking, "What world am I to possess?" instead of, as previously, "What role shall I be given?" (Anderson, 1971, p. 4). In both cases, however, the individual needed society to provide him or her with an identity. The central issue for self-definition was acceptance of one's role in society. If the identity that society offered you was unacceptable, you battled to get society to offer you something better.

Tied in with this struggle for identity was the Romantic value placed on freedom. In freedom one can see the combination of individual assertion and individual dependence on society. If society prevents you from doing what you know is right, or from being virtuous, or from fulfilling your destiny, you do not acquiesce—you struggle to win the freedom to be yourself.

The political history of the Romantic period also exhibits these same themes of freedom, individual dependence on society, assertion of the individual, and discontent with existing social conditions evident in Romantic literature. Rousseau's philosophy, which regarded human beings as innately good but made bad by current social conditions, expressed the dominant political beliefs of the era. France, England, and America all experienced major political reforms that reflected the Romantic ideals, and in the 1840s there were revolutionary uprisings throughout Europe.

While some sought to overthrow the existing governments and social establishments, others sought to create new ones. The nineteenth century saw an unprecedented number of Utopian theories and Utopian experiments. People made substantial personal and financial commitments to these experimental communities which, unfortunately, usually fell short of their idealistic expectations.

Both the Utopian experiments and the political revolutionary movements were based on the belief that contemporary society thwarted individuals, whereas a better society could help individuals to reach fulfillment. Few Romantics reached the conclusion that society was *inevitably* oppressive. All that was needed was the right formula and the means to implement it. Human life individually within society would then be fulfilling. And the Romantics sincerely expected that society would be perfected within a couple decades, if not sooner. Each disappointment, each Utopian failure, was interpreted merely as a sign that the formula had been wrong. It was not until the second half of the nineteenth century that these accumulated disappointments produced more radical and cynical solutions.

Victorian Era

The Victorian era covers an approximate period, from about 1830 to 1900. In America and Western Europe this period was marked by a gradual but decisive shift of the population to the cities. One cause of this urbanization was the growth of industry, which provided jobs that meant leaving a rural life. For the history of identity, the most obvious, and perhaps most important, theme of the Victorian era was the coming to grips with the new relationship between the individual and society that resulted from an urban, industrial life. Other important themes include a further crisis regarding individual self-knowledge, and a recognition of critical breakdowns in consensual, traditional values and beliefs.

A gradual retreat from the Romantic optimism about the perfecting of society can be discerned in certain Victorian attitudes. Outright pessimism about society did not become predominant until the beginning of the twentieth century, for the Victorians generally preserved the belief that an ideal society would eventually be created. But the belief that this society would be in operation within a couple of decades was gradually dropped. The Victorians continued to search for the formula for a perfect society, and they continued to establish experimental Utopias. Their innovations increasingly suggested that conflict between the individual and society was chronic and deeply rooted, that it was not just the existing social arrangements that are imperfect, but many alternative ones as well, and that Utopian hopes and theories had little practical value in the here and now because it might be centuries before the perfect society was established.

Four developments in the Victorian period suggest this loss of faith in the imminent perfectability of society. First, transcendental philosophy advocated the seeking of individual fulfillment outside of social relations. Second, the increasing concern with specific progressive reforms within society implied that society would best be perfected by slow and gradual improvements rather than by sweeping reorganization. Third, the spread of anarchism indicated the growing suspicion that all possible governments were inevitably bad. And fourth, in everyday life people increasingly sought happiness in home and family, which was seen as a refuge from society rather than as an integral part of society.

Transcendentalism. Toward mid-century, transcendentalism emerged as an important movement in American letters. As their name implies, the transcendentalists sought their fulfillment not in everyday social life but in private experience that carried them beyond the oppressive and mundane conditions of society. They kept the Romantic values of personal virtue, resourcefulness, and desire for freedom, but they added a willingness to go it alone. If Emerson was the movement's most respected and articulate thinker and Whitman its most extreme embodiment, Thoreau fulfilled its archetypal ideal most vividly. By cultivating his creativity and finding understanding while living alone in a woodland setting, he seemed to prove that the way to personal fulfillment led away from life in society.

Although the context of transcendentalism was still (as for the early Romantics) the conflict between the individual and society, the transcendentalist solution was more drastic than the Romantic. The Romantic heroes struggled to win from society the freedom to be themselves within society; the transcendentalists preferred to turn their backs on society. Concepts such as rugged individualism took on added importance within the context of the transcendentalist view because the individual was viewed as ultimately alone in the attempt to fulfill his or her potentiality.

During the Romantic era the prevailing conception of individual fulfillment transferred the emphasis from the next world to this one; as a result, there emerged the problem of finding models and techniques for fulfillment. Emerson's project of self-creation reflected a popular, "realistic" solution—pay your dues to society but concentrate on private activities as your means to fulfillment. Whitman expressed and embodied a more extreme view than Emerson, for Whitman's private vision was so intense that it could transform his experiences in society. Thus, his personal failures were actually private triumphs because of what he made of them (Anderson, 1971, p. 93). Obviously, one's personal vision has to be quite powerful to achieve this, and Whitman's approach was not popular with his contemporaries. (Whitman may also have been too sensual for his Victorian contemporaries.) One way of understanding the contrast between the era's acclaim of Emerson and its rejection of Whitman was that people wanted only limited and occasional transcendence. They seemed content to separate public life and private fulfillment, the implication being that life in society was tolerable, although not satisfying.

Although transcendentalism was not as widely influential a literary movement as, for example, Romanticism, transcendentalism is still an important stage for the unfolding of identity. The attitudes of transcendentalists, in their attempt to seek fulfillment in private life, away from society at large, were simply clearer or stronger formulations of attitudes that were indeed quite widespread. The retreat from public into private life was the main feature of the nineteenth century's attitude toward personal fulfillment.

Progressive reform. The Victorian period was a time of social-reform movements. At the risk of oversimplification, one can dramatize the Victorian pattern by contrasting it with the preceding Romantic pattern, which discovered the conflict between individual and society. For the Romantics the practical consequences of that discovery were to struggle individually for the freedom to be oneself or to struggle collectively for the sweeping reorganization of society. The Victorians learned to struggle collectively for the reform of specific faults within the existing society. Thus, their approach was to tackle one problem at a time rather than everything at once. Feminism, the abolition of slavery, the legal regulation of child labor, social democratic reform of the political system, regulation of currency, the regulation and then suppression of prostitution, the standardization and universalization of schooling, temperance and prohibition movements, and even the missionary work to Christianize the foreign heathens—all embodied the Victorian spirit of working within society for specific improvements. They may have believed in the eventual perfection of society, but they did not believe this to be imminent. Since there were many specific areas for improvement, their attitude was *let's get started.*

Anarchism. During the second half of the nineteenth century, anarchism emerged as an important political force in Europe and, perhaps to a lesser extent, in America. One sign of its seriousness was the frequency with which anarchists attempted to assassinate kings and presidents. Thus, in 1878 alone, the German emperor and the Spanish and Italian kings all experienced anarchist assassination attempts, and during the two decades leading up to World War I anarchists murdered six heads of state, including two Spanish premiers and one American president (Tuchman, 1962, pp. 72–82).

Anarchists believed, not unreasonably, that the rich exploited the poor by the means of private property and with the support of laws and governments. Their solution was to abolish private property and government, which would lead to a society in which individuals would work together voluntarily for the common good. Although terrorism and murder may seem peculiar means for implementing such humanitarian ends, typically such "propaganda of the deed" were not the acts of the intellectual anarchist societies but were rather the work of desperate or alienated individuals who read what the societies wrote (Tuchman, 1962).

At first glance it would seem that anarchism and liberal progressivism are opposites. One wants to do away with all states and governments, whereas the other wants to effect specific improvements in the state and government. But both movements reflect the belief that conflict between the individual and the existing society is chronic, harmful, and yet ultimately curable—either by a long regimen of gradual improvement or by the far more radical surgery of anarchy.

Home and family. The Victorians gradually recognized, then, that the conflict between the individual and society was *not* about to be fully resolved in the imminent future. As a result, individuals had to find ways to cope with that conflict in their own lives. Evidence indicates that the most common Victorian solution was to elevate the importance of private life to a refuge from society and as a locus of personal happiness and fulfillment. Middle-class men began to think of home as their castle. In a sense, this solution was a popularized version of transcendentalism: Live in public society insofar as is necessary, but seek fulfillment in your private life.

The importance of private life, at home in the family, increased steadily throughout the nineteenth century. By the end of the Victorian era, it far outweighed the value placed on public life and public affairs. A typical late Victorian sentiment was expressed by d'Avenel: "The public life of a people is a very small thing compared to its private life" (quoted by Stone, 1977). Or, in the words of H. S. Canby, "In the American nineties generally, home was the most impressive experience in life" (quoted by Fass, 1977). A century earlier such sentiments would have been deemed inappropriate if not outrageous.

A provocative account of the shift in emphasis from public to private life advanced by Sennett (1974) runs as follows. The eighteenth century accepted the separation of public and private life but placed greater value on the former. Public life in society was linked to the "higher" values of civilization and culture; private life was linked to nature. (Nature signified the "lower" functions of eating, sleeping, procreating, and so forth.) The nineteenth century gradually reversed the two domains, placing greater value on private life.

One set of changes cited by Sennett in support of his thesis concerns public behavior. In the eighteenth century it was considered proper for people to speak to strangers, without embarrassment, on the street or in public coffee houses. Indeed, in those coffee houses "distinctions of rank were temporarily suspended; anyone sitting in the coffee houses had a right to talk to anyone else"(Sennett, 1974, p. 81). In the nineteenth century, however, behavior in public took the form of "the public silence." Strangers no longer spoke to each other. In public places such as the coffee houses, the new attitude was that people had a right to sit by themselves without talking to anyone. When it did become necessary to speak to a stranger, it was usual to apologize first, such as by begging the stranger's pardon. In the theatres people sat quietly in the dark and watched the performance instead of talking with neighbors and hollering at the actors as eighteenth century audiences had done. Thus, the private realm usurped many of the functions of human interaction and companionship that had formerly belonged in the public realm. For conversation, for example, you stayed at home with your intimates rather than going out to encounter strangers.

One important long-term consequence of the split between public and private domains is the "fragmentation of consciousness" (Brittan, 1977). The modern way of life often divides itself between work, in the public domain, and personal and emotional life, which is centered in private life. The family thus loses its importance in the broader society but becomes an important, self-contained sphere of life (Burgess & Locke, 1945; Fass, 1977).

The various causes of the nineteenth century shift toward an emphasis on private life contribute to a complex and not fully understood process. However, the important point is that Victorian men and women came to perceive human society at large as threatening, oppressive, and unsatisfying. "The feeling of isolation and loneliness, so characteristic of modern man, first appeared in the nineteenth century" (Houghton, 1957, p. 77). As a result, people sought personal fulfillment in private life, particularly at home in the family.

Self-knowledge. In addition to the conflict between the individual and society, the Victorians were beset with problems about self-knowledge. In an important sense, the Victorians were the cultural heirs of the Puritans. The Puritans realized that you could and would deceive yourself. The Victorians carried this one logical step further. If you were motivated to deceive yourself, then other people might potentially know you better than you knew yourself. The belief that others can know you better than you know yourself can be quite frightening.

Whenever you talk to someone it is possible that that person can discern some awful truth about you. Or there might be some immoral trait that you secretly know you have but do not realize that your behavior is revealing.

The immediate causes of the Victorian preoccupation with involuntary disclosures of inner traits and may have lain in social mobility and the bourgeoisie's desire to pass for aristocrats. The real aristocrats resisted and resented such pretensions, and they began to emphasize increasingly subtle and changing signals as indicators of membership in the upper class. Nuances of table manners and clothing, for example, might betray the bourgeois pretender. Circumstance accustomed people to the idea that their behavior might unwittingly reveal their true selves. Once that idea was established, and as personality began to grow in importance as a major component of identity, people began to think that their innermost thoughts and desires were unwittingly revealed. A woman might worry that if she left too few or too many buttons undone at the top of her dress she would be taken for a prostitute or immoral woman. The problem was never knowing the proper "safe" number of buttons. Some Victorians became scrupulous followers of fashion and etiquette trends. Others became fastidious about behaving according to the proper rules in every situation so that their behavior would never reflect personal choice but would always conform to general norms. Others simply became afraid to go out in public. It was not unknown for a Victorian lady to remain at home as much as possible, going out only when veiled and cloaked and riding only in enclosed carriages. Indeed, by the middle of the nineteenth century, urban clothing styles were generally as inexpressive, drab, uniform, and generally concealing as possible(Sennett, 1974). For the most part, everyone wore black from head to foot!

This Victorian fascination with involuntary disclosure of personal traits, and with learning to "read" the "unconscious" expressions of others, is evident in their literature. Doyle's popular detective Sherlock Holmes expressed a typical Victorian attitude:

> You did not know where to look and so you missed all that was important. I can never bring you to realize the importance of sleeves,

the suggestiveness of thumbnails, or the great issues that may hang from
a boot-lace. (quoted also by Sennett, 1974)

Indeed, Holmes's popularity was due in large part to his apparent
mastery of the art of noticing and interpreting nuances of behavior
and appearance. Popular novels were not the only forms that reflected this belief and concern. Freud's development of psychoanalytic theory was probably facilitated by the Victorian interest in
unconscious signals and messages. Freud's own words express the
same belief:

> He that has eyes to see and ears to hear may convince himself that no
> mortal can keep a secret. If his lips are silent, he chatters with finger-
> tips; betrayal oozes from every pore. . . . (Freud, 1905)

Indeed, the Victorian difficulty with self-knowledge became a meth-
odological rule for Freud. He established the principle that no one
(except perhaps Freud himself) could expect to see past his or her
own repressions without external aid. Because of biases that inevitably distort self-knowledge, even an expert psychoanalyst must consult
another analyst in order to pursue self-knowledge, the theory being
that you can't psychoanalyze yourself.

Thus, the problems of self-knowledge were compounded during
the Victorian era. The difficulties of self-knowledge spilled over from
the public sphere into the interpersonal realm and thus complicated all
of social life. The inner self came to be understood as so vast and so
well hidden that some Victorians began to think scientific methods of
study would be necessary even to achieve incomplete self-knowledge.

Repression may have become especially noticeable during the Victorian era because people did actually repress more than in other eras,
although it is difficult to find reliable historical data about how
repressed any people were. One indicator of greater Victorian repression is the lack of openness and license in sexual matters in the
nineteenth century, which is not true of either the eighteenth or the
twentieth centuries (Stone, 1977), to the extent that the word "Victorian" is used as a synonym for sexual prudery. Moreover, personal
moral standards were impossibly high during the Victorian period,
leading to difficult inner gymnastics one of which Houghton dubs

"sincere insincerity" (Houghton, 1957). An example of sincere insincerity might be the Victorian who privately disbelieved in Christianity but felt that Christian beliefs were good for society in general. Therefore, he or she would not want to help undermine those beliefs by refusing to attend church or publicly voicing doubts. As a result, he or she might pretend to believe in it despite private disbelief. What separates "sincere insincerity" from mere hypocrisy is the person's honest wish to believe (Houghton, 1957). Is this self-deception? Either way, a society full of such individuals is ripe for the systematic discovery of repression!

Values. The Victorians also recognized growing difficulties regarding basic values and beliefs. Christianity had begun to lose its grip on society during the early modern period, and by the Victorian era widespread recognition of the decline of Christian belief was a general cause for concern. Particularly troublesome was the fear that people would cease to be moral or virtuous if Christianity should fail because the Christian creed was perceived as the source of moral standards. This is reflected in the fact that a popular topic for intellectual debate was whether morality could survive without religion (Meyer, 1976).

The social weakening of religion, and thus of morality, was especially upsetting to the Victorians because they were not prepared to accept the idea that such beliefs and values are relative. For the most part they thought such things must be universally, objectively, and impeccably true (Howe, 1976; Houghton, 1957). The missionary work and the efforts to reform the poor must be understood in that light—the Victorians thought they were correct and were therefore doing others a favor by imposing their beliefs on them. As doubt undermined the old certainties, society once and for all lost its ideological consensus. One important consequence of that loss was a change in the nature of private doubts. If everyone in a society believed in Christianity, and one person had difficulty in accepting some particular piece of Christian dogma, then his doubt would feel like a failure to appreciate "the facts." The implication is that the person is not fully adjusted to reality. Given this view, reality is objective, and the person is somehow wrong. On the other hand, if some members of the society believe in Christianity and others do not, then one's doubts take on an entirely different aspect. It becomes viable for an individual to believe *or to disbelieve* in Christianity, and which of those one opts for depends on the result of some inner decision. Put another way, identity crises are only possible in a truly pluralistic society—one without consensual belief in the objective truth of a particular set of values, morals, or religious articles. Victorian society found itself reaching that state, and the Victorians were none too pleased about it.

The important point is that the third functional aspect of identity (the structure of values and priorities) became problematic during the Victorian era. Values, beliefs, and priorities became a matter of personal choice. The inner self inherited the awkward responsibility of deciding what to believe in and what values and ideals to espouse.

The Twentieth Century

It is no secret that difficulties with self-definition have become a familiar concern in twentieth century America. Erik Erikson (1968) claims he coined the term "identity crisis" in the early 1940s to refer to a specific, severe form of psychopathology. The term quickly became used to refer to the certain formative struggles, especially those of adolescents, and such crises have even come to be considered an appropriate and normative part of development. The rapid and enduring popularity of the phrase "identity crisis" suggests that a widespread phenomenon already existed; it only needed to be named. In the 1950s scholars began to offer various interpretations of the general difficulty of self-definition (e.g., May, 1953; Wheelis, 1958). A number of recent trends and developments can be understood as attempts to solve these problems of identity. It is clear that by the middle of the twentieth century problems in self-definition had become widely familiar.

The twentieth century witnessed new economic and social arrangements which confronted the individual with a life quite different from that of rural ancestors, as well as a vulnerability to economic depressions that had a variety of effects on individual self-definition. A literary emphasis on alienation suggested that the new economic and social conditions were not fully satisfactory, as did the extensive writing on social criticism. Around mid-century, however, the emphasis on alienation diminished and was replaced by a new attitude of learning to accommodate to life in mass society, while at the same time incorporating the personal struggle for identity. There are contradictory indications about the fate of individuality per se in the twentieth century—we place increasing value on the individual, yet individuality may be increasingly elusive in a mass society. Existential themes, including authenticity, reflect the twentieth century's concern with personal choice and the nature of the self. Yet death, a major existential theme, has been systematically excluded from most of twentieth century life.

Socioeconomic life. The average American was rural in 1800 but urban in 1900. The modal job in the twentieth century is not work on a farm but work in an institution, and increasingly in a bureaucratic institution such as a large corporation. Probably *the* major sociological change introducing the twentieth century was *economic interdependence* far beyond past circumstances. Each person became far more dependent on the system and network of exchange of goods than had been the case in past centuries.

One important consequence of economic interdependence is vulnerability to economic depression. Depressions were nothing new, of course, but their effects were far more dramatic in the urban, industrial society of the twentieth century than they had been in the rural societies of previous centuries. The Panic of 1837 was a major economic catastrophe and caused much hardship, but the agricultural makeup of America enabled the country to get through it quite comfortably, unlike the Great Depression of the 1930s. For one thing, a wholly or nearly self-sufficient farm enables the family to survive regardless of what happens to the money system and the network of exchange of goods. For another thing, in a nation of farmers, if an industrial laborer loses a city job he or she can "return" to the farm to live and work with parents or other relatives. Although this is what happened in 1837, it was not generally feasible by 1930 because the farm population had become too small to absorb the massive urban employment.

Thus, economic disasters of the twentieth century dramatized the helplessness of the indivdual and the consequent utter dependence on society. The traditional ideals of rugged individualism and self-sufficient autonomy became quite literally obsolete. It no longer made sense to think of society as a loose collection of individuals who happened to have some common interests; instead, society was like a machine, with the individual cog useless and worthless except when functioning as part of the whole.

It is not surprising that the individualistic mentality rebelled at being asked to make such an adjustment. In comparison with individualistic ideals, it was degrading to see oneself as weak and dependent, as a replaceable part of a large system that did not seem to care about the individual. Moreover, the catastrophes of depression, war, and labor disputes helped to undermine the nineteenth century optimism about the long-range context of social progress.

The specific psychological consequences of the Great Depression exerted a lasting influence on the mentalities of twentieth century citizens. A central feature of the experience of the Depression, except for those who were somehow untouched by it, was *status inconsistency* (Elder, 1974). Social status in the twentieth century is a blend of education, occupation, and income. The Depression disrupted these relationships. For example, a person might have found himself forced to take a job "beneath him" (i.e., incongruent with his level of education). Status inconsistency bred self-consciousness, as a lack of money forced difficult choices upon individuals. For example, some families elected to have the house painted instead of having good food at family dinners because everyone saw your house but no one knew what you ate (Elder, 1974, p. 53). This self-consciousness deriving from status inconsistency affected the children of these families too, as in the example of high school girls who were ashamed of the lack or inadequate fashionability of their dresses. The self-conscious conformity of the adults of the 1950s can be traced at least in part to their experiences as Depression children.

Researchers predicted that family deprivation during the Depression would cause the children to compensate by developing rich fantasy lives. They found the opposite results—the greater the deprivation, the less the fantasy life in children (Elder, 1974). Deprivation seems to have produced young people who were unimaginative but were very goal-oriented and ambitious in practical ways. Their ambitions for practical success emphasized security over dramatic gain, however. To the 1950s adult the chance for a secure job and suburban placidity probably seemed like a wonderful life in comparison to the turmoil and horror of Depression and war, with which they had lived all their lives.

Other effects of Depression-era deprivation should be mentioned. Unemployed fathers (and fathers whose jobs were "beneath" their qualifications) lost respect within the family. The power of the mother in the family increased with family deprivation (Elder, 1974), and the degree of the father's active involvement in family affairs declined; any conflicts inevitably brought up recriminations about his "failure" and his inadequacies. This kind of family background has been associated with subsequent alienation in the children (Keniston, 1968).

Another important consequence of a depression is found in individuals' careers. Thernstrom's (1973) data suggest that one's career is at a "critical" point when one has started work but has not yet "settled into a stable career pattern" (p. 70). At this point one's upward occupational mobility is critically vulnerable. Men who were at this career stage when a depression struck were never able to recover their chances to climb the occupational and social ladder. Presumably, the end of the particular depression meant renewed opportunities for advancement, but these opportunities went to the younger men. In short, an upward move had to be made early in a career. If your career had reached this point during a depression, you missed your chance. The depression's effect on social mobility was temporary for society but permanent for the individual.

Thus, the depressions of the 1890s and 1930s both produced a generation of men who in an important sense were cheated out of the American dream of upward social mobility. Members of these generations had some right to feel that society had robbed them of their expectations. It is no wonder that alienation spread during these times because all the ingredients—frustration, helplessness, and meaninglessness—were part of the lives of these men. Their expectations and hopes were frustrated by social conditions beyond their control, and their suffering and loss had no meaning or value either for themselves or for society.

Depressions were not the only new economic reality to influence American life in the twentieth century. A basic and far-reaching economic change occurred at the end of the last century (Potter, 1954). Before then, the American economy (like that of the rest of the world) was one of scarcity. The demand for goods generally exceeded the supply, and the limiting factor was production. Given America's then apparently unlimited resources, the only restriction on how much was sold was how much was produced. However, toward the end of the nineteenth century the great advances in manufacturing technology produced a new situation—manufacturers could produce more than people needed. At this point the limiting factor became consumer demand. The main restriction on how much you could sell was now how much other people wanted to buy.

The result of this new circumstance was the rapid growth of advertising, an institution whose purpose is to stimulate demand for products. Advertising is psychologically intrusive; it aims to *make people want* a particular product. Advertising must be considered as one of the most influential institutions of twentieth century America. By mid-century the country was spending more on advertising than on education or religion (Potter, 1954, p. 178). Unlike other major social institutions like education and religion, advertising has a nearly complete "lack of institutional responsibility"—that is, it has "no motivation to seek the improvement of the individual or to impart qualities of social usefulness" (Potter, 1954, p. 177; also see Henry, 1963). Thus advertising is an enormously powerful institution that is largely indifferent to its effects on humanity and society, except for its concern to get people to buy more things.

The extent of advertising's power is suggested by the argument that advertising conquered the Protestant ethic in America. Traditional middle-class values emphasizing "thrift, saving, frugality, and fear of indebtedness" (Larkin, 1979, p. 35) would tend to keep consumption low. The Protestant ethic celebrated earning and saving, not spending and enjoying. But in the twentieth century, increased consumption was necessary for economic growth. Larkin credits or blames advertising with overthrowing the Protestant ethic mentality and replacing it with consumer-oriented values.

Two relationships between advertising and identity can be proposed. Advertising seems to promote conformity because it urges all persons to buy mass-produced goods. "Fads" are the extreme form of this. Fads first became a major phenomenon during the 1920s (Fass, 1977, p. 227); and, then as now, they were "youth-centered and youth oriented." The fads spread from college-age youth to imitative high school students and to adults as well (Fass, 1977, p. 234). Thus, the age of identity crisis and identity formation took on the property of periodic episodes of group conformity in material consumption.

A second relationship between advertising and identity is seen in the growing exploitation of desirable identities. Farberman and others have described how advertisers have marketed their products less and less on the basis of the product's merits and more and more by associating a "dream identity" with the possession of a given product. The suggestion is that the possession of a particular brand of car or cigarette will furnish you with the identity of a successful, attractive, worthy person. The message is clear—accumulating things is an effective means of achieving identity and actualizing one's potential.

Advertising is only a part of the general expansion of the mass media during the twentieth century. Television, movies, radios, magazines, and newspapers are unavoidable—only an extremely rare individual would go for three consecutive days without encountering any of these. Television is perhaps the most powerful and universal medium because Americans regard televisions as a necessity (even the poor own them) and when not working spend more time watching them than doing anything else.

At one level, mass media confront the modern citizen with a complex variety of stimuli. However, at another level, their effect is increased uniformity, not diversity. The issue is the homogenization of experience. The millions who watch a given televison show are exposed to identical experiences. True, they might react differently to it, but the nature of television minimizes individual differences of response because it enforces passivity. If the viewer starts to react to something on television, he or she misses what happens next. "You've got to be silent to be spoken to" (Sennett, 1974, p. 283).

Mass media may thus reduce the chance of individuality. They preempt an individualized stream of thought. What goes on in your mind when you watch a particular television show is probably close to what goes on in the minds of the millions of other viewers. Advertising is merely the most extreme form of this invasion of the privacy of the mind. Advertising invades the mind in order to create new motivations, not just to entertain or inform. Advertising is an intrusive and impersonal form of tampering with the inner self. A successful advertisement will instill an identical desire (for a certain product) within the psyches of millions of persons.

Alienation. With the beginning of the twentieth century, Romantic attitudes and transcendentalist ideals abruptly vanished from serious literature. The idea of the self finding ultimate fulfillment alone but in peaceful coexistence with society was abandoned. Alienation became perhaps *the* major theme in literature (Klein, 1964; Putz, 1979). In fifty years, as it were, the modern individual moved from Thoreau's cottage to Kafka's castle.

Alienation is the combined feelings of powerlessness, meaninglessness, and frustration. To describe the protagonist of early twentieth century literature as alienated, then, is to say that he or she is unable to find fulfillment in the range of options available within society, is unable to bring about a change in his or her condition or in social conditions generally, and cannot be consoled for these failures with a sense of personal worth and dignity or value in the struggle itself.

Why was the theme of alienation so marked in the early decades of the twentieth century? One set of causes stems from the effects of the economic depressions. These were part of a broader context, however, which was the demise of nineteenth century optimism about society. On the one hand, the perfectability of society, which had seemed imminent a century before, seemed increasingly remote. It became apparent that some things were getting worse, not better, and Americans began to look back on the putative "Good Old Days" (e.g., Kett, 1977). At the same time, however, the possibility of seeking fulfillment alone, away from society, was impractical because of city life and economic interdependence. It must have felt as if society permitted no escape. It is important to recall, too, that at the turn of the century society's ubiquitous presence was not benevolent—there were no security and welfare programs, consumer protection laws, federal mediation of labor-management disputes, and so forth. The new, giant institutions intruding into everyone's daily life showed few signs of caring about the individual.

Alienation, then, became widespread because the average person's experience was of being in the grip of large, impersonal forces that permitted no escape but seemed mostly indifferent to personal fate. The typical worker was no longer a self-sufficient farmer or a self-employed entrepreneur, but was rather a replaceable part of a large organization. Another cause of alienation was the deplorable nature of most social conditions. This is connected to the next theme: the endless criticism of society in the early twentieth century.

Social criticism. During the nineteenth century most writers had a rather passive view of society (cf. Anderson, 1971; Trilling, 1971). If society was unsatisfactory, the solution was to seek specific improvements or to win the freedom necessary for pursuing one's own happiness and fulfillment. This passivity disappeared abruptly around the turn of the twentieth century. Writers actively and bitterly chronicled the faults and inadequacies of the existing society. Exposing these ills became an end in itself, exemplified by "muckraking" in journalism and in novels such as Sinclair's *The Jungle*. In other writings such as Dos Passos's *U.S.A.* trilogy, the evils of current social conditions were portrayed as the causal background that produced the alienation of the characters.

After alienation. The literary emphasis on alienation suggests a broad and deep discontent in America and in Western Europe early in the twentieth century. If this was so, then a change in these attitudes occurred after World War II and is reflected in new literary trends. Around that time, "post-modern" American fiction moved away from the themes of rage and rebellion (Klein, 1964; Sypher, 1962). Alienation was still a theme, but it was no longer central. Alienation alone was no longer a satisfactory message for most post-modern writers. Alienation literature allows its protagonists a choice only between being rebels and being victims—an inadequate and unattractive set of options. Post-modern fiction showed a new interest in "accommodation" (Klein, 1964). Accommodation in this literature oscillated between adjusting oneself to fit into society and attempting to assert oneself. These protagonists sought to come to terms with society despite misgivings that such accommodation was merely a disguise for outright capitulation or at the least for more alienation (Klein, 1964). To some, "accommodation" as practiced in the suburbs looked a lot like merely opting for conformity to escape the struggles for authenticity, or blending in with the masses to avoid personal decision and individual responsibility ("survival by camouflage"—Sypher, 1962). Whatever its drawbacks, however, accommodation represented a preference for life, even with compromise, over endless and hopeless rebellious struggles.

The desire to accommodate to society could have resulted from the fact that society ceased to offer a stable target for comprehensive critique. Howe (1959) points out that writers early in the century wrote as if they clearly understood the social structure, but that later writers did not clearly understand the postwar "mass society." Consequently, for these later writers questions of value had to be deferred until an accurate perception of reality could be established. Roth (1961) makes a similar argument, saying that social criticism waned because it was so difficult for a writer simply to understand modern society and describe it in a credible fashion.

The alternative to accommodation in 1950s literature was "beat" literature. One eminent critic characterizes this movement as "yet another venture in losing the self" (Sypher, 1962, p. 138). He sees these writers (such as Kerouac and Ginsberg) as having indiscriminate and insatiable appetites for experience of all sorts—accept everything, love everything, indulge in everything, and merge with everything. Another critic takes a more charitable view and sees value in the assertion of creative, orgiastic independence as opposed to the timid and sterile backdrop of adjustment, conformity, and repression that seemed to represent American society in the 1950s. He notes also that some of this literature, influenced by thinkers such as N. O. Brown, Marcuse, Reich, and even Leary, counteracted the excessive rationality of the times by upholding the positive value of "orgiastic irrationality" (Pütz, 1979, p. 40).

During the 1960s, according to Pütz (1979), the "struggle for identity" took the form of "myth-making"—that is, the individual protagonist projected self-made schemes of coherence onto the world. It was as if he had given up on trying to arrive at an objective understanding of society and to make sense of it had retreated into his own invented schemes. Authors such as Pynchon, Nabokov, Vonnegut, and Barth recognized that these myth-making schemes humorously bordered on paranoia; the protagonists managed to skirt critical tests of their self-invented interpretive schemes. In a curious fashion, 1960s literature can be seen as a revival of the passivity of the transcendentalists and other late nineteenth century writers. Instead of arguing for massive social change, the protagonist either accepted given social conditions or sought to avoid society's intolerable aspects by using imagination to create subjective systems of interpretation. Salvation and fulfillment were again sought in personal vision rather than social restructuring.

Devaluation of the individual self. During the nineteenth century the prestige of the individual self had reached an all-time high. Each self was believed to contain latent creative possibilities, innate good qualities, and a special destiny (although class and racial prejudices sometimes restricted the universality of the excellence of selfhood). The individual self, however, was given a heavy dose of humility early in the twentieth century. For one thing, new social arrangements and events dramatized the relative powerlessness of the individual. Indeed, a devaluation of the self is implied in the literature of alienation and social criticism; to blame one's troubles on society is to assert the powerlessness of the individual. Another contributor to the devaluation of the self was a new, more pessimistic view of human nature. Freud's investigations into the hidden depths of the psyche, for example, discovered filth, sadism, and perversity far more often than latent creative genius or innate virtue.

The influential work of Wylie Sypher (1962) articulates the devaluation of selfhood in twentieth century literature and art. He quotes a famous line from *The Man Without Characteristics* in which Musil's protagonist observes, "The center of gravity no longer lies in the individual but in the relations between things" as representative of the new attitude toward selfhood in twentieth century literature. The prevailing image of man is reduced to that of a "mere functionary," obviously a big loss of status from the "imperial self" (Anderson, 1971) of the previous century (Sypher, 1962; also Pütz, 1979). The same idea is expressed in Grenier's often quoted sentence, "We now walk in a universe where there is no echo of 'I'."

The radical change that occurred in biography at the beginning of the twentieth century (specifically, in 1918) is consistent with the thesis of devaluation of selfhood. Biography now sought to expose the subject's faults, frauds, and frailties. "The muckraking spirit, which had exposed the corruption of such majestic institutions as Philadelphia and Standard Oil, was transferred to national heroes" (Altick, 1965, p. 292). Iconoclasm replaced idealism as the prevailing sentiment.

Not only did the subject of a biography lose any expectations of sympathetic treatment, but the limelight also had to be shared with the biographer. It was not until this period that the interpretive and evaluative function of the biographer was recognized as artistic in its own right. Although the emphasis on "realism" in biography continued to increase, the biographer exerted a kind of poetic license in selecting and arranging the facts. Lytton Strachey, the first and most influential of the new biographers, had few scruples about adapting facts and details to suit his iconoclastic portrayals of eminent Victorians (Altick, 1965).

This trend in biography was not restricted to an obscure and small group of scholars. Biographies competed with novels on the best-seller lists in the period between the two world wars (Altick, 1965, p. 292). An interest in learning about the private and unflattering details of the lives of public figures was apparently widespread in the general population. This decreasing prestige and status of the individual suggest the next theme, the fate of individuality in the twentieth century.

Individuality. Evidence about individuality in the twentieth century points in contrary directions. Various thinkers and social scientists have remarked on the seeming demise of individuality (Adorno, 1951; Fromm, 1941; Habermas, 1973; Landmann, 1971). The "loss of self" that Sypher (1962) describes as characteristic of twentieth century Western art also implies a diminution of individuality. On the other hand, individuality is still valued, uniqueness and the "personal touch" are sought, and privacy is coveted, all of which suggest that individuality is alive and well.

Perhaps the best way to reconcile these disparate observations is to suggest that the appetite for individuality persists, but the possibility of achieving individuality has been greatly reduced. Therefore, semblances of individuality flourish. Narcissism, self-help books, personalized luggage, and the rest may have arisen from a frustrated desire for individuality.

Privacy illustrates the contradiction. The desire for privacy is a sign that people value individuality. And in twentieth century Western society, privacy is highly valued. The term "private property" conveys an almost sacred connotation. The private office is a mark of prestige and status—privacy is one major luxury. The rich tend to build such formidable barriers to keep the public away that one is tempted to speak of "conspicuous privacy" or "ostentatious seclusion." But privacy is not usually used as a means for promoting fulfillment of one's unique potential or for allowing oneself to cultivate one's own personal experience. The average person generally uses the privacy of the home to sit passively and allow television to provide mass-produced, vicarious experience. At the center of this private realm one finds the collective mind.

Several factors have undermined the possibility of individuality in the twentieth century. Economic interdependence has already been mentioned. Modern capitalism is composed of mass markets and bureaucratic businesses. Self-sufficiency is obsolete; success depends on working well with and for others. Thus, capitalism now favors the collective over the individual (see also Fromm, 1941).

The history of personal freedom provides an example of something that once fostered but now undermines individuality. The central idea of Fromm's *Escape from Freedom* (1941) is that freedom has *two* aspects: self-strength and aloneness. Freeing the individual from external constraints enabled him to do what he wanted, but it left him alone in having to decide *what* he wanted. The lonely anxiety of being free to decide one's own fate results in the person wishing to be part of a larger movement or group or context. Fascism in Nazi Germany was one such movement that attracted persons wanting to be part of a larger whole. This may also have occurred in ancient Greece. Basing his analysis on Burckhardt's work, Adorno (1951) argues that the increased freedom of the ancient Greek citizen from the laws of the *polis* resulted in a permissive "individualism" that coincided with the disappearance of genuine individuality.

Why should increases in individual freedom reduce individuality? It is plausible that most people do better with firm external guidelines than when left to formulate their own ideals. The Romantic notion of a creative destiny unique to each individual may be an overgeneralization. A permissive, individualistic society may enable the gifted few to fulfill their potentialities, but the multitudes may fall into uncertainty and hedonism rather than arduous self-actualization.

Some specific developments of twentieth-century society have contributed to the fact that freedom does not necessarily foster individuality. Freedom allows the individual to think for himself and to follow his own desires, but the twentieth-century citizen may in fact be doing neither. Fromm and others have remarked that knowledge has become the domain of specialists. The ordinary person cannot hope to understand the ramifications and complexities of anything important, and so only knows to rely on experts in everything. Landmann's typically pithy assessment sums it up: "Die Vernunft des Einzelnen ist nur noch für den Hausgebrauch" ("The reasoning capacity of the ordinary person is for domestic use only" 1971, p. 117). It might be added that where experts are not needed, the mass media step in and help people know what to think.

The problems of desire are the same as those with thought. Fromm wrote in 1941 that "modern man lives under the illusion that he knows what he wants, while he actually wants what he is *supposed* to want" (p. 278). If it was true in 1941 that motives and desires were instilled in the individual from the external world, it is abundantly more true now, since advertising has begun to accomplish this systematically. If you lack something crucial (like food) you have clear and definite desires. But when you have pretty much all that you need, you may start to want whatever society suggests you want—hence fads and status symbols.

If thought and desire are structured by society, the individual is hardly self-directed. Instead, such a person conforms to Riesman's (1951) "other-directed" personality type who is guided by the behavior of others. Fromm foresaw how this could lead to uncertainties about identity: "If I am nothing but what I believe I am supposed to be—who am 'I'?" (p. 280).

It is clear that a variety of forces are at work in twentieth century society to undermine and attack individuality. However, other evidence shows that the appetite for individuality in some forms is strong. It is plausible that this is more true in America than elsewhere because America's entire history has occurred amid the individualistic trends of recent centuries. In other words, unlike some European societies, America has always had individualistic values. Therefore, one can generalize across national and cultural boundaries only cautiously on this issue.

The continued individualism expressed in the desire for privacy is related to territorialism, the desire to keep others out of one's sphere. A kind of territorialism infests bureaucracies too—each bureaucrat jealously guards his or her sphere of power and may obstruct projects as an exercise of this power. The individual domain is thus favored and protected against the collective domain and the collective enterprise.

The observation that modern technology deindividuates the single person (Landmann, 1971) overlooks the countertrends that have resulted from this deindividuation. Everywhere the "personal touch" or "personal service" is stressed in order to conceal the impersonal nature of transactions. Computerized bank tellers are programmed to say "Thank you." "Dear Friend" or " Dear Customer" from letters have given way to the new form letters that insert the addressee's name, even into the letter's text. Bureaucracies assign customers a "personal agent" or "personal banker" to create the semblance of a human, personal relationship. Respect for the "uniqueness" of every person is ubiquitous and almost sacred. Another indication of the dogmatic valuation of individual uniqueness is its use in explaining all sorts of irrelevant phenomena, such as the tendency of professional athletes to describe and justify their competitive strategies and their personal lives in terms of the necessity of "being myself." Recently, Larry Holmes, the heavyweight boxing champion, defeated a major challenger in a difficult fight. Oddly, his first words to newscasters after the fight were an apology for his lack of glamour compared to previous champions. Still, his justification was ready: "I was born to be myself."

One could also cite narcissism, the attitudes and ideology behind assertiveness training and self-help manuals, and the assertion of existential values as signs that individuality is still highly valued. Even experimental evidence shows that modern Americans desire to present themselves as unique and that they resist being treated as not unique (Fromkin, 1970).

But does this all reflect true individuality, or (as Fromm and others have charged) only a semblance of it? To answer this it is useful to recall Weintraub's (1978) formulation of individuality. In his view, individuality has two parts: placing value on the differences between people, and striving to fulfill one's unique potential by something like the self-actualization of a creative destiny. The modern American attitude seems to include the first part but not the second. Individual differences and uniqueness are strongly valued, although the focus tends to be on personality as the most important thing that differentiates people. (What else could it be? Mass-produced goods, mass-produced and mass-mediated ideas, vicarious experience, and impersonal work leave little room for important differences to emerge among people.)

On the other hand, self-actualization is one of those values that gets lip service but only rare and seasonal exertion. The boxing champion's comment reflects the prevailing form of the notion of individual destiny. "I was born to be myself" implies that individuality is one's birthright, not one's achievement. This seems to be the current attitude. Individuality is not regarded as something difficult to acquire or as the final product of arduous cultivation of one's own potential. Rather, individuality is regarded as something that everyone has. If it requires anything, it requires only occasional choice and self-acceptance.

It is probably no accident that individuality should take this form in this century of advertising, technology, and mass consumption. Advertising teaches people to believe that identity follows naturally from the possession of items, implying that constructing the self is as easy as choosing what toothpaste or car to buy. The social reforms of the last 150 years have portrayed the self as endowed with rights instead of duties, and individuality similarly tends to be regarded as more a right than a duty.

Individualistic child-rearing techniques have probably contributed to the current notion of individuality, too. The modern mother treats each child as special so that it will grow up with a sense of unique worth. A decline of discipline and responsibility in childhood (see Bronfenbrenner, 1974) has accustomed children to not needing to earn their privileges. (Hence the tendency to think of the self in terms of rights, perhaps.)

It is reasonable to speculate that Americans are jealous and almost defensive about being unique individuals. An individuality that is the product of personality quirks, choices, and consumer goods is tenuous. People feel that they are created as unique beings but fear losing this specialness. The experimental results cited above (Fromkin, 1970) are also best explained by the hypothesis that people are defensive about their individuality. The desire for the small signs and indications of uniqueness, which critics like Fromm and Landmann denounce as "sham individuality," is thus inescapable.

Thus the factors that produce the desire to be different are clearly influential in modern, mass society. However, most people are content with expressing their desire for uniqueness in simple ways, or perhaps even in ways that could seem trivial. The type of individuality embodied in the "inner-directed" person, the person who lives life by internal values and goals, is largely obsolete for two reasons. First, the modern ("other-directed") person is crucially sensitive to and guided by the reactions of others. Second, the inner self has fallen under the manipulation of mass society (e.g., by advertising). Two main personal goals and ideals seem to be to earn a lot of money and to become a celebrity. Earning lots of money is a collective goal, what Fromm calls "wanting what you're supposed to want." It focuses on extrinsic rewards in excess of necessity, and the rewards are the same ones everyone else gets. Becoming a celebrity is a matter of being admired or loved for one's personality, which thus celebrates uniqueness that is merely claimed, unlike fame which must be earned or achieved (cf. Lasch, 1978). Thus, there is little sense of individuality as the product of a creative struggle to fulfill one's unique potential.

Existential issues. The emergence of existentialism in the literature and philosophy of the twentieth century has several implications for the study of identity. Existentialsim is a philosophy of personal choice and responsibility, and its emergence is a sign of heightened concern over issues of choice. Indeed, more than in previous eras, the twentieth century has seen the creation of identity as based on choice—that is, on self-definition processes of types IV (optional choice) and V (required choice).

Authenticity is one existential and phenomenological concept that has been influential in many fields. In literature, an analysis of the general trends suggest that in the twentieth century people abandoned "the Romantic quest for freedom" for "the existential quest for authenticity" (Sypher, 1962). The central idea of Lionel Trilling's best-known book (*Sincerity and Authenticity*, 1971) is that around the turn of the twentieth century sincerity ceased to be such an important and prevalent value, and the value of authenticity took its place.

The concept of authenticity was named and explicated by Heidegger (1927). To think and behave in one's own way (as opposed to acting in the commonly prescribed, accepted, and stereotyped way), to accept responsibility for one's own actions, and to experience things in their "true" relation to oneself (instead of in a manipulative, exploitative, or dependent fashion) is the nature of authenticity. Total authenticity is, in the final analysis, impossible; yet man's capacity to question himself and his relation to "his" world makes possible a range of degrees of authenticity. One implication of this is that the question of authenticity is one kind of question of identity (Sypher, 1962, p. 29). To gain in authenticity one must learn in what sense one's experience (and what part of one's experience) is really one's own.

Thus, in a sense, the question of authenticity is a question about the size and scope of the self. The emergence of this question early in this century is consistent with the general devaluation of the self already described. Subjectivity, in general, was fast becoming suspect, tenuous, and almost disreputable. "Being objective" became associated with being correct. More generally, existentialism was a sign that the inner self, including the basis for choice, had become highly problematic.

Death. This overview of the history of identity ends, appropriately, with death. The modern history of death is consistent with the weakening of individuality and with the difficulty of self-definition.

The general treatment of death in the twentieth century has been, at least until the past decade, to avoid and disguise death. For example, the norm for handling death in the family has been "the mutual lie" (Ariès, 1981). The dying person and his or her family all speak as if the person will recover, even if they know otherwise. In addition, the tendency to "medicalize" death treats death as a strictly medical issue (Ariès, 1981). The existential or human aspects of death are concealed and ignored. Death becomes depersonalized, isolated, homogenized. People die in numbered hospital cells instead of at home; antiseptic specialists handle deaths according to standard procedures.

The homogenization of death resembles the homogenization of other aspects of modern life. Death, too, has thus lost some of its individualistic features. It could also be argued that death has taken on features of "sham individuality" or the desire for easy and petty signs of individuality. The American practice of viewing the embalmed and made-up corpse at the funeral (cf. Mitford, 1978) can be interpreted as a way of bestowing celebrity status on each person for one last moment.

The aspect of death touched on in these chapters, however, is not the funeral practice as such but death's meaning and value for the living. Various twentieth century thinkers have discussed the individuating power of an awareness of death (e.g., Heidegger, 1927). In that light, the modern avoidance of death is one further sign of the difficulty of determining individual identity. Death asks hard, searching questions of each individual about the value, meaning, and direction of life. The modern individual avoids thinking about death the way one avoids an asker of rude or embarrassing questions.

Summary

Because of a growing dissatisfaction with Christian ideas of fulfillment, the Romantics experimented with creativity, passion, and cultivation of the inner self as new models. In addition, the desire for unique individuality stimulated an interest in personality. The Romantics also became increasingly dissatisfied with the relationship of the individual to society. This dissatisfaction was expressed as a concern with individual freedom and with the finding of a perfect form of society. In general, the Romantics did believe that an ideal society was attainable.

Later, however, the Victorians would gradually come to accept the conflict of the individual with society as chronic. They retained a certain amount of faith in the eventual perfectability of society, but such Utopian dreams began to seem remote. As a result, some sought fulfillment away from society, as can be seen in the interest in transcendentalism and in the increased emphasis on home and family life. The anarchist movement expressed the radical belief that government, laws, and private property were inherently bad and were responsible for human evil. Thus, the anarchist view of a workable, perfect society required the drastic step of doing away with all such institutions. More widespread than the anarchist position were the pragmatic yet idealistic efforts at progressive liberal reform as a way of addressing specific problems within the existing society. The gaining of self-knowledge came to seem ever more difficult and tenuous during the Victorian period. Moreover, society's consensus about basic truths and ultimate values was lost, and its loss was recognized. Henceforth, values would be personal, not objective and consensual.

During the twentieth century, the individual self came to seem less infinitely potent than it had seemed in the nineteenth century. Economic interdependence, especially during economic depressions, dramatized the helplessness of the individual within society. Feelings of alienation and a bitter dissatisfaction with social conditions reflected the difficulty in adapting to the modern relationship between the individual and society. As the century wore on, though, people gradually became accustomed to the new circumstances. This burgeoning desire for individuality has persisted into the twentieth century, but it has become increasingly difficult to achieve. An interest in personality and in personal choice have become perennial themes.

5

Transformation of Adolescence

This chapter is specifically concerned with the history of adolescence in relation to identity. Today we automatically associate adolescence with issues of identity, including identity crisis, so special attention to the history of adolescence is important in a book on identity. An examination of the life of teenagers in other cultures or in other historical periods yields a picture different from the modern American adolescent, and identity crises often seem rare or absent outside our own historical period and culture. This suggests that the association of adolescence with identity problems may be historically and culturally relative.

A survey of the leading historical works on adolescence does not simplify matters, for there are basic controversies. In particular, historians disagree as to whether adolescence was itself an innovation of the Victorian period. Demos and Demos (1969) argue that adolescence "did not exist before the last two decades of the nineteenth century." In their view, adolescence was primarily an American discovery. Gillis (1974) speaks of the "discovery of adolescence" as occurring between 1870 and 1900, and his work is based extensively on British and German history. Kett's (1977) history of adolescence in America describes the Victorian era's trends as "the invention of the adolescent" rather than as a discovery of adolescence. In his view the conceptions and stereotypes were largely imposed by the culture on the adolescent. In other words, Victorian society had a new awareness of adolescence, but it was not based on an improved understanding of adolescent behavior. Instead, society invented a concept of adolescence and attempted to mold young people into this preconceived stereotype.

Literary evidence also supports the view that adolescence became, in a new way, a concept and a problem late in the nineteenth century. An extensive review of adolescent characters in fiction reveals that the novel of adolescence is mainly a genre of the twentieth century (Kiell, 1959). It was not until around the turn of the twentieth century that literature began to deal in depth with the problems and struggles of the adolescent.

In contrast, the eminent historian Lawrence Stone says, "The idea that adolescence, as a distinctive age-group with its distinctive problems, was a development of the nineteenth century is entirely without historical foundation" (1977, p. 377), and he denounces that hypothesis as "sheer historical fantasy." He quotes Shakespeare to the effect that the ages of sixteen to twenty-three were a deplorable time of "getting wenches with child, wronging the ancientry, stealing, fighting." He says that in the early modern period, citizens of London experienced "constant anxiety" about the dangers resulting from the large number of unmarried apprentices. His evidence indicates that such anxieties were well-founded because the apprentices were indeed a troublesome lot whose disturbances ranged from petty disrespect to full-scale rioting. In America young males were also troublesome. Early nineteenth century youth organizations, such as volunteer fire brigades, would engage in brawls that foreshadowed modern youth gang wars (Kett, 1977).

These conflicting views, however, are not irreconcilable. Rebellious mischief is not identity crisis. It is plausible that adolescence has commonly been a troublesome period in life and has been so for centuries. It is also plausible that the problems of adolescence changed fundamentally late in the nineteenth century.

Before discussing how history and culture transformed adolescence, it is necessary to consider briefly what it is that got transformed. What are the constant features of adolescence? A partial review of cross-cultural evidence about adolescence by Dianne Tice and myself (1985) developed the following picture. Adolescence is innately a time of transition in identity from child to adult. The timing coincides approximately with physical puberty. For various reasons, probably including the sexual and physical changes of puberty, adolescence is often a time of some emotional instabilities, so adolescents are often problematic for the adults who have the responsibility to deal with them. Adolescence is the time for an initiation into the traditions, knowledge, and world view of the culture. Finally, adolescence is often marked by a transitional stage in life, such as isolation during a ritual of initiation. This transitional phase, however, is generally extremely short in comparison to the prolonged adolescence of modern Western life.

The picture just sketched can be applied both to modern adolescence and to adolescence several centuries ago. In particular, it is compatible with either the presence or absence of identity problems. The transition to identity that defines adolescence may be either a smooth, well-defined one or an uncertain and problematic one. The Victorian era saw a change from the former to the latter.

How Adolescence Changed

Four themes stand out in the Victorian transformation of adolescence. First, a new concept of adolescence emerged, which portrayed the adolescent as conforming, vulnerable, passive, awkward, and indecisive about certain issues. Second, the social and economic status of adolescents changed toward greater dependence on adults, toward less responsibility, toward less commitment to the future (adult) identity, and toward having more options for choosing an adult identity. Third, the task of adolescence was changed from that of preparation for a definite adult role to a nonspecific preparation for any of a number of roles, and choices had to be made from among those roles. Fourth, the process of adolescent development became secularized and focused more on identity choice than on building character.

Concept. Prior to the late nineteenth century, Americans thought of adolescence in a way that was both different and more vague than our own. Their concepts were based less on precise age than on physical size, as befits a land of farmers. Indeed, knowledge of one's own age was often unreliable and unimportant. Americans in 1800 did not think of youth as a phase of awkwardness, personal indecision, or uncertainty. Instead, to them puberty signified the fact that the young person was ready and able to do an adult's share (or almost that) of work around the farm, shop, or house (Kett, 1977).

By 1900, however, the new conception of adolescence regarded the young person as conformist, anti-intellectual, and passive (Kett, 1977, p. 243). Americans had come to believe that adolescents needed extensive or even constant supervision by adults. The conformity, anti-intellectualism, and passivity were, after all, applied in 1900 to adolescents who were more typically high school pupils, not the farmhands and apprentices of 1800. The perceived need for adult supervision of teenagers extended even to leisure activities, resulting in such Victorian innovations as the Boy Scouts and the YMCA (Gillis, 1974; Kett, 1977).

This new image of adolescence was considered normal, proper, and desirable. Society came to believe that everyone should experience this passive, vulnerable, and awkward adolescent stage (Kett, 1977; Modell, Furstenberg, & Hershberg, 1976). Thus, the new concept of adolescence was prescriptive, not just merely descriptive—it stated how adolescents *should* be, not just how they were.

Social and economic status. The traditional status of teenagers is usually characterized by modern scholars as "semidependent" (Gillis, 1974; Kett, 1977). Teenagers had few autonomous legal rights, yet in daily life teenagers were neither supported nor supervised by their parents. The practice of "fostering out" was predominant; parents sent their children away at around age seven to live in other households where they were, in a sense, unpaid employees (Gillis, 1974; also Ariès, 1962; Stone, 1977). In the traditional arrangement in Europe, prior to the eighteenth century, the foster household treated these children almost as part of the family, but during the eighteenth century that arrangement deteriorated (Gillis, 1974), and "fostering out" declined. Since this was the age of industrialization, people began instead to send their children away to work in factories. As urbanization progressed, the urban families of the working classes increasingly kept their children in the parental home but the children continued to work in factories.

When children reached their teens and the "fostering-out" phase ended, they were typically placed in another situation of semidependency, such as apprenticeships. The alternatives to apprenticeship included entering a religious institution or the military service. As with the foster period, parents arranged the situation for the child, but once situated the young person was not substantially dependent on the parents. Eventually, the oldest son might return home to take over the parental farm, estate, or shop. Younger sons had to seek their own fortunes if their apprenticeships did not lead to lifelong careers. Daughters were married off whenever possible. Superfluous sons became soldiers or priests, and superfluous daughters became nuns.

Marriage practices also reflected semidependency. Parents traditionally arranged the marriage, although by the nineteenth century the choice of mate was primarily made by the young person. Still, marriage often had to wait until the man was independently established.

The social and economic status of youth before the Victorian era was characterized by semidependency on parents, some responsibilities, generally little power to choose adult identity roles (such as spouse or job), but with the ability to govern one's daily life to some extent, committed by parents to a particular (future) adult identity, and supporting oneself financially by work, yet without much control or money.

In contrast, the new socioeconomic status of youth by the beginning of the twentieth century produced a different picture of adolescence. The average teenager lived with parents or boarded at school or college but, either way, was economically dependent on parents. Other than schoolwork, the young person had few or no responsibilities. The adolescent had the power to choose his or her own eventual occupation and spouse. Typically, there were multiple options for both choices. Commitments to adult roles were either provisional, which meant they could always be revoked or altered, or were lacking entirely. This uncommitted, dependent, and isolated status of youth has been termed the *psychosocial moratorium* (Erikson, 1950, 1968). The change in the social and economic status of the teenager during the Victorian period was thus from semidependent to dependent, from committed to uncommitted with regard to future adult roles, from somewhat responsible to not responsible, and from lacking options to having multiple options for adult identity.

Task of adolescence. Teenagers of past centuries were typically occupied with preparations for fixed, particular adult roles that had been chosen for them. Their task involved two parts. One was to complete the very specific training needed for the allotted adult role (such as in apprenticeship). The other was just to pass the time until the adult role became available. The availability of an adult role might depend on receiving an offer of marriage, graduation or promotion from apprentice to master, or inheritance. If you were dissatisfied with your lot, you either had to learn to accept it, or you might possibly discover a religious "calling" and devote your life to serving God. Such religious awakenings were especially frequent among young men who were discontent with their occupational prospects (Kett, 1977).

Beginning in the Victorian era, however, the task of the teenager centered increasingly around school, where the young person was expected to get a *nonspecific* "liberal arts" education. This broad, basic education was presumed to be a prerequisite for all sorts of occupations, even that of housewife. The precise adult role was often not marked out for the teenager, and educational courses were often not dictated until late in college. Many teenagers could express a specific occupational ambition, but they were simply stating a preference and could change their minds much more easily than could an apprentice in earlier centuries. Indeed, the second part of the modern task of adolescence was gradually to make choices among all the available adult roles. In particular, this meant choosing a specific occupation and working toward it, and choosing a spouse.

Process. The Victorian era also saw changes in prevailing ideas about how personality and character evolved through adolescence. In past centuries the focus had been on religious and moral character development. Religious conversion experiences had been associated with youth for centuries. For many young Puritan males, a powerful religious experience marked the end of the "sins of youth" and the beginning of a life as a pious adult Christian (Greven, 1977). In the early nineteenth century there were many mass revival meetings at which many young people had religious experiences and awakenings (Kett, 1977). Religious development had thus long been an important feature of the process of growth during the teen years.

As for moral development, it too had been an important feature of adolescent development. Around the seventeenth century the "moralization of society" led to a strong concern over instilling character virtue in young people (Ariès, 1962; Stone, 1977). At the beginning of the nineteenth century, the concept of "decision of character" was the American paradigm for adolescent development (Kett, 1977). "Decision of character" entailed personal exertion by the adolescent, especially the male, in order to become a virtuous adult.

It would be an exaggeration to say that religious and moral development has vanished from the adolescent process. Indeed, through much of the twentieth century, churches have had special programs and groups for young people, and schools have sought to cultivate virtue, even to the point of giving grades for "citizenship." But moral and religious development is no longer considered the primary issue of adolescence. Put bluntly, identity crisis has replaced "decision of character."

Modern adolescence is thus centrally concerned with personal values just as pre-Victorian adolescence was, but modern adolescents are either permitted or required to choose and cultivate their own sets of values. For purposes of collecting data, researchers have taken "identity crisis" to mean a period of struggle to adopt a religious and political ideology and to choose an occupation (Marcia, 1966, 1967). Although researchers no longer accept Erikson's (1968) general statement that all modern adolescents have identity crises, there is still a cultural norm that considers them proper and desirable. Evidence also suggests that identity crises may be beneficial to psychological health and well-being. The important point is that identity crises became a feature of adolescence some time around the end of the nineteenth century. That change probably more than any other accounts for the rapid increase in literary interest in adolescents (Kiell, 1959; also Pütz, 1979) and the tendency of some historians to speak of the Victorians as the discoverers or inventors of adolescence. Because of this, an examination of the causes of the Victorian transformation of adolescence into its modern form, which includes identity crisis, is important.

Causes of the Victorian Transformation

My discussion of causes is organized around the following four themes. First, young people increasingly assumed the burden of self-definition as the choice of adult roles was left up to them rather than made for them. Second, family relations evolved in a number of ways that made adolescence more salient (generally, prominently noticeable) and problematic. Third, society created the "moratorium" status for teenagers. Fourth, society's loss of ideological consensus rendered values an aspect of personal identity that needed to be settled during adolescence.

Locus of self-definition. Perhaps the most important factor in the Victorian transformation of adolescence was a shift in the locus and burden of self-definition. In previous centuries society (often represented by parents) had defined the adult identity for the individual. Rather abruptly, however, the adult identity was left mostly up to the adolescent to decide and define.

The change is most apparent with marriage and occupation. These two adult identity components are intimately connected with adolescence. In modern Western societies, as in many others, the adolescent period is considered ended once the young person marries and begins an adult occupational role.

The choice of one's spouse had for centuries resided with one's parents, but the parental role declined through a series of stages (Stone, 1977; Smith, 1973). First, the young person acquired veto power over the parents' choice. Then, by the early nineteenth century, a decisive shift had occurred: The young person became the primary decision maker, and the parents had only veto power (although parents probably acted as advisors and consultants as well). By the end of the nineteenth century, even the parental veto power was in jeopardy. If you and your parents could not agree on your choice of mate, you could actually marry whomever you chose even over parental objections.

With marriage, then, the trend was for the decision to be placed increasingly in the hands of the young person. The old system arranged adult identity for the individual. The new system left it to the young person to arrange his or her own adult identity, and this was to be done during adolescence.

With occupation, the picture is more complex than with marriage, but the outcome is the same. Throughout history, most people had been farmers, and there was little option of becoming anything else. As manufacturing and trade produced a middle class, a variety of job options appeared. Parental connections determined the young person's future occupation by arranging apprenticeships, placing the young person in a trade or profession, and so forth. Upper-class children were also marked for their roles by parental arrangements because parents arranged to leave their estates and titles to the eldest son and arranged military commissions or whatever for other sons. Daughters of the aristocracy were steered by parents into convents or marriages.

For centuries the family filled a vital role—it was the connection between the individual and society (Fass, 1977). The family was what placed children in adult roles. It has only been during the twentieth century that the family's role in this regard has become obsolete. Late in the Victorian era, the young person's occupation began to follow from his or her education rather than from parental arrangements. A thorough study of careers by Thernstrom (1973) showed that by the turn of the twentieth century, in Boston at least, no apparent disadvantage to your career was caused by being from a poor family. Unless you were from the most wealthy segment of the population, your family background had little or no relationship to your occupational level. The new system thus ended one of the family's principal functions and cut a main tie between the family and the larger society (Fass, 1977). The urban, industrial society that emerged in the nineteenth century offered the young person an assortment of career options, and parental influence was at best an ancillary or occasional factor in securing a job.

Thus with occupation as with marriage, the actual adult identity component became something chosen by the adolescent rather than arranged by parental decision and influence within a context of limited options. As the adolescent adopted the burden of determining his or her own adult identity, adolescence became a time for difficult, important, and far-reaching decisions. The adolescent is in a state of noncommitment and transition; he is unformed and needs to find within the self the bases or metacriteria for making those decisions. It is doubtful that the average adolescent was fully ready and mature enough to make such decisions when they were turned over to him or her in the nineteenth century. Probably for that reason, the field of vocational counseling expanded rapidly around 1900 (Kett, 1977), offering expert advice and information to help young people make difficult choices.

Family relations. Numerous changes within the family contributed to the new version of adolescence that emerged late in the Victorian era. There were two broad changes regarding the family itself. First, the family gained added importance throughout the nineteenth century as individuals increasingly sought happiness and fulfillment there rather than in public life. Second, the family tended to become less of an economic unit and more a network of emotional relationships (Burgess & Locke, 1945). The latter occurred partly as the result of urbanization. The traditional farm family worked as a unit to produce goods for consumption, sale, or exchange. Few twentieth century families are engaged in *joint* productive labor. One result of this is that the father has lost his traditional status as foreman or supervisor of the family work activities. As the family became increasingly focused on interpersonal relationships rather than work, families tended to become more egalitarian and democratic.

Other changes directly affected the status of adolescents. For one, evidence suggests that Victorian parents developed closer emotional ties to their children than had parents of earlier centuries. Up until 1800 child mortality was quite high. A new baby's chances of living to age twenty were probably no better than fifty-fifty, and it was not unknown for a family to lose all its children. One generally cited consequence was that it was too risky for parents to love each child very much because of the risk of heartbreak (e.g., Ariès, 1962; Gillis, 1974; Hunt, 1970; Stone, 1977). By the mid-nineteenth century, however, improvements in public health and nutrition had effectively lowered child mortality rates, and parents formed stronger attachments to their children. As a result, the death of a child became a much greater calamity than it had been (Ariès, 1962, 1981).

In addition to increased emotional involvement with offspring, family birth patterns changed. As long as most children died, it was necessary to have as many babies as possible in order to ensure the economic well-being of the family. Children provided cheap labor or extra income, and children were the early modern version of a retirement pension. Typically, a couple married and then began having children as soon as possible and continued to do so as long as possible. This was no longer necessary in the nineteenth century because each child was much more likely to survive. Two stages of birth control for family planning are described by Kett (1977). In the first, parents spaced out births at long intervals. By about 1900, however, parents were switching to the second system, which is the modern system of bearing all the children within a span of a few years and then having no more. As these children grew up, society encountered a novel circumstance—a large number of families in which all the offspring were teenagers at the same time. This undoubtedly contributed to the *salience* of adolescence and adolescent problems (Kett, 1977).

Even more important than birth control for drawing attention to adolescence was the decline of "fostering out" and of the apprenticeship system. It suddenly became common for children to remain in the parental home until marriage. This finding was somewhat surprising to historians, who had shared the general assumption that industrialization had weakened the family. That assumption was contradicted by a fair amount of evidence. In particular, because of industrialization, the average age at which the young left home increased significantly (Katz & Davey, 1978; Modell et al., 1976).

There are four likely consequences of the shift toward having children remain in the parental home until they marry. The first involves the increased parental involvement with children, and family planning based on widely spaced births. The typical children of the middle to late nineteenth century were raised in a rather unusual way. Unlike children of earlier centuries, they received close and emotionally intense attention from their parents for the first two decades of life. And unlike children of the twentieth century they did not have to share parental attention with siblings near their own ages. Much older or younger siblings do not have the same needs and so do not compete for the same kind of parental attention. Given that combination of child-raising practices, the nineteenth century saw an all-time peak in individuality. A more individualistic program for raising children could scarcely be imagined.

The second consequence of keeping children longer in the parental home was, again, a likely increase in society's awareness of adolescence and adolescent problems. To be sure, historians are probably correct in maintaining that adolescent mischief and masturbation had been causes for concern in past centuries (e.g., Stone, 1977). But it seems likely that such concern would be greatly intensified by the decline of fostering out. The everyday impetus for such concern in the seventeenth century might have been the contact between apprentice and master; in the nineteenth century, however, it was contact between parents and children. It is even plausible that the Victorian repression of sexuality was stimulated in part by the intensified parental concern due to increased contact with adolescent children. It may be more worrisome, for example, to be confronted with a daughter than with a servant girl who is out at night with male friends. The adolescent male in particular was the focus and symbol of Victorian fears about sexuality (Smith-Rosenberg, 1978).

The third consequence concerns the emotional development of adolescents. Adolescence may commonly be an emotionally turbulent phase of life, due in part to the physical and mental changes in the individual. A potent focus of the adolescent emotional turmoil is suggested by psychodynamic theory (e.g., Blos, 1962). The teenager is physically ready for adult sexual behavior, but emotionally the teenager is still tied to the parents. The emotional task of adolescence is then to break the emotional tie to the parents so that the individual can love others as an adult would. In previous centuries adolescents typically saw their parents only seldom, and so the emotional turmoil surrounding the attachment to parents might have been minimized. In contrast, Victorian teenagers had frequent contact with parents, which may have made it more difficult to break the emotional tie. The trend toward remaining longer in the parental home may thus have increased the emotional difficulty of adolescence.

The fourth consequence was a probable increase in intergenerational conflict. There is some evidence that such conflict, especially between fathers and sons, was particularly intense during the late nineteenth century (e.g., Smith-Rosenberg, 1978; also Anderson, 1971, Chapter 1). To some extent, an increase in such conflict could have been the natural and inevitable result of an increase in time spent together. It was probably exacerbated, however, by changes in the power relationships within the family. On the one hand parental power decreased. How the power to determine one's adult identity passed from one's parents to oneself has already been described. As adolescents gained the power of deciding who they would be, parents lost that power (see also Smith, 1973). The parents thus lost one potent means for forcing their will on their sons and daughters. Sons in particular could defy their parents because they could become self-supporting via industrial work. Because of job discrimination, a daughter probably could only defy her parents with reasonable impunity if she were about to marry someone.

On the other hand, parental power increased because of the increase in the immediate economic dependency of adolescents on their parents. The "semidependency" of pre-Victorian teenagers meant, in part, that parents had little control over their children's daily lives. The transition to fuller dependency, especially coupled with children more often living at home, however, probably afforded parents an increased chance to regulate their children's everyday affairs.

There were thus two opposing trends. Parents' long-range power over their children's lives was reduced, while their short-term power was increased. Parents stopped being the people who decided your fate and set the course of your adult life. They became, instead, the people who nagged you to clean up your things and to come home on time.

Why should such a pattern increase intergenerational conflict? The answer is that it sets parents up to be perceived as petty tyrants without real, long-range power. The adolescent must tolerate the parental rules for a few years until he or she is ready to strike out alone, at which point parents have little power. The parents have little control over the important features of the adolescent's life unless they use emotional tactics.

The apparent changes in family relationships that presumably contributed to the new awareness of adolescence can thus be summarized: For the adolescents themselves, emotional conflicts with parents increased, the emotional maturation associated with puberty became more difficult, and the emotional demands on them increased. For the parents, concern over their offspring intensified, conflict with adolescent chidren increased, some of their power to resolve disputes with adolescents was lost, and teenage misbehavior became more obvious and threatening.

Moratorium and peer group. The circumstance of the modern adolescent has been characterized as a "psychosocial moratorium" (Erikson, 1950, 1968). This moratorium is defined by three features:

transitional status, lack of commitment, and isolation from society's mainstream. The moratorium took its modern form toward the end of the nineteenth century.

Transitional status, by itself, was not new to the Victorians. Indeed, transitional status appears to be a common feature of adolescence across different cultures, and it may be considered as one of the defining attributes of adolescence. The uncommitted status and the isolation of adolescents were both nineteenth century innovations, however. Both features were shaped by the educational system and other practices that emerged during the nineteenth century.

Age segregation was not very thorough in America early in the nineteenth century (Kett, 1977). The vague and amorphous definition of "youth" produced youth organizations that mixed together people whose ages ranged from preteen to thirty-five. Schooling was somewhat irregular, and it too mixed different ages of pupils in the same room. With each set of reforms or changes, however, age segregation increased, and teenagers were increasingly deprived of unstructured (that is, nonhierarchical) contact with older persons. A thirty-five-year-old and a fifteen-year-old would not ordinarily belong as equals to the same youth group today; the older person might belong as an adult supervisor. The age-segregated school, including the new "high school," spread during the Victorian period. Moreover, fewer children dropped out of school. This happened because of several things, including urbanization and the demise of the apprenticeship system. The view became widespread that schooling improved career prospects for boys and improved marriage prospects for girls. Compulsory education laws and child-labor laws gradually required even the lower classes to send their children to study in schools rather than to work in factories.

It is worth noting that child-labor restrictions were received as a mixed blessing even by those whom they were supposedly intended to benefit. The poor needed their children's incomes and bitterly opposed the enforcement of compulsory education, which must have seemed like an exploitative and oppressive rule (Gillis, 1974). Even today, some historians and sociologists adhere to the view that compulsory education is simply a trick to keep teenagers out of the job market lest they compete for adult jobs and depress wage structures (e.g., Larkin, 1979).

Whether the motives for compulsory education laws were benign and altruistic or exploitative and hypocritical, they were firmly in place by the turn of the century. There is no denying that compulsory schooling and age segregation define the daily lives of modern Western teenagers. Some historians consider these educational practices to be the main cause for the Victorian invention or discovery of adolescence (e.g., Gillis, 1974).

Age segregation has two sides. On one side, it deprives the adolescent of contact with people of other ages. This isolation from the whole of society has been criticized as a cause of youthful alienation (Bronfenbrenner, 1974). On the other side, it increases contact with age peers. As a result, the "peer group" becomes the most important and interesting feature of adolescent social life, indeed, of adolescent life altogether. Several features of twentieth century adolescence are attributable to the importance of the peer group—conformity, susceptibility to fads, and preoccupation with intergroup competition (Fass, 1977).

Age segregation was not of course the only consequence of the expansion of schooling. The uncommitted status of youth was also a result of it. In the previous system based on apprenticeship, a teenager was trained for one specific job. By 1900, however, nonspecific liberal education became the general prerequisite for many different jobs. The Victorians felt that school was a valuable preparation for a career, *regardless of the precise content of what was taught and learned*. That meant no specific career goal was needed to guide studies. Because of this, and since the Victorian period, key choices about adult identity can be postponed until near the end of adolescence.

Loss of ideological consensus. Evidence has been cited that society as a whole turned away from its Christian basis during the eighteenth century. But it took several generations for the realization to sink in. By the Victorian era, however, it was quite apparent that Christianity was losing ground (e.g., Howe, 1976). People wondered and worried about how society would be affected by the decline of Christian faith (Meyer, 1976; also Houghton, 1957).

Three consequences of society's loss of ideological consensus affected adolescent identity development. First, the innate cultural function of adolescence became much more difficult. Second, the selection of personal values and beliefs became a problematic feature of identity formation. Third, the resolution of adolescent crises was made more difficult. Each of these is important and deserves elaboration.

Evidence from different cultures suggests that adolescence is naturally a time for the transmission of the culture's central beliefs and values to the young person. As a culture abandons its certainty in beliefs and values, it becomes much more difficult to know what to transmit to adolescents. It becomes difficult to determine whether a particular adolescent is developing properly or abnormally because the criteria are uncertain. Seven centuries ago, society might have taught Christian theology, Aristotelian philosophy, and Augustinian political theory as truth to its adolescents. Today's universities have to make do with teaching cultural and moral relativism, along with critical thinking. It is unclear as to what version of fundamental truth this culture imparts to its adolescents. A basic feature of the adolescent transition to adulthood has thus become problematic.

Modern adolescents need to develop and choose their own sets of basic values and religious or other beliefs about life (the second consequence). The selection of personal values is *not* a universal feature of adolescence. It is probably a feature only in a pluralistic society. Moreover, values have much more to do with identity in a pluralistic society than in a society with ideological consensus. To understand that, it is necessary to go back to the second defining criterion of identity, differentiation. If everyone in a given society believes the Christian version of truth, then Christian faith does not differentiate. Christian faith may then be part of the context of identity, but it is not a matter of identity per se. In contrast, in modern America Christian faith does differentiate among people. The modern adolescent can decide between Christianity, atheism, scientific agnosticism, and other alternatives, and this choice is part of creating identity.

Medieval society was certainly not completely consensual. In particular, there were Jews throughout Europe. But it is probable that in each city the Christian majority regarded the Jewish minority as ideologically wrong and individually inferior. Few Christians were probably tempted to convert to Judaism. The spiritual career of adolescence typically entailed *learning* Christianity rather than actually *choosing* it. Today, however, choice is necessary for many beliefs and values.

Moreover, choosing is more difficult than learning, so the task of the adolescent has become much more difficult since the Victorians discovered that culture is not made of unshakable truths. Learning, in principle at least, means incorporating a specific body of material that exists outside the individual. In contrast, the modern adolescent faces an identity crisis because no single ready-made system exists to be incorporated. There are several such systems of belief, so metacriteria (identity-related basic values and beliefs) for choosing among them need to be found. The final result is an individual set of "personal values" and "personal beliefs." Beliefs and values did not always have to be personal; when society agreed about them, they were considered objectively true, not personal.

The third consequence of the loss of ideological consensus was that it became harder to resolve adolescence. The old cultural certainty helped adolescents understand and resolve their experiences during that turbulent phase of life. This can best be appreciated by considering the religious conversion experiences, which may have been the immediate predecessors of identity crises. Such experiences often followed a period of youthful indulgence, rebellion, or misbehavior (cf. Greven, 1977). After the conversion experience, the young person presumably became a model citizen, living properly and abiding by the values and standards of the community. Of course, for some young people, several such religious experiences were necessary! (Kett, 1977, p. 82).

These conversions may be analyzed using the psychodynamic model of Blos (1962). The onset of puberty gives rise to desires and feelings stronger than those to which the young person is accustomed. The individual finds it difficult to manage those feelings. A period of indulgence and misbehavior follows, ending when the person finds mature and socially acceptable patterns for expressing the adult needs and wants. At this point the person is likely to experience feelings of guilt because of the recent period of misbehavior.

A firm religious context can enable the adolescent to interpret his or her personal experience in terms of religious symbols, such as the struggle against temptation or toward redemption. The religious framework also provides a clear model of how to resolve the adolescent phase, by providing a model of the proper Christian life. For such adolescents, then, their turbulent phase was one of "sins of youth" but not identity crisis. Fundamental values and beliefs were available to shape the adolescent experience, to interpret it, and to show how to resolve it. These values and beliefs did not have to be chosen, for they existed as if objective truths. The only decision was the "decision of character"—that is, the decision about how far to measure up to the standards. The standards themselves were never in question.

Modern adolescence, in contrast, lacks a secure ideological context in which experience can be guided and shaped. To resolve that emotionally difficult period of life, many adolescents have to begin by deciding what basic beliefs and values will guide their lives. In short, the adolescent construction of adult identity has been considerably more difficult because of Western society's loss of ideological consensus—a loss which was acutely and widely felt during the nineteenth century.

Adolescence in the Twentieth Century

The Victorian transformation of adolescence established our modern form of adolescence, which has persisted throughout the twentieth century. There have been some important changes, refinements, and fluctuations, and these merit attention.

Several developments have intensified the patterns set in the Victorian period. Age segregation has continued to increase during the twentieth century (e.g., Bronfenbrenner, 1963). Whereas colleges and high schools once competed for the same students (Kett, 1977), now they are sequential. College attendance expanded greatly in the early part of the twentieth century (Fass, 1977) and continued to rise intermittently. As a result, more and more adolescents have the opportunity to experience the psychosocial moratorium for several years, as more young people can spend four years free of adult responsibilities *and* free of parental supervision. The establishment of adult identity, in terms of occupation and marriage, can now easily be postponed into one's mid-twenties. Of course, in previous centuries young men often were unable to marry until late in their twenties because they had to wait for an inheritance or another means of support. In that sense, the current late entry to adult identity is not unusual. But the experience of moratorium (lack of commitment, isolation, and so forth) for a lengthy period of time *is* a distinctive feature of youth in the twentieth century.

In the family, too, some relevant Victorian patterns have been continued and expanded. The economic need for large families declined as urbanization progressed, so families became smaller. The new, smaller families did not require such strict parental discipline as had the large farm families. The smaller unit afforded greater opportunity for individual parental attention to each child (although much evidence suggests that twentieth century fathers have not always taken full advantage of that opportunity). As a result of these trends, families have increasingly become networks for emotional relationships and for self-expression, including self-expression by the children (Fass, 1977; also Burgess & Locke, 1945).

Evidence indicates that parental concerns and uncertainties have continued to rise. The uncertainty is suggested by the proliferation of expert advice for parents. Books about child-raising written for American parents began to multiply around 1825 (Demos & Demos, 1977). By the 1920s, they were everywhere. Surveys showed that the average middle-class woman of the 1920s read at least one book or pamphlet on child-raising *every year* (Fass, 1977). Thus, not only did the modern adolescent now face difficult problems (e.g., of self-definition) whose means of solution were uncertain, but the adolescent *was* (to parents) a difficult problem whose means of solution were also uncertain.

Adolescence has expanded to include ever-younger age groups. As older teens more and more have sought "adultlike" behaviors and status symbols (e.g., Kett, 1977), the age associated with the concept and behaviors of adolescence has become younger, now including youngsters in their early teens. Some theorists are therefore reluctant to use the term adolescence (e.g., Larkin, 1979; also Kett, 1977). But the imitation of adults does not make teens into adults; it merely makes them imitation adults.

The Great Depression of the 1930s was one of the most influential events of the century, and it too had its effect on adolescence. Many teenagers were forced by the Depression to help support their families, and others had to take on extra household duties because the mother was working (Elder, 1974). The Depression thus burdened many teenagers with genuine adult responsibilities, thereby destroying the psychosocial moratorium status. Without a moratorium, adolescent identity crises were less likely. Instead, adolescents ended up with "identity foreclosure"—adult identities that were not chosen during adolescent crises but simply followed because of the exigencies of fate and parental guidance (Elder, 1974).

On the other hand, the Depression did reinforce at least one major feature of modern adolescence. The importance of the peer group was intensified in several ways. Elder (1974) found that the more a family had suffered hardship and deprivation from the Depression, the more its children were oriented toward age-mates.

The importance of the peer group to adolescent life has been perhaps the most durable theme in twentieth century adolescence. Its power should not be underestimated. Given the modern family, with extensive and individualized attention (from the mother, if not the father) given to each child, people might have grown up as highly distinct individuals. That they do not necessarily do so may well be due to the conformity pressures of the peer group; these pressures overcome the individualizing influences of the family. The desire to be special and the need for a concept of self as unique persist throughout life. Behaviorally, one learns from adolescent peer groups to fear being too different from others. That perhaps explains why young people will be individualistic and even rebellious only in ways that are approved by the peer group (cf. O'Neill, 1971; also Fass, 1977).

The decline of the belief in moral absolutes persisted into the twentieth century, and it too enhanced the importance of the peer group. As has been argued, a definite sense of firm religious and moral beliefs constituted a powerful guide for behavior and was an influential ally during adolescence. Once lost, a replacement was needed, and to some extent the peer group became the replacement. Various studies and surveys in the 1920s showed that moral standards of right and wrong were much less important to college students than were standards of acceptability and conformity to the group (Fass, 1977, p. 245). By the 1950s social scientists observed that the predominant personality type had shifted from "inner-directed" to "other-directed," guided by how one's behavior appeared to others instead of by internal standards and goals (e.g., Riesman, 1951; Wheelis, 1958; May, 1953).

The peer group has tended to uphold conformity as a value. Sometimes competition, especially between groups such as in intercollegiate football, has also been a value of the peer group (Fass, 1977). Teenagers began to appeal to conformity to justify their behavior as correct and even to oppose parental rules or demands. ("Please, Mom, everyone else does.") Justifications for conformity have varied. Youth in the 1920s justified conformity in terms of the practices of the business world (Fass, 1977). Youth in the 1950s conformed with no apparent ideological underpinning (Friedenberg, 1959). Youth in the 1960s justified conformity within the context of the ideals and ideology of the counterculture (O'Neill, 1971). Conformity has endured even though its alleged rationales have changed. This implies that the rationales are rationalizations rather than truly causal reasons or premises. Peer pressure, not ideology, may be the fundamental cause, although the role of ideology should not be discounted altogether.

A study of the relationships between youth and ideology would be a book in itself, and to my knowledge it has not yet been written, but there have been several excellent and provocative shorter pieces. The general impression seems to be that twentieth century youth, even when it seemed most rebellious, generally did not stray far from basic cultural values. Fass (1977) points out that youth in the 1920s were stereotyped as wild and rebellious, yet that stereotype seems absurd in light of their frequent appeals to the business world to justify their behaviors. A similar conclusion regarding the counterculture of the 1960s emerges from a study by Weaklund (1969). Although the hippie counterculture created the impression of a blanket rejection of American culture as "Establishment," it was actually based on traditional American values—love, equality, tolerance, community and harmony, and individual freedom.

Perhaps it should come as no surprise that the values espoused by adolescents should typically be ones deeply rooted in the culture. Western society lost its ideological consensus, and as a result adolescents had to assemble their own personal value structures, which does not mean that young people had to invent new values or assemble world views out of a void. Instead, the adolescent's task has become one of picking and choosing from the desultory and inconsistent set of values that the culture offers. Ideally, the result would be a coherent and internally consistent subset of the culture's values. But perhaps that is expecting too much. It is certainly easier just to conform. For the foreseeable future, adolescence is likely to remain a mixture of these same two basic ingredients—namely, the pursuit of individual ideals as well as the going along with the crowd. Each has its advantages and its drawbacks.

Summary

Adolescence took on its modern form during the Victorian era, late in the nineteenth century. It was then that adolescence became a focus for problems of identity.

Four themes characterize the Victorian transformation of adolescence. First, a new concept of adolescence emerged, emphasizing youthful conformity, anti-intellectualism, passivity, awkwardness, and vulnerability. Second, the immediate socioeconomic status of adolescents changed in several ways. Increased economic dependence on parents, reduced responsibility, and reduced commitment to future adult roles were some of these changes. Third, the task of adolescence became one of choice among multiple options for adult roles. Fourth, the emphasis on moral and religious character development was replaced, to some extent, by broader issues of self-definition.

The causes of the Victorian transformation of adolescence also involve four social themes. First, the burden of deciding and defining the adult identity was largely transferred onto the young person. Second, changes in patterns of family life made adolescence more salient (prominent and noticeable) and more problematic. These changes included greatly increased and prolonged contact between adolescents and their parents, some shifts in family power relations, an increase in generational conflict, increased emotional investment by parents in their children, and family planning that resulted in families having all teenage children at once. Third, what psychologists call the psychosocial moratorium was socially constructed by a combination of transitional status, lack of commitment to adult roles, and isolation from society's mainstream. An important side effect was an escalation in the importance of the peer group. Fourth, society's loss of ideological consensus made the adolescent transition more difficult in several ways, including the added requirement of choice of personal values.

During the twentieth century, age segregation has continued to increase, further emphasizing the moratorium status of adolescence, as well as enhancing the importance of the peer group. The conformity pressures of the peer group have helped override the individualizing effects of the modern family. The Great Depression infringed on the moratorium status of one generation of adolescents, thus heightening identity foreclosure. Twentieth century youths have often been perceived as rebellious, but this supposed rebellion has generally been grounded in traditional American values. Society's loss of ideological consensus may have caused the appearance of youthful rebellion because as adolescents choose their cultural values they are likely to discover dramatic contradictions and inconsistencies.

6

Recapitulation: Emergence of Identity Problems

Why do people have identity problems? The last few chapters have attempted to sift through historical evidence to answer this question. Our modern difficulty with self-definition can be traced to three trends. First, traditional means of self-definition have failed, and their replacements have relied on more complex and problematic processes of self-definition. Second, identity has become an increasingly abstract, elusive entity. Third, the desire for individuality—the desire to be special or unique—has become more widespread and difficult to fulfill.

The failure of traditional means of self-definition is alone sufficient to explain why identity has become a dilemma. The evidence for this failure seems clearer than evidence for the other two trends.

To describe how traditional means of self-definition have ceased working for us, it is necessary to return to the model of identity discussed in Chapter 2. Remember that continuity (unity) and differentiation are the two *defining criteria* of identity—something contributes to identity if it unifies one over time and differentiates one from others. These two ends are achieved by the identity *components*, which are the basic units of self-definition. They include religion, sex, parentage, and so on.

Components produce identity to the extent that they make the person the same across time and differentiate the person from others. If the components fail to provide continuity and differentiation, then the individual will lack a stable identity. This is exactly what has happened. The events of the last few centuries have steadily undermined the capacity of identity components to provide continuity and differentiation.

There are two processes by which components have been rendered ineffective in producing identity.

The first process, what I shall refer to as *destabilization*, is the failure of the *unifying* function of the identity component. A way of defining the self provides continuity only if it remains the same throughout life. If the component of identity changes, the unity of the self over the lifetime is lost. Actual change is not necessary to weaken the ability of the component to unify identity; the possibility of change will do the same. Actual change separates the present and future self from the past self. Possible change—as in expecting to change, or considering that one might change—separates the present and past self from the future self. One example of an identity component that has undergone destabilization is identification with where one lives. The home is one source of identity, and living one's entire life in the same home is a powerful source of continuity in the sense of self. But the increases in geographical mobility have *destabilized* the home: few people live an entire life in the same place any longer.

The second process, what I shall refer to as *trivialization*, is the failure of the *differentiating* function of the identity component. A way of defining the self provides differentiation only if it furnishes some fairly important distinction between the self and others. As distinctions cease to matter, their contribution to identity disappears.

In the trivialization of an identity component, it becomes less important to be A rather than B. There are several variations on this. One is that the component ceases to affect what is possible for you. For example, who your great-grandfather was used to be important in determining what would be possible for you to do in your life, but today it is generally irrelevant. A second variation of trivialization consists of increased uniformity. It doesn't matter whether you are A, B, or C if they are all pretty much the same. It can be argued that bureaucratic growth has made many jobs similar to each other, thus trivializing the distinctions among them. (In contrast, the spread of "specialist" fields in medicine presumably increases the degree of differentiation, thus facilitating self-definition for physicians.) A third variation of trivialization consists of what might be called loss of *legitimation*. This occurs when people in general have ceased to regard some criterion of differentiation as important. What has happened to the role of religion is a good example of this. Certainly the distinction between Catholics and Protestants has been trivialized. It used to be a matter of life and death and a source of tremendous animosity. Today, Catholics and Protestants live together peacefully—at least in America. (In Ireland, that difference has not been trivialized.)

The next step in describing the failure of traditional self-definition is to list the major identity components that defined personal identity in a previous era. The Middle Ages can be used as a starting point. What then, were the major components of personal identity during the Middle Ages?

Names furnish one source of evidence because a name identifies you. Everyone had a first name or "Christian name," usually that of a biblical character. Although it is not clear what personal significance was attached to being named John as opposed to Matthew, the Christian naming does affirm the importance of religious models in defining the medieval self. Religion, then, was an important component of medieval identity. There were several models for proper Christian lives, and the individual molded his life to fit one of them. The Christian faith provided an important basis for the unity of the single life. And when the Protestant Reformation occurred at the end of the Middle Ages, adherence to one or another Christian sect became an important (life versus death) identity component.

There were several types of last names. During the Middle Ages, there were four main types of surnames (Dellquest, 1938; Withycombe, 1947). One was based on one's geographical home (e.g., William of Orange). A second was based on one's family (e.g., son of John, or Johnson). A third was based on one's job (e.g., John Smith or Peter Tailor). The fourth type was based on salient physical (or personal) characteristics (e.g., Louis the Fat; Frederick Red-Beard; Ivan the Meek; John "Cruikshanks," which meant "crooked legs"). These four types imply four identity components—geographical home, family membership, job, and physical appearance or nature. Family membership should probably be subdivided into two identity components, ancestral family and marriage. The importance of identification with the ancestral family is attested to by the practice of giving babies the same last name that their parents, grandparents, and earlier ancestors had. The importance of identification by marriage is attested to by the practice of changing one's surname when marrying, a practice that survives even today.

Consideration of the medieval social structure yields a few more identity components. Social rank and role (e.g., duke or serf) was a crucial determinant of who you were and what you could do with your life. Gender was clearly important. Age was probably also important, although age is a peculiar identity component because it keeps changing—it obviously cannot provide continuity over one's entire life.

Finally, moral status must be included as a major component of medieval identity. It seems likely that the medievals' concern with morality in self-definition derived from their religious faith. It is mentioned separately because religion and morality later became separated. Renaissance and early modern citizens were concerned with "honor" and "reputation" (for virtue) as important component of self-definition (Ariès, 1962; Stone, 1977). Extreme examples of the importance of honor can be found in military history. The Order of the Star was a medieval society of French knights, and one requirement of membership was an oath never to retreat more than a certain distance (about 500 meters) from a battlefield. The Order came to an end when most of its members chose to be slaughtered rather than retreat from an ambush (Tuchman, 1978; also de Rougemont, 1956). By the early modern period, armored knights were obsolete, but similar examples exist of honor outweighing both personal survival and strategic military advantage. At the battle of Fontenoy (1745), an English column advanced to within fifty paces of the French lines, and both sides aimed their rifles. The opposing officers saluted each other, and the British captain gallantly invited the French commander to give the order to fire first. "No, sir, you shall have the honor," replied the French count. As a result, the French were mowed down before they fired a shot (de Rougemont, 1956).

Having assembled a list of the major identity components for people living in the Middle Ages, what has happened to each of these components in subsequent centuries?

1. *Geographical home: Destabilized.* Although medieval Europe had its share of traveling minstrels, peripatetic students, and roving soldiers, one must assume that it was nonetheless common for persons to live their entire lives in the same locale. The end of serfdom, urban migration, the shift from agricultural to industrial jobs, and the vastly improved technology of travel have all increased geographical mobility. The amount of times people change residence, described by Thernstrom (1973; and depicted in the novels of Dos Passos) as typical of late nineteenth and early twentieth century New England, far exceeds anything the medievals imagined. Today it is regarded as unusual, if not exceptional, for a person to live his or her entire life in the same home. Thus, one source of continuity that enhances self-definition has been lost.

2. *Ancestral family: Trivialized.* Strong identification with a network of kin and ancestors has nearly vanished in America. To the propertied classes of the Middle Ages (and the centuries immediately following), the lineage had a certain reputation and honor that the current family members had to uphold. One inherited the vendettas, respect, obligations, and so forth, along with the family estate. Today inheritance has shrunk to a one-time transfer of transient property, and the parental homestead is likely to be sold by the heirs. No one worries about avenging an insult done to one's grandfather, and few worry about how their behavior will reflect

on the memory of their ancestors. With a very few exceptions, it just doesn't make any difference who your grandfather was. Lineage and family descent have become trivial as means of defining the self. The brevity of the "Roots" fad testifies to this trivialization. Although genealogical knowledge seemed to promise self-knowledge, it failed to provide it. Stone (1977) suggests that the "decline in respect for lineage and ancestry, in the concept of self as a trustee for the handing on of blood, property, and tradition, resulted in some loss of identity" (p. 426).

3. *Marriage: Destabilized.* The history of marriage is complicated by several trends that have worked in opposite directions. However, it does seem clear that marriage as a possible means of self-definition has been destabilized during the past century.

The early medieval status of marriage was a chaotic mixture of bigamy, desertion, secret marriages, and quasi-divorce arrangements (Stone, 1977). The Church finally succeeded in taking over the control of marriage around the thirteenth century. In principle, this meant that marriage was indissoluble until death. Through succeeding centuries, legal reforms consistently enforced the permanence of marriage.

All sorts of problems followed from this impossibility of divorce. Certain types of marriages (e.g., those of underage persons) were declared illegal, but if you had one, it was (despite its illegality) binding for life—you could never marry anyone else. A nobleman whose wife committed adultery prior to bearing him an heir could get a separation but was not allowed to remarry, which meant that he could not have an heir for his name and property. Some noblemen became desperate enough to have special and expensive Acts of Parliament annul their marriages (Stone, 1977).

Among the landless poor, of course, marital permanence could scarcely be enforced. Discontented husbands simply ran away and were never heard from again. Obscure practices such as the "wife-sale" persisted into the nineteenth century. To enact a wife-sale, the husband put a halter around the wife's neck just as if she were a cow, led her to market, and auctioned her to the highest bidder. (This was a ritual; normally the wife consented and the purchaser had been arranged in advance.) But, for the majority, marriage was for life. In Stone's words,

> In the late seventeenth and eighteenth centuries, therefore, full divorce and remarriage were possible by law for the very rich and by folk custom for the very poor, but impossible for the great majority in the middle who could not afford the cost of the one or the social stigma and remote risks of prosecution of the other. (p. 36)

You stayed married until you died. However, it must be kept in mind that people died earlier then. Stone goes so far as to suggest that remarriage was as frequent in the seventeenth century as it is in the twentieth (1977, p. 48); he considers the liberalization of divorce laws as the historical consequence of lowered mortality rates. In other words, a marriage might not last an entire life because one spouse might die before the other was old. Obviously, though, death is hardly equivalent to divorce for the one who dies. Moreover, you choose to get a divorce, but you do not choose to have your spouse die young.

In general, marriages lasted longest during the Victorian era. In the latter part of the nineteenth century, people lived long lives, but divorce was still difficult or impossible. American publications debated the pros and cons of liberalizing divorce laws (Ditzion, 1969). The rising demand for liberalization testifies to the fact that permanent marriage was considered a burden. Indeed, Ditzion quotes one wag who proposed that the government collect a tax from those desiring divorce; this would enable the government to pay off the entire national debt even if all other taxes were abolished (1969, pp. 109–110).

Reformed laws have made divorce more and more available during the past century, and divorce rates have continued to rise. People today marry somewhat younger than the Victorians, a change that occurred rather abruptly in the "marriage rush" following the Second World War (Modell, Furstenberg, & Strong, 1978). The tendency toward "hasty" marriage may itself have fueled increases in divorce (Ditzion, 1969, p. 398). The wartime experiences of veterans increased their authoritarianism, a trait which produced conflict in the newly democratic family (Burgess & Locke, 1945). Whatever the cause, it appears that the postwar trend toward earlier marriage has not led to longer marriage.

It seems apparent, then, that the proportion of persons who died while married for the first time has declined substantially over the past centuries. In view of the modern divorce rate, it is unrealistic to expect a marriage to last from youth until death. Marriage no longer furnishes the continuity over one's entire adult life that it once did. More important perhaps is the increased awareness of the possibility of divorce. In addition to the loss of actual continuity in marriage, the *promise* of continuity has been substantially undermined.

In addition, it is plausible that modern marriage practices have removed a link between the adult identity and the childhood identity. If it is true that some marriages during the Middle Ages were arranged by parents when their children were still quite young, then those children had an important identity component established early in life. But marriage no longer has the same power to link the identity of the twenty-five-year-old bride or groom to that same person at sixty, or at six.

4. *Job: Destablized.* Medieval aristocrats did not really have "jobs," unless their administrative and leadership roles are considered jobs, which they were not. However, guildsmen, serfs, and peasants certainly had jobs, and the majority were set on their occupational paths rather early in life. The vocational system was not flexible and allowed little room for choice. This was still probably true in the early modern period (sixteenth to eighteenth centuries), although there were exceptions. One such exception was the death of the oldest son, which enabled the second son to become prime heir to the family estate. A military or theological career, the common fate of younger sons, did not then have to be pursued (Stone, 1977). In general, though, whether aristocrat or serf, one's occupation was determined early in life and remained constant.

Even when occupational decisions were reached late in life, the choice differed from today's model. In some cases, for example, the occupational plan changed after a religious conversion (Kett, 1977). Still, the person had had a plan and then altered it, which is not the same as not having any serious occupational plan prior to adolescence.

Today, it is common and even expected for people to change jobs. Several signs point to an increasing acceptance and increasing frequency of major career changes among persons in their forties. Those who do not change their occupational fields tend to get different jobs because of the nature of bureaucracy. One gets promoted, and one's occupational activities (and status) change. Even if not promoted, the reorganizations periodically assign new duties. The medieval model in which you made shoes at age twenty and were still making them at age sixty is obsolete. Your job activities, your role in the organization, and your status and salary continue to change over the course of a modern career, even if one does work for the same company from college until retirement. Identity must therefore be an abstract synthesis of different jobs.

This destabilization may be fairly recent. Kett (1977) observes that "most people in preindustrial American society did not have careers; a man was likely to be making as much at 40 or 50 as he had been at 18 or 20" (p. 151), and he cites evidence that among factory workers this was still the case into the twentieth century. Widespread bureaucratization and permanent inflation seem to have been the factors that led to the modern notion of a career with continually rising status, salary, and responsibility. Bureaucratization and inflation only became ubiquitous in the twentieth century.

The link between childhood and adult occupational status was probably cut prior to the twentieth century. Before this, as long as apprenticeship was the definitive preparation for a career, you were steered into your vocation rather early in life. Apprenticeships tended to begin around age fourteen (Kett, 1977), and parents probably had planned them even earlier. In a rural society, most farmers' sons knew they would become farmers. In contrast, the modern adolescent often graduates from high school at age eighteen (or even college at twenty-two) with only a dim glimmer of vocational goals.

Of course, there are numerous exceptions to the destabilization of modern jobs. For example, the decision to practice medicine as a career needs to be made while the person is still in his or her teens, and the professional activities may become rather stable after the practice is established (by the early thirties). The job of physician is thus probably a more effective identity component than is the job of a bureaucrat.

5. *Social rank: Destabilized and trivialized.* Social rank (class status) was an extremely important identity component in the Middle Ages and remained so well into the early modern period. It was (along with gender) the first thing you knew about someone—you could tell it by the person's appearance, before a word was spoken. Society was highly and rigidly stratified. Your social rank was your place in the hierarchy, and it influenced just about every aspect of your life. It was also very difficult to change this component of your identity.

The enormous increases in social mobility after the Middle Ages undermined the *stability* of social rank. It became possible to change one's social rank during one's lifetime. Indeed, the American Dream "promised" unlimited social mobility for everyone. Although rags-to-riches success stories have been rare, modest but significant rises in social class were common by the turn of the twentieth century (Thernstrom, 1973).

Thus, social rank has been destabilized. Underneath this destabilization, however, there has been a prolonged conflict concerning the legitimacy of the system of social rank.

Medieval social rank was determined by birth: Status was based on "blood" or lineage. Social mobility was created by the possibility of acquiring wealth, not of changing one's "blood." The early modern period saw a conflict between wealth and blood as the essential criteria of social status.

In a sense, wealth won out. Today, social class is a function of wealth; social scientists refer to "socioeconomic status" instead of social rank. Blood (lineage) has very little to do with social status, except insofar as wealth is inherited. In addition, the significance of social status has simply diminished. The significance that "blood" lost was not all gained by wealth; rather, it was just lost. Modern social status (wealth) is recognized as a mark of achievement, but it does not denote an intrinsic difference in personal worth the way it once did. The French and American revolutions denied the legitimacy of the hierarchy of social rank as a just determinant of individual worth. That "all men are created equal" was, indeed, a revolutionary idea. The medieval mind took it for granted that the aristocracy were better people than the serfs. Their noble birth was, after all, God's will.

Nietzsche's research on the linguistic evolution of moral terms—his "genealogy of morals"—sheds further light on the medieval mind. He found that all words denoting moral goodness and virtue derived from words that described the upper class. (Even today, we describe an unusually virtuous action as "noble.") The medieval mentality, of course, placed great emphasis on moral goodness as a determinant of personal worth, due in large part to Christian ideology. A link between moral goodness and noble blood is evidence that the nobility were regarded as intrinsically better people than the common folk.

This view was repudiated in the American Declaration of Independence. And in the past two centuries, it has gradually disappeared from our society—the civil rights legislation of the 1950s and 1960s is an example of the same removal of institutional credence in innate human inequality. The point is that social rank lost much of its legitimacy as an identity component. In that sense, it has been trivialized as well as destabilized.

6. *Gender: Partially trivialized.* Modern society can hardly claim to be utterly without discrimination on the basis of gender. However, it seems very close to that ideal when compared with medieval society. Modern women have the same rights as men—to vote, to get an education, to have a career, to own property, to initiate lawsuits. Medieval women had practically none of these. Many of the consequences of gender have thus disappeared. Obviously, not all of them have. Although sex roles have changed from institutions to expectations, from structural opportunities and life paths to personality types, they do persist. It is best to describe gender as partially (although substantially) trivialized as an identity component.

Motherhood is one exception to the trivializing of gender. The ability to bear children is still exclusively the province of women, and it often is centrally important as an identity component. Being a mother is a common means of self-definition for a woman.

In fact, it is plausible that motherhood is more powerful as an identity component today than it was in the Middle Ages. Modern mothers have much more contact with their children than did their medieval predecessors, in that modern mothers care for them as infants and live with them at least until adolescence. One possible explanation for this increase in the importance of motherhood is the secularization of fulfillment concepts during the Romantic era. When people started looking for fulfillment on earth, men sought it in work and creative endeavors; but these means of fulfillment were unavailable to women. Women may therefore have intensified their involvement in the activities open to them, of which motherhood was central. Thus, through the eighteenth century, more and more women began to seek satisfaction and fulfillment by showing off their children to others (e.g., Stone, 1977). In fact, by the end of that century some women's lives seemed dominated by their determination to raise child prodigies.

7. *Age.* Age cannot undergo destabilization because it continually changes. For the same reason, therefore, it is at best only a temporary or transient identity component. However, age has gained in importance since the Middle Ages. If Ariès (1962) is correct, age meant nothing (except perhaps some added experience and wisdom) after early childhood. The age stratification of society is a modern innovation. The value attached to the elderly (experience and wisdom) has diminished because their "wisdom" is seen as obsolete in rapidly changing times. Today, the young are the ideal.

Thus, although one identity component has gained importance since the Middle Ages, it is a component that by definition cannot provide continuity.

8. *Bodily characteristics.* It is doubtful whether the occasional occurrence of names like "Louis the Fat" really signified that obesity (or other such characteristics) was an important identity component. Withycombe (1947) suggests that this type of surname was the least common of the four main types.

However, the importance of physical endowments for personal self-definition in an agricultural society should not be underestimated. Size and strength were certainly decisive attributes on farms, especially before motors and other technology.

Urbanization has undoubtedly trivialized size and strength as identity components. Physical strength may make it easier for today's urban citizen to open pickle jars, but it does little to decide how much food he will get or how successful she will be at a desk job.

This is not to say that physical attributes are irrelevant to modern identity. The demise of the system of arranged marriage has increased the importance of physical beauty and charm as a means of attracting members of the opposite sex. Many people exert considerable effort to make themselves attractive, and it seems likely that one's attractiveness is an important component of one's self-concept and self-esteem.

Thus, although some physical qualities have been trivialized, physical attractiveness has probably gained in importance since the Middle Ages. However, physical attractiveness (like age) is not a constant throughout life; it often does not appear until late adolescence and declines with age. Again, this is another component that has gained in importance but cannot guarantee continuity of identity.

9. *Moral goodness: Trivialized and destabilized.* Morality has had a complex history. For my purposes, it is sufficient to observe that morality was a decisive component of self-definition in the Middle Ages and again during the Victorian era, but that its importance has diminished in the twentieth century.

Several factors have contributed to the decline of morality. Urbanization has long been associated with vice, probably because city life seems full of sinful temptations. However, an additional feature of urban life may be even more important than "temptations" in undermining morality. The city places the individual in a large and changing social environment that is not conducive to moral self-definition. Moral qualities are not quickly or easily communicated to others. A reputation for honesty, for example, has to be developed over a long period of time. In a small town in past centuries, everyone knew who was honest, sexually proper, and so forth, because in general, everyone lived his or her entire life there and because there were few enough people that one could, to some extent, know them all. In the modern big city, however, there are far too many people to know, and the high mobility means that those you do know may be gone in five or ten years. This new type (large and transient) of social environment fosters an emphasis on identity components that can be simply and rapidly communicated to a stream of new acquaintances—components such as physical (especially sexual) attractiveness, income and possessions, age, and charm. Persons meeting at a convention or singles bar can quickly grasp these characteristics of each other but not moral qualities such as loyalty or honesty.

The general point is that personal virtue has lost much of its importance in determining how one is treated by others. One's access to certain social circles, one's marriage options, and one's business success once depended on moral qualities; people refused to associate with someone who lacked certain moral qualities. The decline of all of this constitutes a trivialization of morality as an identity component. Indeed, during the 1960s, the widespread fascination and identification with the rebel, the bad boy, the outsider (Thompson, 1979) made it no longer necessary to be stringently moral by traditional standards in order to win some sort of approval.

Individual identity is first shaped by the child's experiences in the family and at school. These institutions placed increasing emphasis on the moral education and guidance of the young, beginning in the fifteenth century and becoming widespread by the seventeenth century (Ariès, 1962). This "moralization of society" (Ariès, p. 412) culminated in the strict discipline of the nineteenth century but has diminished or has been reversed in the twentieth century. Modern American schools place ever decreasing emphasis on the moral guidance of pupils (Bronfenbrenner, 1963; Larkin, 1979). Early in this century, the dominant aspect of family relationships shifted from an emphasis on duty and obedience to a new emphasis on emotional communication and nurturance (Fass, 1977). The two main architects of individual identity have thus moved away from their former primary concern with morality.

The increasingly impersonal nature of business transactions has also reduced the importance of morality. Trust was presumably a more critical aspect of buying on credit at the old general store than it is in using Master Card at today's department store. (See Harris, 1981, for a more thorough discussion of this.) The era of doing business by one's "word" and handshake, without signed documents, was a time during which morality was implicit in business relations; obviously, no one does business that way any more. Again, personal morality has lost its differentiating consequences, which means it has been trivialized.

It could also be suggested that morality has been destabilized. Today, persons do a variety of things that traditional morality condemned—lying on one's tax returns, engaging in ("promiscuous") premarital sex, using illegal drugs, and cheating on highschool exams. Unfortunately, morality *requires* continuity in order to provide self-definition. All positive moral attributes tend to follow the model of virginity—that is, one breach permanently removes that identity. Last month's swindler can hardly identify himself as an honest man, even if he is telling the truth this month. Morality is not a form of self-definition that is well suited to the flexible, adaptive, or other-directed person of today. Destabilization of moral behavior eliminates the viability of morality as a means of self-definition.

10. *Religion: Trivialized.* Religious faith was of extraordinary and fundamental importance for the self-definition of medieval man. Religion provided the unifying purpose of life and furnished the models for living. Variations in religious faith were taken very seriously, and people were readily put to death for them. The papal schism in the fourteenth century, followed by the Protestant schism at the end of the Middle Ages, ushered in a period of mutual persecution and religious warfare. Faith became a matter of life and death.

During the eighteenth and nineteenth centuries, however, religious tolerance began to spread. At the same time, the general intensity of religious faith declined. (The two trends may well have been related.) Together, these trends constituted a trivialization of religion as an identity component. Today, in most places, Protestants and Catholics coexist peacefully and even amicably; they no longer murder one another over details of creed. Moreover, the majority of people live their lives according to very secular goals, models, and patterns. The secularization of the Protestant work ethic and the Romantic concept of individual (secular) potential drastically reduced the role of religion in the search for the meaning of life.

There are numerous and various exceptions, of course. Jews have been cruelly persecuted during the twentieth century and perhaps even very recently (e.g., Timerman, 1981). Periodic bursts of piety such as these shown by the "Moral Majority" indicate a sizable minority of mainstream Americans who are devout and intolerant Christians. In Ireland and in the Middle East, there is armed combat between religious groups. However, it is clear that religion is overall a much less common and less powerful component of personal identity than it was in the Middle Ages.

There are two parts to the trivialization of religion. One is the decline of consequences associated with its distinctions; Catholics are not excluded from Protestant neighborhoods or from jobs when the employer is Protestant, and vice versa. The other is loss of legitimation; as the general population becomes increasingly agnostic, it ceases to recognize the validity of articles of religious faith as bases for meaningful distinctions.

Modern Sources of Identity

It is not surprising that identity has become a problem in the twentieth century. Eight of the ten means of self-definition that formed personal identity during the Middle Ages have lost much or all of their effectiveness through trivialization or destabilization. The other two (age and physical attributes) are by nature unstable and are thus unable to provide continuity of identity over the life span. It is a wonder that modern man has any sense of identity left!

As the effectiveness of socially defined identity components has decreased, there is an increasing need for people to generate a self-definition internally. But a few other things have become available as means of self-definition to fill the void created by the collapse of the traditional means. The infiltration of personality into identity has been discussed in Chapter 4. People define themselves partly by how they do things and how they get along with others. Personality is probably not one identity component but a group of components. Personality may help provide self-definition by giving the self content, by distinguishing the self from others, and by creating some continuity over time. However, making one's identity out of lots of personality traits may create a lack of unity. If each X that one can fill in the phrase "I am X" is considered an identity component, it will be difficult to grasp their unity.

Along with personality traits, ownership may have gained in importance for self-definition. Status symbols and "conspicuous consumption" (Veblen, 1899) define the self through its material acquisitions. These visible signs of wealth and taste are taken to indicate one's personal quality or value. In addition, as noted earlier, modern advertising fosters the impression that identities are created by buying certain products. Of course, no product can provide an individual identity; it simply assigns one a spot among the prefabricated set of social identities.

Personal accomplishment as a means of self-definition has also probably gained since the Middle Ages. Even a single accomplishment can give you a valuable identity component for the rest of your life. Being an Olympic medalist or Nobel Prize winner has that effect. Obtaining an education (to a certain level) also has that effect. Being a college graduate, for example, is something that has lasting meaning regarding the self. Getting a Ph.D. or M.D. is sufficiently important to change one's name—people will address you as "Doctor" for the rest of your life.

A fourth modern source of self-definition is participation in some idiosyncratic organization or activity. The spread of leisure time to all levels of society has enabled people to take part in a wide variety of activities, and these hobbies and memberships help define the self. One is not just a clerk; one is a jogger and a guitarist as well as a clerk. Although most of the activities are done by many others, they provide a kind of local differentiation because there are so many possible combinations that one's own combination seems unique among one's acquaintances. There are millions of clerks, millions of joggers, and millions of guitar players; one knows several of each; but one may be the "only" one who is all three things. With the other joggers, one is the guitar player; among musicians, one is the clerk (with the "daytime job"); at work, one is known as the jogger or guitarist.

Thus, several new types of identity components have come forward to fill a void created by the decline of the traditional means of self-definition. The new methods have some obvious limitations, however. In the first place, they do not take form until adulthood. Personality and hobbies are in flux until at least late adolescence, accomplishments accumulate during adulthood, and the acquisition of status symbols is a game for established adults. It is no wonder that adolescence is viewed as a time plagued by identity problems, because the modern means of self-definition stabilize only after adolescence.

In addition, these new means of self-definition require effort and choice. Accomplishments, hobbies, and the acquisition of possessions all require decisions and then willful implementation of those decisions. Even personality is seen as something you cultivate, as the multitude of self-help and pop psychology books testifies. You have to create your identity. The new means of self-definition are harder to use than the traditional ones.

Finally, it is plausible that the modern means of self-definition would tend to promote fragmentation or compartmentalization of identity. Personality is not just one identity component but several of them. The same holds for accomplishment and for ownership, and often for hobbies and activities as well. The "well-rounded" individual, one who creates identity by being a unique combination of common attributes, tends to need a lot of identity components (as in the jogger-clerk-guitarist example) because it is the number and diversity that create the differentiation on which identity is based. Having lots of identity components creates anew the problem of finding a unity among them to establish a clear sense of identity.

Self-definition Processes

In Chapter 2 five types of self-definition processes were discussed. Type I identity components are acquired passively, usually by circumstances of birth, and they normally remain stable throughout life. Type II involves acquiring an identity component by means of one well-defined achievement or transition. Type III components measure the self along a hierarchy or scale of criteria, and one can always move up or down the scale. Type IV involves optional choice—an identity component is given, but the person may choose to change it. Type V forces the person to make a choice among various alternatives. (For examples, see the table at the end of Chapter 2.)

The five types were arranged along a continuum of how difficult and problematic they are to use. It is easiest to acquire identity by having it assigned to you; it is somewhat more difficult to achieve identity according to well-defined standards, procedures, and criteria; it is problematic to acquire identity by acts of choice, especially in the absence of guidelines. The history of self-definition has been a gradual shift toward the more difficult and problematic self-definition processes.

Medieval identity was defined mainly by Type I and Type II processes. The person was defined by the kinship network and social rank into which he or she was born. Gender decisively determined the course of one's life. These components—home, ancestry (lineage), gender, social rank—reflected Type I processes. Several well-defined transitions marked the Type II acquisition of new identity components—becoming an adult, marriage, and parenthood. In the same way, there were well-defined transitions that marked succession to new roles or titles because of the death of an incumbent, such as when the son acquired the family title, or because one completed a requisite training and ceremony, such as that for a knight or priest.

Some traces of Type III and even possibly Type IV processes can be observed in medieval society. The concern with honor, glory, virtue, and morality reflected the fact that the self could be redefined at times. In particular, gaining glory through feats of arms was in a sense hierarchical and competitive although there was no clear standard of measurement. Morris (1972) suggests that some men could choose among different occupations or among different forms of monastic life. Given that these choices were within the general context of Christian faith and values, and given that the men presumably had gotten started in one direction before confronting the alternative possibilities, these choices would seem to be Type IV processes. Still, such processes were probably rare in medieval life. In general, medieval self-definition was accomplished by means of the simplest and least problematic (Types I and II) processes.

In the early modern period, self-definition became centrally concerned with the problems characteristic of Type III and Type IV processes. The rise of the middle class entailed an increase in the use of wealth as a standard of self-definition, with its attendant issues of competition, uncertainty, and discontent. Toward the end of this era, wealth began to replace lineage as the defining standard of social status, which caused even the aristocracy to become concerned with wealth as a factor in self-definition (cf. Stone, 1977; also Sennett, 1974).

During the Protestant schism, and then in the subsequent eras that witnessed a decline in Christian faith, Type IV processes were most widespread. Protestantism confronted persons with an alternative to their most fundamental beliefs. Christian faith had always served as the ultimate arbiter of questions about proper and correct action. Now that there were rival forms of Christian creed, a new criterion was needed to decide whether Protestantism or Catholicism was the true religion, but obviously there was no such criterion. To say that the schism *forced* individuals to make choices seems misleading, however, because most individuals were brought up in one or the other faith. Some could repudiate it (i.e., make their own choice), but they could also remain foreclosed in the faith of their upbringing. The Protestant schism was therefore conducive to Type IV self-definition because it made personal choice possible but not obligatory. In the same way, the decline of Christian faith made its rejection an option for individuals, but they did not have to confront that choice; they could adhere to it in a foreclosed fashion.

Choice did not inevitably mean repudiation of the faith in which one had been brought up. One could certainly confront the alternatives and make a decisive personal choice in favor of that faith. But just making such a choice was a self-definitional act quite different from the adherence to such faith without ever questioning it. The difference lies in the problematic and difficult nature of the process of self-definition that is involved.

The decline of Christian faith continued during the Romantic era. It is important to emphasize that most persons still professed belief in Christianity, but their belief had less and less influence over their daily lives. More generally, the Romantics believed that there were ultimate values, whatever they might be, but increasingly recognized the necessity for the individual to make choices for the sake of self-definition. The Romantic attitude toward society reflects the Type IV process. Society was perceived as oppressive, and a need to reject some of society's dictates was recognized. But these acts still took place within an overarching scheme of belief, faith, and value.

During the Victorian era, increasing numbers began to recognize that they did not believe in Christianity. The failure of this basic value was experienced as critical. Without such a framework, choice is highly problematic; individuals are forced to choose, yet no guidelines or criteria for choosing are available. Such choice was increasingly experienced as problematic. The increasing artistic and philosophical concern with choice early in the twentieth century, such as the existentialist concern with authenticity and responsibility (cf. Sypher, 1962; Trilling, 1971), attests to this. It is also attested to by the newly problematic nature of adolescence.

Desire for Individuality

At the beginning of this chapter, three developments were mentioned to explain the emergence of identity problems in the modern era. The first has already been examined—the decline of traditional, simple, and effective means of self-definition. Now to the other two.

It seems likely that an increased desire for identity has contributed to the urgency of identity problems in the modern individual.

The increased desire for identity appears to be an increased desire for differentiation, not continuity. Two trends have probably made people more desirous than their predecessors of being special, unique, and different—an increase in individualistic child-raising and a cultural shift toward valuing individuality.

It seems quite likely that child-raising practices can foster or inhibit the appetite for individuality. If you are brought up to believe you are unique or special, you will tend to think of yourself that way as an adult. If as a child you received love in connection with your being special or unique, you will probably value differentiation and seek it for yourself as an adult. The issue is this: Have child-raising patterns evolved in recent centuries in such a way that gives children increasing affection in connection with increasingly individual attention? The answer appears to be yes.

Back in the days when most children died, it was emotionally risky to become too emotionally attached to any particular child. Stone (1977) describes parental practices of the early modern period in England that strike the modern sensibility as callously indifferent to the children. For example, parents in the upper classes persisted in sending newborn infants out to the country to be suckled by strangers, despite the knowledge that the risks of infection and death were much greater than in the parental home.

Gradually, during the seventeenth and eighteenth centuries, parents became more affectionate with their children (Ariès, 1962; Stone, 1977). In the nineteenth century, child mortality declined permanently, due to various improvements in public health, hygiene, and medicine. The death of a child became a terrible tragedy rather than an expected event (Ariès, 1981). The practice of giving several sons the same name (in the hope that at least one would survive) died out. Both of these developments indicate that parents were investing increased emotion and importance in each individual child. By the nineteenth century, each child was special and important.

Social changes vastly intensified the impact of these new parental attitudes on children. The nineteenth century saw the disappearance of the long-standing practice of "fostering out" children (i.e., sending them to live with other families) and the disappearance of apprenticeships. Rather abruptly, children now lived in the parental home from birth until marriage.

The decline in early mortality applied to adults, too. Adults now had a good chance of living to old age. As a result, fewer children grew up as orphans. The picture of the (early modern) family as a brief, transient union became obsolete; Victorian marriages lasted, on average, longer than any others in recent centuries (Stone, 1977).

The result of all this was that by the nineteenth century the typical child grew up in the presence of adults who were specially and strongly concerned about him or her. The child received individualized attention and affection. Because of this, persons probably grew up with a serious emotional investment in being special.

This argument provides an effective and consistent basis for explaining an important subsequent development. According to Burgess and Locke (1945), early in the twentieth century the family moved from placing primary emphasis on duty and work to a new emphasis on intimacy and emotional relationships. Lasch (1978) and others have observed that the type of individuality desired by twentieth century persons had changed, too. The desire for achievement through work and for fame based on this has given way to a desire to be a celebrity—that is, a desire to be loved and admired for oneself or for one's personality regardless of one's achievements (or lack thereof). G. B. Trudeau parodies this modern trend in his "Doonesbury" comic strip by portraying a talk show on which the "celebrity of the week" has forgotten what he did that made him a celebrity. "Okay, not important," says the interviewer.

Thus, a change in what parents emphasized in family relationships was accompanied by a change in the type or basis of individuality sought by adults. Both changes emphasized personality, including interpersonal and emotional patterns.

Overall, then, it seems quite likely that changes in child-raising patterns have produced people with an increased desire to be special, different, and unique. A second probable reason for the presumed increase in the desire for differentiation was contained in the evolution of general cultural values and ideology. This evolution raised the value of individuality.

The emergence of individuality as a major value has been discussed in detail by Weintraub (1978). The medieval citizen could live by the well-known models of the proper Christian life. Fitting the model was important; details and particulars were not. As society became more complex, offered choices, and embodied change, the traditional models stopped working—they no longer provided all the answers.

Toward the end of the Middle Ages, increased social mobility and increased trade had raised plenty of possibilities for deception and misrepresentation of self. Indeed, the concern with differences between appearances and underlying realities was a major theme of sixteenth century culture (Trilling, 1971). Necessity dictated distrust of the "outer" self, and the "inner" self was born. Individuality was discovered as something inside the individual—that is, something hidden.

This does not mean that the inner self initially was given a great deal of value. The sixteenth century stress on the value of "sincerity" may have meant that the inner self should be equivalent to the outer self (Trilling, 1970). The interest in one's own particulars (individuality) may have been a kind of curiosity and not the result of a serious value commitment (see Weintraub, 1978, on the sixteenth century). Individuality was discovered before it was valued (see also Morris, 1972). People were fascinated by the discovery of their special characteristics, but there was no apparent sense of why these were important.

That, however, changed. Protestantism was developing at that time, and Protestantism (especially Calvinism) emphasized the inner life. The gradual erosion of religious faith also contributed to individuality; the emerging concept of secular fulfillment rested on a notion of individual creative potential. The general public became interested in the personal lives of writers and artists (Altick, 1965), presumably because their lives exemplified the new ideal of secular fulfillment through creative destiny. The Romantic period placed ultimate and secular value on what was inside the individual, such as traits and emotions. Perhaps inevitably, this led to the prevailing attitude (reflected in literature) that the individual and society were in chronic conflict with each other.

The point is that Western culture increasingly placed a value on private, inner experience, and this value was connected to individuality. Inner experience meant the personal, special, unique quality of an individual's life. As culture came to place more value on this, people presumably began to want to be special and unique; individuality was thus more desirable.

The Romantic era (around the beginning of the nineteenth century), then, embodied both an ideological and a sociopsychological shift. The ideological shift located the value of the individual life within the individual, not within God or society at large. The sociological shift was marked by a gradual decrease in society's capacity to provide the individual with the meaning of life. Society became somehow too impersonal, complex, uncertain, and threatening. People turned away from public life and sought fulfillment in personal religious experience, individual creative development, and (for the masses) private family relationships. Indeed, during the Victorian era (the late nineteenth century), the private family home became a bulwark against the chaotic and threatening world of public society. Rugged individualism, disillusionment with society, the secularized work ethic of competitive capitalism, and the emphasis on family life—all of these express the belief that it was now up to the individual to define the meaning of his own life; society had let him down by failing to do it for him. Fulfillment was associated with private, even inner, life—with individuality.

As stated earlier, life in the twentieth century has been marked by a peculiar contradiction: individualistic values amidst collective life. The spread of urban, industrial, bureaucratic life and the development of a consumer economy with mass media and advertising have resulted in the "mass society" with its collective behavior patterns. The individual lives in the midst of society and is totally dependent on it. Society provides the individual with a means of livelihood, information, food and clothing, entertainment, and so forth. But society refuses to provide a meaning for life other than the system of extrinsic rewards (as in earning lots of money). If the individual is at all sensitive, he or she feels that society is indifferent to his or her fate. (Society seems especially indifferent when compared with the parental home! Growing up in the modern family, with its individual concern and affection, must make people all the more sensitive to society's seeming indifference.) In the early part of the twentieth century this reached crisis levels. Alienation, labor movements, the demand for increased public welfare, and other similar trends all expressed the view that society was intolerably indifferent to the individual's fate.

Society did take some steps. The New Deal was the most obvious. In the New Deal, the government agreed to take on a drastically expanded role as a sort of parent, to promise minimum levels of security and subsistence for the individual. This assuaged the feeling of being at the mercy of powers indifferent to one's fate, but it obviously did not solve the problem of providing a meaning for life. The "accommodation" trend of postwar letters was a coming to terms with the new reality—the need to create one's own individual meaning in the midst of life in a mass society. "Myth-making" and identity searches in the 1960s literature (Pütz, 1979) are a continuation of the same trend toward resolving the issue of finding individual meaning within collective life.

In Europe the picture was far more complex than in America. Totalitarian movements rejected individuality and self-definition by personal achievement and choice, and returned to Type I identity components such as ethnic heritage (Arendt, 1951). Events ranging from career advancement to imprisonment and execution were (are) determined in totalitarian society by ethnic membership. Arendt emphasizes that many Europeans eagerly and passionately identified with their ethnic groups, even when incarcerated for belonging to those groups. (She suggests that such membership was often the sole remaining source of identity for such persons, who by then were often deprived of rights and citizenship.) She also emphasizes that all personal achievements, behavior, and actions are profoundly irrelevant to one's fate in a totalitarian society—and that people acquiesce remarkably well to that reality. There has thus been some movement away from individuality in the twentieth century. People may have continued to value their individual qualities, but they were attracted to social movements that were not individualistic in practice.

America was founded at a time when the fashionable views about secular creative potential demanded that the individual be free to pursue individual goals. The basic American ideals of equality of rights and freedom from constraint have shaped our government ever since, and reforms have extended these rights to segments of the population (women, blacks) initially denied them. The sense of individual rights is as vital in twentieth century America as it has ever been. Part of the reason for the persistence of the value of individuality is its connection with individual rights. Individuality itself has become a "right" rather than a duty or achievement.

Thus, individuality has continued to be an important value in twentieth century America (and presumably Western Europe, too) because of society's failure to provide a meaning of life and because of the link between individuality and the concept of human rights. However, collective life in mass society has made the *practice* of individuality considerably more difficult, as numerous observers have suggested. (For example, high-school peer-group pressures and bureaucratic practices promote conformity to collective norms of appearance and behavior.) This then is the problem: Individuality is encouraged in theory (as an ideal) but is discouraged in practice. The proliferation of artificial individuality and of semblances of individuality (Fromm, 1941) are results of that disparity.

The general consequence, however, is the concern with identity. Modern child-raising techniques and the modern valuation of individuality lead to a desire for differentiation. The obstacles to individuality created by living in a modern collective society make the appetite for differentiation difficult to satisfy. The quest for identity expresses that problem and that appetite.

Identity as Abstraction

The third development that helps explain the emergence of identity problems is the change in the nature of identity from a set of concrete givens to an increasingly hidden and abstract set of priorities and values. Identity has come to depend more and more on a reification of abstractions.

As already mentioned, medieval identity was often largely determined by birth (e.g., social rank, lineage) and most of the remainder of identity was determined by parents during one's early years (i.e., marriage, occupation). Few options were available to any one person. Identity was the content of these components. Today, however, a tendency to regard identity as the precondition of these components has emerged. Medieval man *was* his occupation; the modern individual self *is expressed by* occupation.

To an extent, this is a reiteration of the earlier discussion of self-definition processes: The formation of identity has come to rely more and more on the complex and difficult processes that involve choice and achievement; medieval identity emphasized the simple and passive Type I processes. But there is more to it than that. The person's identity was once equated with surface phenomena; now it is equated with hidden, presumed causes of those phenomena. As MacIntyre (1981, p. 56) suggested, the individual came to be thought of as existing prior to and apart from all roles. Identity became an abstract, hidden matter.

The cause of this change probably lies in the drastic changes in social organization and individual freedom. A major social trend over the last half dozen centuries has been to offer the individual an increased range of possibilities for what he may be and to leave it up to him to choose among them. If you have no option except to be X (as in the Middle Ages), then your identity is X. If, however, you can be either X or Y or Z (as today), then you must choose. In order to choose, you need to find a criterion for comparing and evaluating X, Y, or Z. Thus, you need to identify with some value (criterion) prior to becoming X, Y, or Z. You need to "find yourself" before you can choose. Identity is a precondition to becoming X; it is no longer just being X.

Actually, since each of the choices has its own criteria, identity has become a matter of *metacriteria*. One needs metacriteria to help decide whether to define oneself according to this or that set of criteria. For example, the criteria for becoming a physician involve receiving an M.D., getting a license to practice, completing an internship, and so forth. Becoming a scientist involves meeting the criteria of having a Ph.D., obtaining a laboratory, developing theories to test, and so forth. But one first needs metacriteria to guide the choice as to whether to be a physician or scientist.

Obviously, not everyone goes through this. A substantial number of modern persons simply become physicians or accountants or mothers without much thought. The modern dilemma of identity only applies to those who seriously confront the plurality of options available in modern life.

The introduction of choice into identity has thus brought about the need for metacriteria that help individuals choose. Unlike the medieval identity, most components of modern identity reflect implicit or explicit choices (that is, Type IV or Type V self-definition). As the Middle Ages ended, and with it, the unity of Christian faith, one needed criteria to decide between Catholic and Protestant (and then perhaps between Presbyterian and Lutheran, and so on) faiths. The decline of parental authority enabled (and required) individuals to choose their own spouses. Later, it required individuals to choose their occupations. Geographical mobility made one's home a matter of choice, often a series of choices. Leisure time brought up the choice of hobbies and pastimes. Personality became an important source of identity components, and with the new value on personal "flexibility" (Wheelis, 1958), personality, too, became something that one chose, or at least periodically adjusted.

The conception of identity as an "inner" self was fed by these developments. The appearance of new manifestations to express the inner self meant that new dimensions were attributed to the inner self. Thus, your leisure activities were presumed to "express" you. That suggests that there was now something in your inner self that was not directly knowable but that dictated your leisure activities.

How to make all these choices? The presence of many choices entails a need for many metacriteria. Unfortunately, perhaps, the modern individual often seems to have given up on finding firm, unimpeachable metacriteria. The modern individual trusts only science and medicine, and these have little to say about how to choose spouse, career, faith, and home. The traditional basis for final, firm metacriteria—religion—is no longer an unimpeachable authority. Many persons who still cling to Christian faith spend a fair amount of energy arguing and justifying their beliefs on "scientific" grounds and in "scientific" terms. By definition, faith that requires external justification is not unimpeachable authority. It is this loss of unimpeachable authority that helped cause the shift from Type IV to Type V self-definition. Choice could no longer be avoided. The necessity of making choices, in turn, made it necessary for identity to contain metacriteria.

Obviously, many of the main choices are made during adolescence. The search for metacriteria for making choices has become an important part of the adolescent "identity crisis." This is important to keep in mind. The adolescent in an identity crisis is not simply comparing different occupations—the identity crisis must be largely resolved before vocational counseling can help. Instead, the adolescent is searching for metacriteria by which to choose occupation, spouse, and so on. Because of this, the identity crisis is perceived as an inner rather than an external conflict. The crisis is a matter of identifying oneself with some value from which the choices can be derived.

It is plausible that there simply aren't enough good metacriteria on which to make all these choices. A choice between a medical and a legal career cannot be made on a purely objective basis—neither field is completely superior to the other. And many persons would probably be equally happy in either field. Still, somehow, the choice must be made. The comment by Habermas (1973) and others that meaning is a scarce resource that is becoming ever scarcer could be applied to the difficulty of individual decision-making. In the absence of both internal and external criteria for making choices, identity becomes quite difficult to assemble. It therefore seems likely that making identity a precondition of certain choices has contributed to the emergence of identity problems.

Summary

This chapter summarizes the historical emergence of problems of identity, in terms of identity components and self-definition processes.

The major components of medieval identity have ceased to function effectively for the modern individual. Social change can make a type of identity component ineffective for producing identity in two ways, and these are based on the two defining criteria of identity.

The first, *destabilization*, means that the identity component tends to change during a lifetime. The defining criterion of *continuity* is thus not satisfied. The second, *trivialization*, means that it no longer matters whether someone has that particular identity component or not. The defining criterion of *differentiation* is also not satisfied, or at least not in a way that makes any difference.

Of the ten major components of medieval identity eight have become wholly or partially ineffective in creating identity because of either destabilization or trivialization. Geographical home, marriage, job, and social rank have undergone destabilization. Ancestral family, social rank, gender, moral virtue, and religion have undergone trivialization. The other two (age and bodily characteristics) are by nature unstable, and are therefore unable to satisfy the *continuity* defining criterion. Thus, traditional means of self-definition have failed in establishing identity.

New major components of identity have emerged to replace the older ones, but these are harder to use. In general, self-definition processes have changed from the simple, passive, well-defined processes (Types I and II) to the complex, problematic, and uncertain processes (Types III, IV, and V). Modern self-definition requires choice, achievement, and frequent redefinition of self; medieval self-definition generally did not. The historical movement toward the more complex and difficult self-definition processes is a major reason for identity being a problem

People also want to be different, in the sense of unique or special, probably because of a cultural evolution that places increasing value on individuality and inner experience, and because of individualistic child-raising techniques that teach children that they are special. Differentiation is one of the defining criteria of identity, so its increase means that people have a greater need for identity than in previous eras.

A last major cause of identity problems is the fact that identity has become an abstract, elusive entity that is supposed to contain one's personal and unique answers for life's difficult questions. As self-definition required more and more personal choices (i.e., Type V self-definition), people needed guidelines (metacriteria) for making these choices. Identity used to mean one's roles or attributes; it now meant the underlying entity that is expressed by these roles or attributes. Identity became equated with one's set of metacriteria, which may or may not always exist. Hence the appeal of images like "finding oneself" or "searching one's soul" for questions about identity. The appropriate metacriterion is presumed to be there somewhere inside, but one doesn't know just where or what it is. So one hopes to establish the metacriterion by searching for it. Equating identity with abstract, elusive metacriteria has helped to make identity hard to know and define, and has thus contributed to the problems of identity.

7

Functional Aspects of Identity in Historical Perspective

This chapter attempts to expand the psychological understanding of identity by examining the historical evolution of the three functional aspects of identity: The interpersonal self, the sense of personal potentiality, and the personal structure of values and priorities.

Interpersonal Roles

It is necessary to consider first the interpersonal aspect of identity, namely, the set of roles for relationships and the "public self." Among sociologists, the term *identity* seems to refer exclusively to the social roles of the person. This includes formal roles, which are defined by relationships—mother, policeman, teacher, boss, friend. It also includes what might be termed the public part of personality, or "public self-image"—the creation of an impression of oneself in the minds of others as having particular traits or qualities (e.g., Baumeister, 1982; Goffman, 1959; Schlenker, 1980).

Equating interpersonal roles with identity was probably quite accurate for medieval humanity. People were differentiated mainly by certain roles—family, social rank, occupation. The other two aspects of identity (values and potential) were less important for differentiation. Strong Christian morality created a general consensus concerning values; values did not differentiate persons. The important potentiality to fulfill was salvation, with access to heaven, and this too was the same for everyone (i.e., it did not differentiate). Some persons certainly had individual goals, but these generally fit into the collective patterns (Weintraub, 1978). Moreover, there was little or no privacy, and little or no belief in an "inner self"—the public self dominated.

The medieval person's identity was defined by society within a firm network of culture, institution, and tradition, and thus medievals seemed to have little or no need to seek or create any identity for themselves over and above that furnished by society.

The early modern period (sixteenth to eighteenth centuries) saw profound disturbances in the relationship of the single person to society, and at this time the interpersonal aspect of identity started to become problematic. Perhaps these disturbances did not yet add up to a crisis, but they were substantial. The obsession with deception, false appearances, and role-playing suggests an incipient breakdown of trust in general. Accelerating urbanization increased contact with strangers whose identities and inner motives remained unknown. This uncertainty was disturbing and perhaps threatening. As a result, the sense of community had to be restricted to one's circle of acquaintances. The defining of the individual by society became a problem because the *social* identity components (family lineage, social rank) began to undergo trivialization and destabilization. Persons found it necessary or desirable to shield part of their lives from public scrutiny, and privacy was cultivated. Most people probably still accepted society as defining their identities, but all these trends seem to indicate that the way in which society defined identity was less and less satisfactory.

The relationship of the single self to society certainly did reach a crisis during the nineteenth century. The belief in a chronic conflict between the individual and society held that something was fundamentally wrong with the way society defined identity. Perhaps the problems in the preceding (early modern) era could be shrugged off as regrettable exceptions or tolerable imperfections, but now it seemed that there were so many "exceptions" or "imperfections" that the system itself was unacceptable. Anderson's (1971) treatment of nineteenth century literature shows an evolution from struggling with the necessity of accepting one's place in society to seeking to define a place for oneself apart from society. This was a critical step: The individual began to assume the burden of defining himself, because society was such a failure in doing this. The ascendancy of the private over the public domain of experience reflects the same sort of shift toward seeking one's own meaning of life instead of accepting it from society. The sense of community declined still further, becoming restricted to intimates.

What happened in the nineteenth century was a breakdown in the network of culture, institutions, and tradition that society had used to furnish meaning to individual life. Religious faith eroded past the point of no return. Morality was strained to where it fostered hypocrisy. The structure of social rank lost its stability and even much of its legitimacy. The disruption of this network left society unable to furnish individuals with meaning, for, as Habermas (1973) says, sources of meaning are difficult to replace.

The twentieth century began by exacerbating the crisis. The relation of the individual to society was frustrating, even catastrophic. The transcendentalists had tried to go it alone, but going it alone became impossible in the urban, industrial, bureaucratic world of the twentieth century. Economic interdependence revived the problem of the Romantic era: Although life in society was intolerable, there was no alternative. That was the meaning of alienation. The alienated person rejected society but had no alternative to it. Someone who objects to city life is not described as "alienated" if he or she moves to a farm and lives happily ever after; he is only described as alienated as long as he persists in the city life that he cannot tolerate.

Another way in which the twentieth century exacerbated the crisis was by undermining the connection of the family to the larger social institutions (e.g., by the diminishing importance of family connections in securing employment; Fass, 1977). The private realm was thus losing its connection with the public.

As suggested in Chapter 6, later developments during the twentieth century could have been attempts to resolve the crisis. The literary themes of "accommodation" and "myth-making" indicate efforts to find individual meaning amid collective life.

None of this should be taken to mean that this first functional aspect of identity (roles in relationships) is unimportant in the twentieth century. On the contrary, there are various indications that the interpersonal self is extremely important today. Riesman's (1950) discussion of the "other-directed" person emphasizes the trend toward increasing concern with acting in ways that will be acceptable and pleasing to others. Lasch's (1978) observation that success does not count unless publicly acknowledged testifies to the dependence of achievement on the interpersonal (public) aspect of identity. In fact, there is considerable evidence that modern human behavior is widely and consistently influenced by concerns with creating and maintaining the public self (Baumeister, 1982).

Nor is it correct to say that modern persons create themselves because society does not determine them. The twentieth century mentality recognizes that the individual is strongly influenced by society. This can be seen with personality. Personality became a major identity component during the last century. Prior to that, personality was regarded as the result of innate predispositions and characteristics. That view was reflected in the pseudoscience of phrenology, which examined bumps on heads in the hope of divining dispositions. Phrenology persisted into the nineteenth century, but with the increasing sense that persons could shape their own personalities. The concept of "decision of character" (see Kett, 1977) reflected the view that traits could be self-determined. During the twentieth century, the prevailing "scientific" views (especially behaviorism) have portrayed personalities as resulting from environmental forces. The "loss of self" (Sypher, 1962) portrayed in twentieth century art may reflect the view that persons are the consequences of society rather than the other way around.

The key point, however, is that society's influence on the individual is not guided by a benevolent intention. When society affects your life, it is not necessarily for your good. The various beliefs in divine providence, in relentless social progress toward Utopia, or in society and its leaders provided contexts for the effects of society on individuals. These belief-based contexts made individual suffering tolerable, understandable, and justifiable. The twentieth century person has largely lost or abandoned these beliefs. In the modern view, the influence of society on the individual personality is arbitrary, unplanned, and even uncontrollable. It is a cause that produces an effect, not a context that furnishes meaning.

The modern citizen then is aware of himself as a product of his society, as extremely dependent on and enmeshed in society, and as living by and for goals and values that emphasize the recognition and approval of others. However, the modern individual also feels the need to furnish the meaning of his own life unless he is content and fulfilled with the definition of self as bureaucrat, parent, and spectator. Society furnishes the options, but it is up to the individual to create a coherent life from them, which suggests the second functional aspect of identity—potentiality.

Sense of Personal Potentiality

If society will not provide the individual with a coherent meaning of life, then the individual has to provide it. Empirically, life-meanings have two parts: justification and fulfillment. Justification (or legitimation) will be covered in connection with the third functional aspect of identity, namely, values. The concern here is with fulfillment. The question of fulfillment raises the question of potentiality, for it is one's potentiality that is fulfilled. The need for persons to create their own meanings of life has led to a concern with how to discover and cultivate potentiality in order to achieve fulfillment.

To the medieval mentality, the only really important potentiality was salvation. What you achieved or failed to achieve in life was secondary to eternal bliss. Indeed, "secondary" may be too kind a word. Other forms of fulfillment were suspected of being detrimental to salvation because they might be sinful. This tension can be seen in the life of the great fourteenth century scholar, Petrarch (cf. Weintraub, 1978). Although he had extraordinary creative talents, his writings about himself reveal that he frequently felt he should abandon his creative efforts and concentrate on piety. He worried that his pursuit of fulfillment in this world might jeopardize his fulfillment in the next. Arguments like "God gave me this talent, so God must want me to use it" were unconvincing. Petrarch persisted in his creative work, but his worries and ambivalence persisted too (Weintraub, 1978).

Petrarch may have continued to pursue fulfillment in creativity, but he was probably quite unusual. One possible reason for the "Dark Ages" being so dark is the fact that creativity took a back seat to salvation. The dominance of Christian ideology affected nearly everyone, and it decreed that fulfillment came after death.

The sixteenth to eighteenth centuries saw an enhanced awareness of individual growth and change. This led to an expansion of the sense of potential for life here on earth. The new concepts of late childhood led to an awareness of, and concern with, how experiences occurring while young could shape the character of the adult (Ariès, 1962). This cultivation of personal potentiality was recognized primarily in terms of morality. There was, however, an increasing awareness of the creative potentiality. The Romantic concept of the creative destiny of the individual was a culmination of the trend toward perceiving value and fulfillment in cultivating one's potential during his life.

The decline of Christian faith in the eighteenth and nineteenth centuries placed a great deal of emphasis on such secular forms of fulfillment as creativity. People were no longer willing to postpone fulfillment until heaven. Misery and frustration became intolerable given the absence of the consoling expectations of heaven. There are indications that the conflict between self and society apparently became worse around the beginning of the nineteenth century. In actual fact, it does not seem that society became more oppressive. If anything, society became less oppressive. Dissatisfaction with social conditions increased because people's expectations increased, due in large part to the erosion of Christian faith. The demand for fulfillment *in this life* (instead of the next) was bound to make people much less tolerant of existing social conditions, especially those that seemed to thwart fulfillment.

Artists were admired and their fulfillment envied, but not everyone could be an artist. The secularization of the (Protestant) work ethic made secular forms of fulfillment available to every man. The increased role of mothers in raising children provided women with a secular form of fulfillment. Education was promoted for everyone as a means of discovering and cultivating one's potential. This is illustrated by the Victorian concern that inadequate schooling destined males for "dead-end jobs" (Kett, 1977). The fear of the dead-end job expresses the notion of fulfillment in terms of career potentiality, and it expresses the faith that education (the cultivation of one's potential) will facilitate fulfillment. The medievals did not fear dead-end jobs; indeed, there were none because all jobs included the possibility of earning heavenly rewards.

The fulfillment provided by work in the nineteenth century was an "inner" success, namely, the triumph over oneself (e.g., Larson, 1978). The *process* of work provided fulfillment—the exertion, the self-discipline, the perseverance, and so forth. The enjoyment of the results of work was based, at least in part, on their constituting a sign of success in the inner struggle.

In the nineteenth and twentieth centuries, however, several trends undermined the chance to derive intrinsic satisfaction from work. Work became organized more and more around extrinsic rewards. This change indicated that the work itself had lost its capacity to provide fulfillment.

Three trends have diminished the chance to find fulfillment in work. The first is a fundamental change in the nature of work. Braverman (1974) provides a thorough analysis of this change. He begins by observing that "division of labor" has two possible meanings, one old (social) and one new (task). Even primitive societies often have a *social* division of labor. In that arrangement, different people to different jobs. The various members of a society each contribute a different product or service. But each person normally does his or her entire job. In contrast, modern business management practices have produced the task division of labor, in which each job is subdivided into its component parts, and each part is assigned to a different person. The factory assembly line is perhaps the most familiar example of task division of labor.

The task division of labor developed as modern management grasped and used the theories of Babbage (1832). Babbage proposed, correctly, that profits could be greatly increased by subdividing each task and assigning the parts to people of appropriate skill levels. If one mechanic built the whole machine, then that mechanic had to have enough skill to do all the most complex parts of the job and therefore had to be paid well. Moreover, he would be paid the high wage rate even when doing the simplest parts of the job. Instead, Babbage suggested that the expensive mechanic be assigned only the complex activities that required his expertise. Lesser skilled workers could be hired, at much lower wages, to do the simple things. Babbage's theories were correct, and management soon learned to save substantially in labor costs by dividing each large job into its component tasks (Braverman, 1974).

But as Braverman makes painfully clear, there is a dramatic, hidden psychological cost in that reorganization of labor. Everyone's work becomes repetitive and monotonous. This includes even the work of the most skilled and expensive mechanic who now does the one complex part of the task over and over all day. Moreover, everyone's work loses its visible identification with the task as a whole and with the product. The satisfaction of building a cabinet yourself and of seeing it take shape provides you with pride in the finished cabinet. This satisfaction is much harder to get if you just saw the boards while someone else drills them, someone else screws them together, and yet someone else varnishes them. Braverman's essential point is that the possibilities of enjoying and taking pride in one's work are degraded by the task division of labor.

Factory manufacturing is not the only type of work to have undergone this subdivision into components. White-collar work has undergone it, too, although this began in the twentieth century, after blue-collar work had already been adapted to it (see also Larkin, 1979). Today, it could easily involve two dozen employees to mail a customer a bill for a credit-card purchase in a store if you count the sales clerk, the computer programmers and operators, the accountants, and so on. In the nineteenth century a clerk knew the entire operation of a bank or company; today the clerk knows only the smallest part of the operation. Consequently, it is difficult for the modern clerk to find meaning, value, or personal fulfillment in what he or she does.

The reorganization of work according to the task division of labor is one reason work has lost its capacity to provide intrinsic fulfillment. A second, related reason is that the social bond between producer and consumer has become distant and impersonal (Harris, 1981). When primitive man made a spear for his own use, he made certain that it was well made and would not fall apart in the hunt or the battle. If he made the spear for his neighbor, a fellow tribesman, he was equally or almost as careful. In contrast, today's workers make things for strangers they will never meet face to face. Or they provide services for people they will probably never see again. Harris argues that today's poor workmanship and today's rudeness or uncooperativeness among service personnel are caused by the impersonal nature of their relationships to the consumer. It is hard to care deeply about the needs of total strangers, and this apathy leads to careless labor, shoddy merchandise, and poor service.

The third trend may be partly a consequence of the first two. Lasch (1978) suggests that the meaning of success has changed. It no longer means an inner, almost spiritual triumph as it did in the previous two centuries. Instead, it depends on recognition by others and on equaling or surpassing the accomplishments of others. In Lasch's words, "Success in our society has to be ratified by publicity"; if not, it does not count as success. Moreover, because most people have bureaucratic desk or service jobs, personal accomplishments are difficult to recognize and measure. To some extent, people simply have begun to use salary as the measure of success. Salary, obviously, is entirely extrinsic to the work activities, so using it as a measure of success renders the intrinsic work secondary. Lasch suggests a further consequence. The desire for public recognition has changed from a desire for fame to a desire for celebrity status (see also Trilling, 1955). To use Lasch's terms, fame implies respect and recognition for one's accomplishments, whereas celebrity status implies love and admiration for one's personality, regardless of specific achievement. A celebrity is celebrated for who he is, not what he has done. That, says Lasch, is the epitome of the modern concept of success.

Due to these three trends, work has shifted its basis from intrinsic to extrinsic motivation. There may be an additional reason. Experimental research has shown that when extrinsic and intrinsic rewards are both present, the extrinsic rewards predominate. If you like doing something, and you get paid for it, eventually you come to feel that you do it in order to get paid, not because you like it (e.g., Deci, 1971; Lepper, Greene, & Nisbett, 1973). For all these reasons, then, the general trend is to view work primarily and essentially as a means of earning money. In terms of identity, people think of their potentiality in terms of how much money and status they can earn (e.g., "salary potential").

Fulfillment, however, seems dependent on intrinsic rewards. Even our current, materialistic mentality refuses to recognize someone as "fulfilled" simply on the basis of having earned lots of money. "Fulfilled" is reserved for those who get satisfaction out of the process of doing what they do, and perhaps out of the intrinsic result. But that sort of satisfaction is elusive and difficult to find given the modern conditions of work.

If fulfillment through work is hard to come by, where does the modern individual find fulfillment? A second source of fulfillment is love. During the last two centuries—that is, ever since our culture began to seek secular modes of fulfillment—we have come to regard love as an essential feature of a fulfilled life. Someone who goes through life without love will commonly be regarded as unfulfilled. Contrary to earlier attitudes (cf. Stone, 1977), passionate love has now become viewed as a good basis and even as the quintessential basis for choosing a mate.

Love does have some drawbacks as a model of fulfillment, the main one being the impermanence of passion. People do not remain passionately in love over long periods of time. Fiedler (1966) observes that, although many novels end with marriage and with promises of everlasting happiness, no one has been able to write a good novel about a happy marriage. Marital bliss is dull, not passionate, at least to readers of novels. Fiedler's point is consistent with the behavioral evidence that frequency of sexual intercourse diminishes substantially over time, even in relatively happy marriages (e.g., Mann, Berkowitz, Sidman, Starr, & West, 1974). Although in our society we use romantic passion as the main criterion for getting married, it may be neither necessary nor sufficient for a happy marriage. Although passionate love may be a viable model of human fulfillment, it is not one that is conducive to prolonged and stable satisfaction.

Still, people are very concerned with love in connection with the second functional aspect of identity, namely, potentiality. Many young people worry about whether they will be able to attract a spouse and, if so, whether this person will be a suitable and attractive spouse. As recently as the 1950s, this was probably the most important identity element for young women and a major one for young men, because society discriminated against those who were unmarried. Today it is socially acceptable to be unmarried, but people still place much weight on their potential for attracting lovers. Being unable to love is regarded as a disastrous psychological affliction. Thus, one modern attitude is that one's sense of potential ought to include being able to attract others and to feel and express love. Given the modern difficulty of finding direct fulfillment in work, love has probably become the most important domain of potential and fulfillment.

Outside love and work, the possibilities for fulfillment appear to be limited. The feelings of alienation and "loss of self" express the attitude that one cannot make a difference, cannot have a meaningful impact on society. Raising children is seen as a way to counteract this. However useless or frustrating one's life has been, it can seem meaningful as long as one has raised children who may yet achieve or experience something of value. In a sense, this "solution" resembles that of the medieval Christian. Fulfillment is postponed indefinitely, even into the next life. This time, though, the "next life" is that of the offspring. Along the way, there are moments of substantial pride and satisfaction. These furnish enough fulfillment to allow one to get by.

Until and unless one really settles for being a parent, however, fulfillment is a problematic aspect of modern life. The search for identity is the search for one's potentiality so that one can then begin progress toward fulfillment. The desire for fulfillment was shaped ideologically by the secularization of human potential into the Romantic notion of creative destiny, and is shaped psychologically by modern child-raising techniques that foster narcissism and individuality. Everyone knows he is special; he just isn't sure *in what way* he is special. It is hoped that this can be discovered, and that the discovery will show the way to a meaningful and fulfilling life.

Values and Priorities: The Inner Self

The spread of belief in an "internal self" may have been part of the emergence of identity problems, because identity acquired the additional obligation of deciding one's activities. Inside identity, there had to be bases for making many different decisions. As moral and traditional rules became lax and relative, each identity had to contain an inner structure of values and priorities. This is the third functional aspect of identity.

The "inner self" was not really created or discovered. The proper term is "reified," which denotes a process of coming to regard something abstract as concrete. The "inner self" does not really exist. It is a useful concept for describing important parts of human experience and behavior, but no one has ever really seen an inner self nor determined exactly what it is inside *of*. It is certainly not "inside" the head or brain, because the contents of the inner self are essentially contents of *meaning*, whereas the brain is physical matter. Physical matter and meaning are quite different types of phenomena, and it is likely that neither can be reduced to "nothing but" the other.

The medievals seem to have gotten along fine without much sense of an inner life or a hidden self. As Ariès (1962) and others have pointed out, privacy was nonexistent; in general, no one was ever alone. Even if one did happen by chance to be alone for a moment, it did not count, for God was the most important audience, and God was omniscient. All of one's thoughts and acts thus had a witness.

If one happened to sin, it might be kept secret, but this was disapproved of. The Middle Ages developed a practice for dealing with sin. The first step was to make it public—to confess it. Secrecy was the domain of sin, and the attack on sin began by removing sin's secrecy. Foucault says the result is that "Western man has become a confessing animal" (1980, p. 59). He notes that sex, the most commonly private act, has been systematically transformed into something to talk about. In the modern era, people continue to deal with fear and anxiety and guilt about sex by talking about them.

Medieval life was also rather rigid. The average person had few major choices to make. He was what he was because of the circumstances of his birth. However, when the rigid feudal system broke down, people began to have alternatives. They could change the circumstances into which they had been brought at birth. They were what they were because of their choices and achievements. Causes now seemed to be located somewhere in the persons themselves. The inner self began to be reified.

It is important to distinguish between a phenomenon and a metaphorical concept used to refer to it. Saying that medieval persons did not have inner selves does not mean that they lacked thoughts and feelings. Of course they had thoughts and feelings. But they may not have regarded thoughts and feelings as items with a hidden existence in some mysterious, inaccessible container called the self. They did not conceptualize a person as a being who carried around a large stock of latent thoughts and feelings that were important even if the person's behavior gave no sign of them. Today we do think in those terms and in that sense, we have acquired a belief in the inner self that was generally absent during the Middle Ages.

The concern with deception fostered (and probably reflected) the growth of the inner self. Deception can logically be analyzed in terms of inconsistency of behavior. But the prevailing model regarded deception as hiding, not as inconsistency. One pretends to be or to intend one thing, but the hidden self is or intends something else. The true self thus came to be regarded as the hidden self; the preaching of sincerity as a virtue exhorted people to show their true (i.e., inner) selves.

As mentioned earlier, Puritanism gave rise to a concern with self-deception. Again, the real was the hidden self; this time, though, it was hidden even from oneself. Moreover, the hidden part of the self was the evil, sinful side. Puritans feared that sinfulness lurked behind their outer appearance of virtue.

The spread of the desire for privacy accompanied the growth of the belief in the hidden, inner self. Aristocrats wanted to have sexual adventures but wanted to keep them from servants who might disclose the knowledge to others (Stone, 1977). Sin and deception were thus involved in the growth of privacy, which enabled one to sin secretly and to maintain the deceptive public appearance of virtue.

The tension between hidden sinfulness and deceptive appearances of virtue reached extremes during the Victorian era. Victorian standards of conduct were perhaps simply too high for human nature, resulting sometimes in outright, deliberate hypocrisy (duplicity), sometimes in self-deception and "sincere insincerity" (Houghton, 1957). "Sincere insincerity" meant that the Victorian wished he had better and nobler private feelings than the ones he actually had, and insofar as the wish was sincere, he was justified in advocating values and beliefs he lacked. The Victorian extremes of self-deception reached a point at which they could be explored systematically. This was Freud's achievement. Freud's ideas greatly fleshed out the hidden or inner self. Indeed, the hidden (unconscious) self became larger than the visible self.

The point in the preceding paragraphs has been to suggest the link between the origins of the inner self and morality. The inner self began, perhaps, as secret sinfulness that was concealed. Others were deceived, and then even the self was deceived. The hidden self was equated with the "real" or "true" self. In the brutal kind of arithmetic that prevailed, secret wickedness plus the semblance or appearance of virtue amounted to wickedness. The understanding and discovery of self became a difficult but important project.

Morals, of course, are one kind of values. The inner self was always associated with the structure of values. The inner self was associated with choice, but choice was a moral issue, and the prevailing moral standards meant that one of the alternatives was the "correct" one. This gradually ceased to be the case. Religious faith declined, and since the consensus about moral values had been based on religion, it suffered, too. During the twentieth century, issues of personal choice have ceased to be approached in primarily moral terms.

The proliferation of choice in numerous spheres of life has called for individuals to develop and use values other than morality. One may choose between being an accountant, a physician, and a scientist, but that choice cannot properly be made on the basis of morals. Similarly, the choice of leisure pastimes is generally not made on a moral basis. Acts express values and priorities, and moral values are no longer either necessary or sufficient to make choices and decisions about how to act. The inner self has thus taken on dimensions of value other than moral.

The decisive historical event concerning this third aspect of identity was the decline of religion and its morality. This decline left the structure of private, individual values in a state of anarchy. Before that, one knew what was the right decision in most situations that called for decisions. If one sinned, one knew that it was wrong—it was a weakness or failing or slip, not an affirmation of sin as a personal value. Taking choice out of the moral context has necessitated finding other criteria of value. As fewer choices are obviously wrong, it becomes perhaps more common to regard choices as an expression of values. The intrusion of personality into identity facilitated the use of personal preference as an explanation for behavior. Clothes, possessions, and hobbies are seen as expressions of personal preferences. But where does one get all these preferences? Personal preference is probably inadequate to make many decisions. Indeed, there are probably just not enough criteria to make all the decisions that confront the modern person. Yet they do get made, even if casually or arbitrarily. Once made, however, they are taken as further expressions of the inner self.

Current research in social psychology supports the view that behavior is often guided by situational factors of which people are scarcely aware. Yet, after the fact, people tend to explain their behavior in terms of their values and dispositions. Thus, behavior comes first, guided by situational causes, and then people attribute inner states to themselves to explain their behavior (e.g., Bem, 1965; Nisbett & Wilson, 1977).

The inadequacy of established criteria for making decisions has to result in the increasing acceptance of whatever criteria one finds. Personal preference is thus an accepted and acceptable reason for making a choice. Similarly, the prospect of personal advantage seems an eminently sensible and acceptable criterion for making choices. To a strictly moral Christian of centuries past, however, neither of these was an acceptable criterion, especially if the decision could be interpreted in moral terms. You were supposed to do what was right, not what you wanted to do.

The acceptance of multiple criteria or multiple schemes (dimensions) of value drastically increases the possibility of internal conflict. Or, rather, it makes it more difficult to resolve inner conflict. Clearly, the rigidly moral Puritans were loaded with inner conflicts between their moral/religious values and their sinful appetites. The correctness of the correct choice was never at issue, however; it was only in doubt as to whether they would make the correct choice. This sort of choice conforms to the model of Type IV self-definition, in which the right course is known, but one *may* choose to do something else. Moral and religious values took precedence over others. The acceptance of other criteria, however, removed the consensual hierarchy. If a merchant's error gave a Puritan too much money in change, the Puritan may have been torn between greed (keep the money) and moral duty (return it), but he or she knew the correct decision was to return it. Today greed is an acceptable motive, and some would call you foolish to return the extra money. It is nonetheless immoral to keep it. The conflict between moral duty and personal acquisitiveness *has no* correct resolution. This sort of choice resembles Type V self-definition. What you do will express something about you, to be sure, but what metacriterion can you find to decide between moral duty and acquisitiveness? Somehow you just do one or the other—very likely under the influence of situational pressures—and your "choice" leads to a reification of something about you that supposedly caused the decision.

Once alternative values are acceptable, the ability of morals (or religion) to furnish a justification for one's choices is lost. In Habermas's (1973) terms, a legitimation crisis is produced. If morality is just one among an assortment of possible criteria, then morality itself requires justification. This calls into question the hegemony of the moral-religious values to serve as ultimate arbiter of the justification of one's acts and presumably aggravates the problem of the meaning of life all the more.

Moreover, of course, the lack of firm inner commitments makes it difficult to do something others aren't doing. Maybe they know something you don't; maybe they have a basis for decision that you have not discovered. If you fully accepted morality as the final criterion, then once you had a moral interpretation of a situation you knew what to do. More information was not needed. Others could not have knowledge you needed unless there were something that was relevant to morality and that you hadn't noticed in that particular situation. But if you did not fully accept morality as the final criterion, then you were not sure how the decision had to be made. *Anything* that others knew about the situation might help. Your informational dependence on them was increased ("informational social influence" in the words of Deutsch & Gerard, 1955), and thus your conformity increased. The uncertainty of decision criteria is probably an important part of the modern loss of self as well as an important cause of modern conformity. The latter hypothesis is especially supported by the prevalence of conformity among adolescents, the persons who have (almost by definition) not resolved the inner anarchy of values.

It was previously suggested that the decline of religious faith contributed to the emergence of the modern form of the adolescent identity crisis. The religious conversions of adolescents of previous centuries may have been forerunners of identity crises. To the extent that the adolescent identity crisis is prompted by a need to define one's own identity, it is a problem of making choices. Making choices requires criteria—the establishment of values and priorities. A religious conversion was an affirmation of one's commitment to religion. Once that affirmation was made, order was established, and moral and religious values took priority over other values and desires. The inner anarchy was replaced with a stable and workable hierarchy of metacriteria. Choices and decisions could then be made.

The religious conversion, then, was a means of solving the problem of adolescent choice. The decline of religious faith and religious experience among youth deprived them of a means of solving identity crises. An effective replacement solution has yet to be found.

Summary

The first functional aspect of identity is the interpersonal self—the roles of the person in relation to society at large and to other particular persons. The part of personality perceived by other persons has also become an important part of this aspect. The medieval person's place in society was defined by a rigid social structure based on birth and heritage. The social identity was thus predominantly determined by society—that is, by circumstances beyond the person's control. Increased personal freedom and related trends began to leave the person more and more latitude for defining himself or herself. Persons began to be chronically dissatisfied with the identities society had given them. The spread of alienation denoted a failure on the part of society to provide meaning for individual lives. During the twentieth century, people retained their involvement in society (social definition of self) but began to assume the responsibility for defining the meaning of their own lives. One's interpersonal identity had to be adopted and created rather than just accepted. Its importance was central. One consequence of the modern "loss of self" resulted in a dependence on others for self-validation.

The second functional aspect of identity is the sense of personal potential. Two developments raised the importance and difficulty of this functional aspect. Society's refusal to provide individuals with a satisfactory meaning for life forced persons to seek personal fulfillment as a satisfactory purpose and meaning. The decline of Christian faith resulted in a demand for fulfillment in this life rather than the next. (It is likely that the two developments were related.) To seek fulfillment, one needed to know what one's potentiality was that could be fulfilled. Creative work was soon recognized as a valid and viable means of fulfillment. However, not everyone had the potential (talent) for creativity. Fulfillment was sought in work of all sorts. Fulfillment denoted intrinsic satisfaction in some activity. Extrinsic satisfactions gradually replaced intrinsic ones, however, and twentieth century trends have increasingly emphasized extrinsic rewards. The possibility of fulfillment in work may therefore be diminishing. In its place modern persons seem to value intimate relationships. The burden of fulfillment gets placed on the family. The desire to find and cultivate one's personal potential remains widespread and is an important part of the modern quest for identity.

The third functional aspect of identity is the structure of values and priorities. This seems to have evolved out of the inner, or hidden, self. The inner self began, perhaps, with deception and immorality—the necessity or desirability of concealing one's sinful behavior. Protestant self-consciousness led to the concern with self-deception. The hidden (sinful) self was the real self. As morals became increasingly strict and demanding, secrecy and sin became increasingly common and unavoidable. The Victorians gave morality a bad name; the reaction against the Victorians denounced the hypocrisy to which the Victorian's impossibly high standards had compelled them.

Because morality became linked with hypocrisy and because religious faith no longer furnished a firm justification for moral values, other values were tolerated. The increasing range and scope of choices required nonmoral criteria for choosing, and this too encouraged the adoption of values other than moral ones. This resulted in a kind of inner anarchy—an inability to decide among the conflicting prescriptions of the different value schemes. The search for identity has taken on as a part of itself the need to form a stable order of values and priorities so that choices can be made effectively.

8

Development of Identity

How is it that children grow up to have identities? This chapter tries to provide some answers to this question. The field of developmental psychology does not have one generally accepted concept for how identity develops. Therefore, I have constructed a model out of past research, observations, and speculations. The need for a model arises because past research on identity development has mainly focused on two-year-olds and adolescents, whereas I wish to emphasize the years in between those ages as well.

This chapter also compares the individual development of identity with the historical development. In the preceding chapters, a progression of steps was outlined by which modern identity and its problems took shape. The prevailing self-definition processes shifted from the simplest (Type I) to the most difficult and complex (Types III, IV, V), showing a progression from self-definition by passive assignment of identity to self-definition by achievement and then to self-definition by choice. The three functional aspects of identity became problematic in a sequence that started with the interpersonal aspect of identity, then turned to the potentiality aspect, and ended with the values-and-priorities aspect of identity. In examining the research on child development, it is important to keep in mind the question of whether there is any evidence that this progression mimics the historical sequence. Any similarities will help confirm this account of modern identity and its dilemmas.

Organismic Unity

The German philosopher Hans-Georg Gadamer noted that life separates itself from its surroundings. Thus, the differentiation between self and environment is actively accomplished by each living thing. Biological processes differentiate, and living things typically seem to have an apparent unity of process. Plants, for example, respond as totalities to events like watering and pruning. What affects part of the plant affects the entire plant.

The unity of the organism persists across time. The process of life lasts until a definite endpoint (death), at which time the entire organism ceases to be alive. Your death encompasses all of you and nothing else; in that sense, it precisely marks off the boundaries of you.

Thus, the two defining criteria of identity (continuity and differentiation) are expressed in biological processes. One might say that there is a biological basis for identity. Still, identity is not a biological thing. Biology makes identity possible. Identity is, however, a unity of meaning, not of biology. Identity starts with the biological body but then develops far from there.

Infancy

Infancy highlights the argument that biology provides a basis for identity but is not sufficient for identity. Babies are full-fledged organisms with functioning bodies, but one can hardly describe the newborn as having a sense of identity. If babies have any identity at all, it is only insofar as parents reserve identity for them. For example, parents care about leaving the hospital with their own baby, but if an inadvertent swap were made we could hardly expect the baby to know the difference.

Most researchers and theorists have focused on the infant's developing awareness of its body as the first step in the formation of a self-concept. Although there is some controversy as to how completely and how long this body awareness dominates the early self-concept, it seems clear that self-awareness begins with the infant's awareness of its body. After all, there are not many alternatives. Needless to say, the infant has few skills, and without language it cannot grasp most identity components.

Studies of self-understanding in infants are limited by the infants' inability to talk. Still, there have been studies of infants' capacity to recognize themselves in mirrors. Lewis and Brooks-Gunn (1979) summarize this research, including much of their own, in the following manner. First, the infant is interested in and attracted to images of other infants. By the time the infant is three months old, though, it has a special interest in its own mirror image, presumably because it discovers the contingency: The mirror image moves whenever the infant moves. The next big advance in self-knowledge occurs at around eight months, when the infant acquires the capacity to understand object permanence, or the concept that particular things continue to exist across time. Only then can the self be known as something that persists across time.

Lewis and Brooks-Gunn go on to say that self-permanence is a prerequisite for knowing the self's characteristics. They report observations showing that infants only begin to recognize themselves on the basis of facial features during the second year of life. In other words, during the second year infants begin to recognize their own images on the basis of distinctive features and characteristics rather than just through contingency.

The capacity to recognize oneself can be taken as a sign of the development of rudimentary self-awareness. Kagan (1981) has similarly argued that the second year of life is marked by the development of self-awareness. For Kagan, the development of self-awareness starts with comparing one's acts with meaningful standards and rules. The child in the second year becomes able to understand and appreciate standards and to use them to make judgments (e.g., broke, dirty, bad). Scrutiny of the speech of children in his studies revealed that children began using standards between nineteen and twenty-six months of age. *All* children in his studies made utterances involving standards, which is a sign that they are an important feature of the child's world. Why is this true? There is little mystery here. Kagan cites cross-cultural evidence that the words "good" and "bad" are always among the most common words adults say to babies and young children. Moreover, toilet training occurs during the second year, and the struggle over it acquaints the child with the need to conform to standards imposed by adults.

Related to the appreciation of adult standards and rules is the evaluation of one's own acts as good or bad and the development of some concept of mastery. Kagan says that near the end of the second year children start to smile when they do something properly or successfully. Mastery smiles, he says, indicate that the child conceptualized a goal (a standard), strove to reach it, persisted, succeeded, and recognized its success. Thus, an important step in the beginnings of self-awareness is self-recognition of active agency judged according to meaningful standards.

The second year of life is also marked by the acquisition of speech. It is unlikely that the co-development of self-awareness and speech is coincidence. And since identity, as suggested above, is an entity consisting of meaning, the self may not be able to exist or to be known without language, or at least without the linguistic capacity to process meaning.

It has already been suggested that the child's active use of meaning seems to be an important ingredient in Kagan's account of the development of self-awareness. Indeed, the child comes to expect things and events to have meaning. Kagan refers to a "disposition to impose meaning" in children during the second year of life.

As the child learns words and comes to expect and impose meaning, it develops a curious habit: It begins to narrate its own actions. At first these utterances are quite simple, like saying "up" while climbing up into the mother's lap. There are many things in the environment that the child could talk about, but the child specifically and preferentially talks about its own actions and behavioral intentions (Kagan, 1981). This narratization of one's own actions would seem to be the beginning of the incessant babble of thought that is the nearly unbreakable habit of most adults.

What are the first contents of the self that the very young child grasps? The most important (to the child) early categories for classifying self and others are familiarity, age, and gender (Lewis & Brooks-Gunn, 1979). Familiarity is mainly applied to others, as in the distinction between parents and strangers. Age and gender, central components of self-knowledge, are used by infants "to identify themselves," beginning around the age of fifteen months (Damon & Hart, 1982). In support of the notion that infants acquire very early in life a highly developed sense of age, Lewis and Brooks-Gunn cite Fagan's (1972) demonstration that six-month-olds can already distinguish pictures of adults from pictures of other infants. The capacity to distinguish males from females appears slightly later. Still, knowledge of one's own gender seems to be firmly in place by the middle of the second year of life.

So it seems appropriate to regard self-knowledge of gender and age as the beginning of identity. Both gender and age are features of the physical body, but they already go beyond mere awareness of one's own body. Gender, for example, is not just the discovery of one's own genitals and hair. Gender only has meaning within the context of the distinction between two categories (male and female). The distinction is learned, and the self is classified as one or the other.

At the beginning of this chapter, I asked whether it was possible that self-definition in the modern child follows the same course as the historical progression through self-definition processes. In this connection, it is important to observe that the main identity components early in life reflect Type I self-definition. Gender and age are both components that one simply discovers one has. One does not earn, choose, or change them. (Age will gradually change, of course, but the infant does not yet know this. Moreover, its change is based on neither achievement nor choice.) Thus, identity begins with the simplest kind of self-definition, the mere passive acknowledgment of assigned components.

But identity does not remain at the passive level for long. In fact, the active side of identity soon predominates. This suggests that research on the development of self should focus more on how sense of self connects to *behavior* and less on how it might connect to *the body*. Some observations by Kagan (1981) are relevant. He says that the pronoun "I" is first used by children toward the end of the second year; the same goes for the child's use of its own name. These developments occur after the child has already learned some verbs, although the earliest words tend to be nouns. More important, the first usages of "I" or of the child's own name are two-word sentences consisting of "I" followed by an action predicate (e.g., "I go," "I play"; Kagan, 1982, p. 67). These observations are consistent with the argument that identity occurs through learning to interpret behavior, rather than simply learning to understand one's body. The requirements of language, stipulated perhaps by the physical organization of the brain, lead us from behavior to identity.

Toddlerhood: Age Two

By the second birthday, the toddler has the makings of an identity that is far fuller and more complex than that of the infant. The two-year-old can speak, so it can begin to use linguistic concepts of identity. It is developing active skills; it has long since mastered walking, for example. The symbolic power of learning to walk is significant in the development of the infant's self-awareness. Learning to walk is a major achievement of self-definition. It broadens one's horizons and possibilities, it makes one less at the mercy of the environment and more in control of it, it facilitates the growth of a sense of initiative, it makes one independent of adults (in one respect, at least) and similar to them, and probably it is also just simply exhilarating (Erikson, 1968; Mahler, Pine, & Bergman, 1975). Being able to walk is perhaps the first Type II component in the identity. Such components will soon (ages three to five) become centrally important in identity.

Two years of experience, and the development of language, enable the toddler to form a stable concept of self. Mahler, Pine, and Bergman (1975) say that during the third year the "establish-ment of mental representations of self as distinctly separate from representations of the object [i.e., the parent] paves the way to self-identity formation" (p. 117). The child thus can conceptualize it-self, including the knowledge that it is not part of the mother. Some writers (e.g., Damon, 1983) have speculated that toddlers love to say "No!" to parental suggestions because that is a way of differen-tiating themselves from the parent. Rejecting the parents' directives may be an early form of autonomy.

Two-year-olds can also perceive their limitations, at least in the sense of being able to recognize that they cannot perform certain desirable acts. In Kagan's (1981) studies, children cried when the experimenter performed acts that the children could not yet do. These acts were symbolic acts with toys, such as making one block "drink" a bottle, washing a toy horse with a cloth, having a doll use a toy shovel to dig an imaginary hole, or having a doll simulate horseback riding using a wrench for a horse. Children between the ages of eighteen and twenty-six months tended to cry when they watched the experimenter perform such acts. By around thirty months when the children could duplicate those acts, they no longer cried when the experimenter did them.

Kagan also recorded that children dramatically increased the frequency of self-descriptive statements (e.g., "I go, I play") at about age two. These included both statements about one's physical properties and one's action competencies. The two-year-old makes such statements *spontaneously*. As Kagan and others argue, one can-not make self-referent and self-descriptive statements without some concept of the self, so two-year-olds must indeed have some con-cept of self. It is a concept they use spontaneously, not just when adults ask questions. Moreover, this concept of self does seem already to include the potentiality aspect, at least in the sense of what actions one can versus cannot do.

Self-evaluation also seems to appear at around age two. Damon and Hart (1982) cite evidence that two-year-olds show pride and shame, as indicated (respectively) by strutting and by embarrassed blushing.

A last feature of self-definition among two-year-olds is the development of concepts of ownership. Ownership, by definition, presupposes the persistent existence of an owning self (and of an owned object). Moreover, ownership is based on a strict and clear differentiation of self from others: My toys belong to me, and no one else may touch them except as I allow. Both defining criteria of identity are thus centrally implicated in ownership.

Research evidence links sense of ownership to sense of self. Levine (1983) administered several measures to assess level of self-definition development in two-year-old boys. She then covertly observed their play with a peer. She found that boys who scored high in self-definition claimed toys more than did other boys. For example, the more self-defined boys were more likely to say "mine" more frequently than the other boys. She noted that this claiming of toys was not a negative or hostile behavior. Instead, the highly self-defined boys began by asserting their ownership of their toys as a means of defining boundaries and structuring the interaction with the peer. They would then interact in a positive and desirable fashion with the peer. Thus, Levine stresses that claiming toys "appeared to be an important part of the child's definition of himself within his social world" (p. 547; see also Garvey, 1977).

Early Childhood: Ages Three to Five Years

As has been stated, theorists have generally emphasized body awareness in the development of infants' self-concept. Some theorists (Erikson, 1968; Mahler et al., 1975) have observed the symbolic importance of learning to walk. Keller, Ford, and Meacham (1978) studied the relative importance of body image and action competencies in the self-concepts of three- to five-year-old children. Their results provided clear support for the predominance of action competencies over body knowledge. Again, sense of self connects most importantly to behavior, not to body.

Keller, Ford, and Meacham used several types of measures to assess the relative importance of various categories of self-definition. These measures ranged from the open-ended question of what would be the best thing for the experimenter to write to "tell about you," to the binary forced-choice measure such as, "Now I'm going to say two things about you and you tell me which one is the best one to put in what I write about you." The forced-choice instruction was then followed by a pair of statements, one of which referred to the child's body image and one to an action competency (e.g., "Timmy can brush his teeth" versus "Timmy has a nice face"). The two statements were always taken from things the child had previously said about itself in answers to questions.

Of all measures, the action competencies were the preferred category for children at each age (three, four, and five years). Moreover, Keller and her colleagues retested six weeks later to investigate the stability of responses. Not only were the action competency responses always the most popular, they were also the most stable (i.e., the most likely to be mentioned both times). Other categories of self-description, including body image, interpersonal relationships, possessions, age, gender, and various others, were comparatively uncommon and were variable in frequency. Thus, action competencies seemed to be not only the most important features of the children's self-concepts, they also had the most to do with stability across time. Action competencies are thus important for both of the defining criteria of identity—continuity and differentiation. It seems fair to conclude that action competencies are the most important identity components to children at this age.

Keller et al. note that the only other fairly popular category (other than activities) of self-description responses was that of material possessions, and this only among the three-year-olds. It may be that the sudden and powerful importance of ownership in the formation of identity is linked mainly to ages two and three, and declines thereafter. Then again, maybe people simply become reticent about citing their possessions as the centrally important features of themselves. That reticence could account for the empirical observation that older children are less likely than three-year-olds to describe themselves in terms of their possessions.

Although three-year-olds may prefer to be known by their action competencies, they do not understand the abstract idea of a self except as part of the body. Broughton (1978) asked children direct questions such as, "What is the self?" and concluded that children tend to think the self is part of the body, usually the head. But such responses probably just reflect the child's inability to deal with the abstract terms (e.g., an inability to distinguish between self, mind, and body) rather than a predominance of body awareness in self-concept.

Altogether, then, one can see a movement toward action competencies as decisive components of identity during early childhood. These competencies are acquired by a single (though possibly time-consuming) learning process and are stable thereafter. They are thus Type II self-definition processes involving a single-criterion transformation of self. They also clearly seem to involve the second functional aspect of identity (potentiality) even if only in a rudimentary fashion.

Late Childhood: Ages Six to Twelve

The sense of identity develops greatly in late childhood. Between the ages of six and twelve, children become able to grasp the idea of what a self is in psychological terms. Damon and Hart (1982) cite various studies indicating a "shift from physicalistic to psychological conceptions of self" during this period. At this time some concept of an inner self develops. The child is also very concerned with accumulating skills and competencies. Brim (1976) cites evidence that sense of personal control increases steadily from first to tenth grade. (By tenth grade, presumably, the sense of personal control has benefited from increased awareness of choice as well as increased competency.) Erikson (1950, 1968) has also emphasized the acquisition of competencies as a distinctive feature of the late childhood/preadolescent stage.

To find out what categories children would use to describe identity change, Mohr (1978) asked first, third, and sixth graders to imagine changes to their identities. For example, he asked, "What would you have to change about yourself for you to become your best friend?" It is difficult to judge just how children would interpret his questions, so one must be cautious in generalizing from his conclusions. (Still, his observations seem verified by the work of others.) He found that the youngest children in his sample (first graders, about 6 years old) conceptualized identity change in terms of "external" characteristics such as name, age, physical qualities, and possessions. By third grade they had shifted to an emphasis on behavioral patterns and habits. (One cannot tell from Mohr's report whether competencies were a frequent type of response, but one assumes they were.) The sixth graders used both behavioral and internal characteristics. Examples of internal characteristics were feelings and thoughts. Mohr's findings thus confirm a "developmental sequence of external, to behavioral, to internal bases for making self-identity judgments" (p. 428).

In previous chapters it has been suggested that belief in inner self is somewhat historically relative. People have not always had inner selves. They have probably always had thoughts and feelings, but they did not think of themselves in terms of hidden or inner qualities. If inner selves are not universal, it seems necessary to ask how we teach our children to have them.

Research has scarcely begun to address this question, but some speculations are plausible. The inner self is the repository of hidden metacriteria that supposedly form the structure of one's motives and intentions and explain one's acts. It therefore follows that we teach our children to have inner selves by forcing them to develop and to elaborate just such a set of metacriteria. One simple way to do this is to ask the child what it wants. Instead of just giving the child something to eat, we ask it whether it wants to eat a hamburger or a hot dog. Most children have certain definite preferences as to what they will and won't eat. But the child faced with such a question will try to find an answer even if no preference existed a moment before. Sometimes, therefore, such questions will cause the child to create an "inner" preference—a metacriterion. The next time a similar choice is faced, the child may tend to give the same answer as the last time. Adults may even help the self-attribution process along by remembering the child's choice the last time and saying, "You like hot dogs better, don't you now?"

The manufacturing of a complete and consistent set of intentions is even more important to the creation of an inner self than is the development of a set of preferences. Adults facilitate the child's development of the set of abstract intentions by always asking the child to explain why it did something. In order to respond to "Why did you do that?" a child must come up with a reason from which the behavioral intention was presumably derived. Often children deny they had a reason, but the adult may insist. Ultimately the child is forced to invent a reason. But the child probably tends to believe the parent—that the reason really did exist first, inside the child, and the child's act resulted from the reason. The lesson is that acts derive from inner states, and the child learns to think in those terms.

One day last summer my neighbor's preschool child spilled its milk. The mother was exasperated and began to yell, but she wanted to be fair. She wouldn't punish the toddler for an accident. So she insistently and repeatedly asked the child whether it had knocked the milk over on purpose or not. The child was completely helpless to answer this question, for it had no idea what "on purpose" meant—no understanding of intentionality. From the look on the mother's face the child knew that a spanking rode on whether it said yes or no, but it lacked any way of determining either the correct or the optimal answer. To me, this child's dilemma vividly illustrates the pressure we use to require our children to learn to think in terms of inner states.

There is some evidence about the acquisition of the inner self in Rosenberg's (1979) work. Rosenberg questioned a large sample of children and adolescents about their beliefs regarding the self. He was surprised at the extent to which children apparently believe their parents know them better than they (the children) know themselves. Even between the ages of eight and eleven years, children said that in the event of some disagreement between themselves and a parent about some trait of the child, the parent would probably be right. Most striking was what happened when Rosenberg asked his most extreme question: "'Who knows best what kind of person you really are, deep down inside?'" (p. 247). Even here, over half the children eight to eleven said the mother or father knew better than the child.

Clearly, children's knowledge of the inner self is felt by them to be less certain than their parents' knowledge of it. The implication is that children learn about their inner selves from the parents. As adults, we presume to have privileged access to our inner selves, but children do not yet have that presumption. This does not mean that children do not know when they are angry. Rather, they have not yet mastered the concept of an inner self, with its hidden contents that supposedly cause certain behaviors to happen. They have not learned how to talk about their feelings and actions in terms of the inner self, so they defer to the adults' superior knowledge while they learn.

It appears that action competencies—the behavioral self—continue to be important to self-definition throughout the late childhood stage. There is an important change, though, from the way in which competency is implicated in identity in early versus late childhood. Instead of evaluating competencies against explicit, fixed standards or criteria, the child begins to evaluate its competencies in comparison to and in competition with other children. To put it another way, there seems to be a shift from Type II to Type III self-definition as the child becomes older. Damon and Hart cite several studies (e.g., Secord & Peevers, 1974) showing that older children evaluate their abilities in comparison with other children. As an example, they cite the contrast between the young child's "I can ride a bike" and the older child's "I can ride a bike better than my brother" (Damon & Hart, 1982, p. 854). In particular, a study by Ruble (1982) showed that younger children make almost no use of information about how other children do; young children evaluate their performances on absolute standards. Older children, in contrast, engage in considerable social comparison and evaluate how they did by comparing it with how others did. Erikson (1950) makes a similar point by characterizing late childhood as concerned with avoiding inferiority. Competence has become a comparative and hierarchical concept, subject to competitive redefinition, instead of a criterial concept. The hierarchy is a sign of Type III self-definition processes.

A last feature of late childhood deserves comment. Damon and

Hart (1982) considered the "social self" to be a late-developing aspect of the self. Their thinking on this was apparently shaped by the adolescent's concern with interpersonal skills and traits. Therefore, Damon and Hart were apparently surprised to find evidence of this "social self" prior to adolescence; it seemed out of place there. They cited evidence that older children often describe and define themselves in terms of belonging to various social groups— "a Boy Scout", "a Catholic" (1982, p. 854; also Livesly & Bromley, 1973).

Yet perhaps these responses are not so surprising. Remember that the interpersonal aspect of identity is probably the first of the three functional aspects to appear; the family defines who the child is long before the child has developed potentialities or values. More important, though, is the fact that self-definition by group membership is relatively simple and clear-cut. One acquires such an identity component by joining the group; therefore, it is single-transformation (Type II) self-definition. The interpersonal skills and traits of adolescence are a complicated and hierarchical type of self-definition (Type III), subject to frequent change. It is to be expected that they would be preceded by one of the simpler, less problematic forms of self-definition.

From age six to age twelve, then, the child's identity seems to emphasize Type II and increasingly Type III processes of self-definition. Also, the potentiality aspect of identity becomes much more clearly defined. Six-year-old boys often still believe they can grow up to become mothers or members of a different race (Brim, 1976), while twelve-year-old boys have clear conceptions of what they can and cannot do and how they compare with their peers in terms of such competencies. They have often formed clear expectations about their futures as adults, although these expectations may undergo drastic revision during adolescence.

Play

Play is the universal business of childhood. To discuss childhood without discussing play is not taking childhood on its own terms but using adult categories instead.

It seems likely that the development of play is intimately linked to the development of identity. Not all types of play, of course. Play that boils down to mere enjoyment of motion, such as spinning around or swinging, has little relevance to identity. But many children's games seem to be essentially concerned with the defining criteria of identity. Moreover, in the developmental sequence of preferred children's games, the successive stages of self-definition processes can be detected.

Many games are based on the assignment of roles to participants. For the duration of the game, each participant has a role to enact. The role entails continuity of purposive activity, or at least continuity of functional activity. Moreover, the various participants in the game normally have different roles, so differentiation is also sustained for the duration of the game. Thus, the nature of playing games fundamentally involves the two defining criteria of identity.

Solitary play may be an exception. Role differentiation is possibly lacking in solitary play. However, Garvey (1977) stresses the essentially "social" nature of play: Solitary play is derived from interactive, group play.

The earliest game in the life of the modern child, perhaps, is Peek-a-Boo. Garvey (1977) records that most mother-infant pairs she observed played Peek-a-Boo. She points out that even Peek-a-Boo has a clear differentiation of roles and a structure of moves appropriate to each role. Peek-a-Boo is probably played so early in life because adults play it with their babies, and the adult ensures that the roles are assigned. To learn about the development of identity, though, it is necessary to emphasize the games children play with each other.

"Pretend" games can already be observed among toddlers. Hogan (1982) cites observations of thirty-six-month-old toddlers at play. In his account, the pair of toddlers does very little until one of them proposes something like, "Pretend you're Batman and I'm Robin." Then there is a flurry of activity as the toddlers seek to enact these roles. In such games there is no well-defined endpoint, no object, no score—indeed, Hogan suggests that such games simply continue until the toddlers have exhausted their ideas of how to enact the roles. The point is that "pretend" games are nothing more than the adoption and enactment of identities for short periods of time. They are exercises in continuity and differentiation of roles.

The assignment of identity is a difficult task in the play of young children. I have watched the children in my neighborhood spend longer debating who gets what role ("No, *I* want to be the daddy") than they spent playing the game. Hogan (1982) records observations of intransigent protests over the roles assigned (such as when a boy is assigned to be the mother). Garvey (1977, p. 53) observed several pairs of three-year-olds each of whom "became so engrossed with apportioning props for a tea party that the party itself was forgotten." (Again, note the close connection between ownership and identity at age three.)

The play of young children thus often centers around the assignment of identity and the enactment of continuous, differentiated roles. Such play resembles the Type I self-definition of the children's identities. Games resembling Type II self-definition are popular among early elementary and pre-school children. Garvey (1977) suggests that organized play of games with rules starts at about age 6.

One example of such "Type II" games is "Follow the Leader," in which one child performs a series of acts and the others all repeat the same acts. Although this may take the form of simple or silly acts, it can easily develop into a pre-competitive exercise of "Can you do this?" Each child in turn establishes itself as a competent player by duplicating each of the leader's acts. The decisive feature of the game is a Type II self-definition—being able to do each specified act.

Another interesting game from this phase is "Mother May I." Several children take turns asking one child (the "mother") whether they may take a certain number and type of steps. The "mother" arbitrarily assents or refuses each request. The one who covers the allotted ground first becomes the next mother. As a race, this game has competitive overtones, but the competition is absurdly unfair: The outcome does not depend on fair competition but on the whims of the "mother." (An amusing aspect of this game is the apparent portrayal of the utter arbitrariness of parental exercise of power, which is presumably how the child views the matter!)

Reaching the criterion is thus not a properly competitive achievement. All the game offers is the occasional, single-criterion transformation into "mother."

Garvey says that the first peer games children will play tend to be cooperative ones such as Ring-around-the-Rosey. The competitive games appear later between the ages of seven and nine. Ring-around-the-Rosey, however, does not differentiate the roles. Every participant does the same thing. Yet the game does get the children to play interactively, something that may often be lacking in the games of younger children. (Games of "Batman and Robin" or of "playing house" can be surprisingly disjointed when played by younger children.)

As a transition to the competitive games there are several pseudo-competitive games. These assign incompatible goals to the different roles, an essential feature of competition, but they do not have an endpoint. They are cyclical; no clear conclusion arises from the game as to who succeeded and who failed. One such game is "Tag," in which one child is "it" until it can manage to touch (tag) another child, who then becomes "it." Everyone who is not "it" at the moment runs around trying to evade the tag. Another such game is "Hide-and-Seek," in which "it" closes its eyes for a time while the other players hide and then "it" tries to find and tag them before they run back to some designated spot. The first player tagged by "it" becomes "it" the next time. Thus, both these games involve single-criterion transformations of identity (becoming "it") but do not offer any hierarchy of criteria by which identity is measured. At the end of an hour's play of such games, no winner or loser has been established, unless "it" completely fails to catch anyone. Even then, this persistent failure usually signifies the collapse of the game, not its outcome.

Other such games are "Red Light, Green Light," which is very similar to "Mother May I," except that there are fairer competitive rules, "Red Rover," which does have an endpoint, but one that is reached by getting everyone onto the same team, "Dodgeball," and "Duck Duck Goose." These games are all based on single-criterion redefinitions of self, and they are played around the time children begin elementary school.

The truly competitive games mark the transition to playing at Type III self-definition. Such games offer clear measures of the players' skills and achievements. The measures may be quantitative, as in a game's score, or spatial, as in position in a race. The measures are often not individual but sum up the whole team's achievement, as in team sports. Still, the essence of the game is achieving a measurement that compares favorably with the measure tallied by one's opponent.

Some games change in character as the children get older. These games for young children resemble Type II processes, for they are one-criterion demonstrations of competence. For example, the younger child learns to jump rope, play hopscotch, and perhaps master devices such as hula hoops or pogo sticks. Among older children, however, these same activities gradually acquire a hierarchy of skills and thus seem to invoke measurable, comparative components of self. Instead of merely being able to jump rope, one has to master all sorts of refinements, such as alternating feet, turning around, and jumping rapidly. Late in elementary school, children compete as to who can sustain the hula hoop or pogo stick in motion the longest. When the play reaches that stage, it resembles the graded or measured self-definition of Type III processes.

The games of toddlers simply assigned roles and allowed them to enact them in any way they wished. In contrast, the competitive games of late childhood are designed to make it difficult to enact one's role. For the small child, just keeping to a continuous and differentiated identity for a while is difficult enough. The older children can stay in role without difficulty, so their games build in obstacles to fulfilling the roles. Specifically, each role has an assigned goal, and the only way for one child (or team) to fulfill its goal is to prevent the other from fulfilling its. In competitive games, one has to assert and fulfill one's role (situational identity) in the face of determined efforts by others to stop one from doing so.

The developmental sequence of child's play thus resembles the movement through the first three stages of self-definition. It seems best to stop there and make only a few observations about possible parallels between subsequent play and Types IV and V self-definition processes. Very little play involves choice in a fundamental way; play choice is at best the choice of optimal means toward specific and explicit goals, such as choice of strategy in chess. Such choice does not accurately resemble the choice in self-definition Types IV and V.

There can be an element of choice in deciding what game to play. When the choices become habitual, they *may* be seen as expressions of inner preferences and priorities. To some extent this seems to happen during adolescence. Peers begin to make inferences about an adolescent's inner self based on whether he or she devotes free time to playing football, the swim team, playing chess, or collecting stamps. Although preadolescent children do engage in these activities, the activities are perhaps not taken as expressive of children's inner selves as they are in adolescence. The difference may have something to do with the adolescent's greater freedom to choose activities and greater awareness of alternatives. (Thus, possible choice evokes Type IV self-definition.) It can be argued, then, that choice of hobby does come to resemble self-definition by choice, at least during adolescence.

A number of aesthetics theorists have linked art to play (e.g., Lange, 1960). If one accepts this connection, it is easy to see art as the version of play corresponding to Type V self-definition. The artist, especially in modern art, has few firm rules to obey; the choice of how to create art is radical and cannot be dodged. Moreover, it has been assumed, since at least the Romantic era, that art expresses the inner self. Thus, the artist's choice of how and what to create does have clear elements of self-definition. Developmentally, artistic pretensions seem to emerge during middle or late adolescence. Children draw pictures, but it is not until high school that young persons think of their products in terms of artistic creation and expression. And adolescent poetry is notorious.

Adolescence

Erikson made famous the importance of adolescence for identity formation. His concept of "identity crisis" conveyed the notion that self-definition must be accomplished during adolescence. The discussion here of identity crisis is restricted to a few observations about self-definition during adolescence, in order to complete the developmental scheme; the next chapter is entirely devoted to a consideration of identity crises.

One key development of adolescence is that the third functional aspect of identity (structure of values and priorities) becomes problematic. The other two aspects have been problematic for self-definition in earlier phases of development, but they become problems in a new way during adolescence. Values and priorities become a problem for the first time. Adolescence is the stage of choice when values and priorities are called into question. It is the questioning of these values and priorities that makes adolescence centrally concerned with issues of choice. Self-definition confronts the problems of choice, as reflected in Type IV and Type V processes.

Prior to adolescence, children do have values and priorities. Children have likes and dislikes very early in life. Even three-year-olds will occasionally describe their personal preferences as a way of talking about themselves (Keller, Ford & Meacham, 1978). Older children are aware of various values, even ideological ones, such as beliefs that Catholicism is the one true religion or that Communists are both bad and wrong. The values-priorities aspect of identity does not first appear during adolescence, but it does first become a problem then.

Several features of adolescent development support the argument that it is then that values first become problematic. Damon (1983) reviews the studies of moral development, following the work of Piaget and especially Kohlberg. The general consensus is that moral thinking reaches levels of complexity and abstraction during adolescence that do not appear among younger children. Adolescents are thus able to appreciate moral dilemmas and search for firm, abstract, ultimate principles in ways that children cannot. Universal moral principles are, in fact, difficult to find, so adolescents often have to struggle with this.

Damon also observes that political and other ideological concerns first appear during adolescence. A child may call itself a Catholic, but its capacity to understand Catholic ideology (theology) is limited. The child probably knows that it belongs to a Catholic family and is Catholic by virtue of that membership. Adolescents question their ideological commitments, which often leads to trying out new religions, new political views, and so forth.

Given that moral and ideological issues concern adolescents, it can be concluded that the values aspect of identity is problematic during adolescence. Such concerns are relatively absent earlier in life; the third functional aspect of identity (values) may be problematic for the first time during adolescence.

Evidence exists that a number of specific changes related to self occur during adolescence. Self-consciousness apparently increases dramatically (e.g., Elkind & Bowen, 1979; Simmons, Rosenberg, & Rosenberg, 1973; Tice, Buder & Baumeister, 1985). Some have even argued that self-consciousness reaches its developmental peak early in adolescence and declines thereafter (Simmons et al., 1973; Tice et al., 1985). It seems likely that the increased self-consciousness follows from a developmental advance in cognitive capacity. Adolescents are able to think about and evaluate themselves much more so than younger persons. The self can therefore be much more of a problem for adolescents than it is for children. Adolescence increases one's *capacity* to have problems of the self.

Sense of personal agency also increases during adolescence (e.g., Damon & Hart, 1982). And Brim (1976) has argued that sense of personal control reaches its peak during adolescence and declines throughout the rest of life. Adolescents, in other words, feel more in control over their lives and fates than do the members of any other age group. The co-occurrence of peaks in self-consciousness and in sense of personal control may well be more than just coincidence. Recall that Kagan (1981) noted early peaks in rudimentary self-awareness and sense of control occurring together at the end of the second year of life. So it seems that self-recognition of identity is closely linked to agency, the active sense of self.

Furthermore, adolescent agency embodies a strong sense of choice. Damon and Hart (1982), in integrating past research, speak of "the adolescent's new respect for the volitional powers [of the self]" (p. 856). In other words, the sense of choice is conceptually related to the sense of personal agency.

Damon and Hart also reviewed additional evidence that the advent of adolescence is further characterized by an increased awareness of how the self extends into the past and future, and by an increase in the levels of abstraction for thinking about the self. Both of these developments indicate a shift away from the child's concrete, immediate, here-and-now sense of self, which is centered in bodily existence and physical activity. The self is understood by adolescents in terms that begin to resemble adult conceptions of identity: continuity across time, and abstractness. But the decline since early childhood of the importance of body awareness as a basis for sense of self is briefly reversed at the beginning of adolescence. Adolescents are (self-) conscious of their bodies. It is likely that the rapid bodily changes that mark puberty are responsible for the developmentally brief focus of attention back onto the physical body.

Trends that occur throughout the adolescent stage are also reviewed by Damon and Hart and are based on previous investigations (especially Montemayor & Eisen, 1977). First, as adolescents grow older (from age nine to age eighteen), they describe themselves more and more in terms of ideological beliefs. Second, their spontaneous self-descriptions refer increasingly to a sense of self-determination. (This increase in self-determination seems to be further evidence for the adolescent's strong belief in personal control and agency.) Third, self-description with reference to one's possessions and to one's bodily characteristics declines throughout the course of adolescence.

The interpersonal aspect of identity also becomes a new sort of problem in adolescence. Nearly every personality theorist has remarked on the immense difficulties adolescents have in cultivating new social skills to meet the nascent inclinations toward heterosexual companionship. Apparently the concerns of the interpersonal aspect of identity spill over to affect the potentiality aspect. Damon and Hart review evidence that shows that unlike younger children, when asked what they would like to become, a majority of adolescents answer in terms of interpersonal traits.

Comparison of Historical and Developmental Patterns

Several parallels between the historical scheme and the developmental scheme become apparent. One is the evolution of self-definition processes, which in both schemes moves from Type I to Type V. Another is the sequence by which the three functional aspects emerge and become problematic.

The review of historical evidence suggested that the interpersonal aspect of identity was the first to become problematic, during the early modern period. Developmentally, it is also the first. During the first couple of years of life the child has to learn that it is an entity separate from the parents but is a member of the social system that includes them (perhaps along with siblings and pets). Both developmentally and historically, the early form of the problem is not one of personality or social style but is one of conceiving a place for oneself as an individual within a system of other individuals who have different roles and intentions. In both schemes, personality does not enter until later.

Historically, the potentiality aspect of identity became a major concern during the Romantic era, when the Christian version of potentiality lost its power and appeal. Developmentally, the potentiality aspect is also the second to become problematic. It is a major concern during ages three to five, when the child's self-concept focuses on what the child can and cannot do. In late childhood the problem becomes more complex as the child increasingly compares its capacities and competencies to those of other children.

The values aspect of identity was the third one to become problematic in our history. This appears to have happened during the Victorian era and the early twentieth century. Developmentally, this functional aspect appears to become problematic during adolescence.

The fact that two schemes coincide does not prove that the sequence necessarily follows in that order. Still, it seems more than coincidence. It could be that the three different functional aspects of identity become problematic because of links with particular types of self-definition processes. Changes in self-definition processes led to problems with certain functional aspects of identity. For example, it is plausible that the issue of one's potentiality becomes problematic in connection with self-definition based on achievement (Types II and III). In other words, people may start to question and evaluate their potential because they want to define themselves according to some achievement-based criteria. By the same token, it is plausible that values become problematic when self-definition is most concerned with choices and decisions. However, this is speculative; there is no direct or clear evidence of such connections between shifts in dominant self-definition types and the emergence of problems with a particular functional aspect of identity.

Summary

The development of identity seems to follow a course from awareness of one's body, to classifications of one's body, and finally to a sense of personal agency. Agency is reflected in competence and achievement during childhood. During adolescence, agency is also reflected in choice.

Self-definition early in life is centered in the Type I processes, which are the simplest. Age, gender, and material ownership are the first important self-definitions. By the fourth year of life, however, concern with competency in activities becomes paramount for self-definition. The acquisition of an action competency is a Type II self-definition process. By late childhood, however, competencies are measured and are competitive; they thus belong to Type III self-definition processes. The young child understands its identity in terms of what it can and cannot do. The older child defines its identity in terms of how well it can do things compared to various standards and to other people.

During adolescence, a sense of self through personal agency begins to address issues of choice. Choice brings Type IV self-definition processes into play. Issues of choice are most clearly implicated in the typical adolescent's identity crisis, which is discussed in the next chapter.

9

Identity Crisis

Surprisingly little is known about identity crises. Research has only begun to clarify what the causes and consequences of such crises are. In this chapter I shall integrate what is known about identity crises into two coherent models. Since the research is limited, much of this is speculative.

Erik Erikson (1956) claims that he and his colleagues coined the term "identity crisis" in the 1940s to refer to a specific, narrow type of psychopathology they observed at the mental hospital where they worked. The term became popular, and with popular usage it began to refer to a wide range of existential ailments. More important, it became used to refer to formative struggles of "normal" (non-pathological) persons.

Erikson concludes that identity problems must have been widespread in our society by the time he coined the term. The widespread occurrence and importance of such problems would explain why society seized on the term "identity crisis" and began using it in many contexts, despite the lack of clear definition or empirical understanding.

Although our knowledge about identity crises has increased significantly in the past decades, there is still no clear definition or model of what an identity crisis is, for good reason. The most common research method used to study identity crises starts by classifying people according to whether they have had identity crises or not, and then proceeds to compare the different groups of people along a certain dimension—how they respond to external influence, for example (e.g., Toder & Marcia, 1973). Despite the value of such research, however, it can tell us very little about the *process* by which identity crises are initiated and resolved (Bourne, 1978).

Another reason for the lack of a process model for identity crisis is that *perhaps all identity crises do not have the same kind of process.* Erikson and subsequent writers seem to have assumed a single, definable phenomenon constitutes identity crisis. But identities can be in crisis in more than one way. In a recent paper, J. Shapiro, D. Tice, and I have proposed that there are basically two distinct kinds of identity crises.

We took as a point of departure the recent philosophical work by Habermas (1973). Habermas argued on conceptual grounds that there must be two and only two types of identity crises. He called them "legitimation crisis" and "motivation crisis." Habermas was mainly interested in the crises of countries and other large social systems. Therefore, we had to extrapolate some in order to apply his ideas to individuals.

The *identity deficit*, which corresponds to Habermas's "motivation crisis," refers to the inadequately defined self, characterized by a lack of commitment to goals and values. Without such commitments, the person lacks internal, consistent motivations. The person thus has no basis for making consistent choices and decisions. The stereotypical adolescent male identity crisis fits into this category. The adolescent does not know what he wants to be or how to decide. He questions himself and the world, looking for new sources of meaning, fulfillment, and value.

In identity deficit, the problem is having *not enough* identity. But having *too much* identity can also be a problem. The *identity conflict* (related to Habermas's "legitimation crisis") refers to the multiply defined self whose multiple definitions are imcompatible. More simply put, the different components of someone's identity are in conflict. The person suffering from identity crisis (unlike identity deficit) has firm commitments. But the different commitments make impossible or incompatible demands. The situation makes it impossible to choose and to act consistently with all the person's values and goals; one commitment may have to be betrayed. An example of this would be a person committed to both career and motherhood who is suddenly confronted with an opportunity for promotion that will require a substantial reduction of time spent with her children. Both commitments are important, but one of them must be partially sacrificed or compromised.

Identity deficits *can* seem to involve conflict. The key to distinguishing between the crisis and the deficit is to determine whether there are commitments. An adolescent torn between various options and possibilities is usually not committed to any of them. The identity deficit is a reluctance to give up any options; the identity conflict is a reluctance to betray actual, felt commitments.

To understand the two crises more fully, I will look at the causes, subjective experiences, behaviors, and resolutions associated with each type.

Causes of Identity Crises

Erikson has argued that some form of identity crisis is a normal and possibly universal part of human development. He suggested that adolescence is the common time for this crisis, in part because adolescence is characterized by a "psychosocial moratorium"—an opportunity to experiment with different possible identities, free from the necessity of making a definite, firm commitment to one of them.

Erikson's seminal ideas have been qualified on several counts. First, the universality of identity crises has not been found in research studies. Erikson did say that the identity crisis is often totally unconscious; put in these terms, it is hard to refute. Still, researchers generally seem to agree with the idea that some people go through a difficult period of questioning and redefining their identities and others do not.

The overview of the historical trends also leads to the conclusion that identity crises are not universal. The association of identity crises with adolescence must be recognized as a product of cultural, historical, and social factors. In other eras or other societies, adolescence was not a "psychosocial moratorium"and was not a time of chronic identity crisis. Part of the cause of identity crises in general thus seems to be the set of social conditions that facilitate them. Erikson would probably agree, because he was one of the first psychoanalytic thinkers to acknowledge the central role of cultural and historical factors in human development.

Erikson's writings focused on the identity crises of adolescence, but he believed that identity crises could occur at any stage in life. In particular, other authors (e.g., Rubins, 1968) have recognized the mid-life crisis as an identity crisis. No empirical justification exists for denying the possibility that identity crises can occur at various points in life.

One last comment about Erikson's ideas deserves mention. Even if not everyone has an identity crisis, such a crisis may still be part of normal development in our society. If so, then much does not need to be said about what precipitates that type of identity crisis (identity deficit). It simply occurs in the normal course of life, like learning to walk or talk. It may occur in adolescence simply because only then are the person's cognitive capacities sophisticated enough to engage in complex self-questioning and consideration of alternatives, and because in our society the choices and commitments that form adult identity are made during adolescence. One question does remain concerning causality: Why do some people and not others have identity crises?

As far as I know, no major theory of developmental psychology has argued that identity conflict crises (unlike identity deficits) are a normal stage of typical human life. It is nonetheless possible that many people have them. They may be precipitated by situational causes to a much greater extent than identity deficits are.

Causes of identity deficit. Why is it that not everyone seems to have an adolescent identity crisis? One approach to this problem used a research strategy developed by James Marcia and his colleagues, which was based on Erikson's theories. In the Marcia approach, an interview is used to determine whether the subject has had an identity crisis (including one in progress) and whether the subject is committed to some ideology and occupational goal; the method then ascribes one of four classifications to the subject. If the answer is Yes to both, the person is classified as *identity achieved*—someone who has had an identity crisis and has resolved it by a commitment to definite goals and values. Crisis but no commitment constitutes a *moratorium* status. Moratorium subjects are usually currently in the midst of an identity crisis, hence the lack of definite commitments.

The other two classifications of identity status refer to people who have not apparently had an identity crisis. People who show evidence of firm commitments to goals and values, without having had identity crises, are called *identity foreclosures*. These persons are typically committed to the values and goals their parents taught them; they have never had to reject, revise, or even seriously question the basic framework of these values, although there may be small differences between theirs and their parents. Most children presumably have "foreclosed" identities up to a point—that is, to the point at which they either have an identity crisis or abandon their parents' values.

The final category, *identity diffusion*, refers to persons who have never had an identity crisis and are also uncommitted to any definite set of goals and values. Consistent with Erikson's ideas, this category is generally regarded as the most maladaptive, and even pathological, of the four.

The typical research practice is to classify persons according to this scheme of four categories and then look for patterns associated with the differences among the four types. In terms of the causes of identity crises, for example, several studies have sought to compare how the various groups got along with their parents. Obviously, it is difficult to get reliable information about how someone's parents treated him or her. Bourne (1978) reviewed the literature on this question and concluded that the results of only one study could be trusted (Jordan, 1971). (A later review by Bernard, 1981, describes several other studies that point to conclusions similar to Jordan's.) Jordan's investigation, unfortunately, studied only males. It found that one important factor associated with the occurrence of identity crises was whether the son perceived his parents as accepting or rejecting. Jordan did verify the accuracy of the sons' perceptions by surveying the parents themselves. Sons who had had identity crises in the past (identity achieved status) or were currently having them (moratorium status) saw their parents as having been inconsistent and ambivalent; sometimes their parents were accepting, at other times rejecting. Sons with foreclosed identities, in contrast, were typically close to their parents, especially to their fathers, and perceived them as consistently supportive. Consistently disapproving and rejecting parents were associated with adolescents with "diffuse" identities.

Clinical case studies are consistent with the picture of parental ambivalence as a cause of identity crisis. Erikson's (1968) clinical observations support the picture of clinging, intrusive mothers and ambivalent fathers as the typical background for identity deficits in their sons during adolescence. Levi, Stierlin, and Savard (1972) report a series of cases of adolescent identity crises among males. In these, the father typically has conflicting feelings about the son, including envy and admiration, the desire for a protegé, feelings that his own values are repudiated by the son, and enjoyment of his son's failings as consolation for ways in which he (the father) feels inadequate. The mothers in these cases tended to proffer support and demand appreciation from their sons in ways the sons rejected.

Psychoanalytic theorists (Blos, 1962; Falk, 1976; Schafer, 1973) suggest that the identity crisis is provoked in part by the son's ambivalence toward his parents. During adolescence, he feels contradictory impulses. One is the desire to go back (regress) to being a child, completely submerged in the parents who both dominate and care for him. The other is to grow up and break away from the parents. The unconscious emotional attachment to the opposite-sex parent (the oedipal complex) is revived at puberty because of the strong emotions that accompany sexual maturation. This oedipal love contributes to the desire to regress and merge with the parent. The impossibility of this love contributes to the feeling that one must break away from the parents.

There are thus several indications that ambivalence in the relationship with one's parents increases the likelihood of identity crisis, at least among males. (Unfortunately, relatively little is known about causation of identity crises in female adolescents.)

On the face of it, the adolescent male's identity crisis begins with a rejection of parental goals and values. If such a rejection never occurs, presumably the person has a foreclosed identity (or diffuse identity, if perhaps values or goals were never gotten from the parents). Repudiating parental values might then leave a vacuum, which is the identity deficit. But why is there a crisis? How does this vacuum differ from that of the diffuse identity?

For the person to struggle to create a new identity rather than be content with identity diffusion, he must have some positive forces or motivations. Undertaking a struggle requires a certain amount of faith or hope that a satisfactory resolution is worth striving and suffering for. Consistent with this, Erikson (1968 and elsewhere) discusses the importance of "basic trust" in the formation of identity. Also, religious faith was seen as an essential ingredient in the Christian conversion experiences that I have suggested were the nineteenth century precursors of adolescent identity crises.

What does all this have to do with ambivalence in the relationship with parents? An adolescent's capacity for hope, faith, and trust is probably greatly dependent on there having been some powerful positive elements in the relationship with the parents (Erikson, 1950; also Rogers, 1961, on the value of "unconditional positive regard"). Negative feelings toward the parents help set off the repudiation of parental values, and the positive influence of parents produces the inner resources needed in the struggle to achieve a new identity.

Parental ambivalence (as perceived and reciprocated by the son) could contribute to identity crisis in the son in a second way (in addition to the way described in the previous paragraph). The rejection of parental teachings and influences is rarely total. Some of these teachings and values are kept, while others are questioned and abandoned. The point here is analogous to Weaklund's and O'Neill's assessment of the "hippie" youth counterculture of the 1960s—the apparent rejection of the "Establishment" concealed the fact that many traditional and even contemporary values were retained by the young rebels.

As Habermas suggests, a crisis is a state of a system. If you reject the entire system you have no crisis—you have nothing. A crisis occurs when you reject, or at least put on trial, a large enough part of the system that the system may have to change fundamentally. But there still has to be some continuity, to judge the trial and guide the changes. Despite what he may say, it is probably impossible for an adolescent to reject everything he has been taught and begin a new identity from nothing.

In that case, then, the typical adolescent identity crisis probably consists of a need to overhaul the identity, retaining some parts of it and changing or replacing others. The identity is in a state of deficit but is not a complete blank or vacuum. Ambivalence about parents meshes quite well with the process of retaining and discarding different parts of what they taught.

Thus the adolescent identity crisis is brought on by a partial rejection of parental values, which leaves the young person without enough goals and values to construct an adult life. Even if this view is completely correct, there are still some unanswered questions. In particular, what specific event precipitates the crisis? Why does it start at some particular point in adolescence instead of much earlier or later? Two speculations can be made in reply to these questions.

One possibility has to do with cognitive development. Elkind (1978; Elkind & Bowen, 1979) has suggested that an important increase in mental capacities occurs at the onset of early adolescence, thus making a dramatic increase in self-consciousness possible. Adolescent self-consciousness is hardly a novel observation. But it has an important consequence. The increased ability to reflect on oneself and to imagine how one is perceived by others probably increases the ability to exert control over oneself. One can evaluate one's behavior and appearance with some "objectivity" and can then change them to match (or deviate from) various norms and standards. Confronted with the possibility of changing oneself, one almost has to decide whether such changes are desirable. The self is a problem for the adolescent because adolescence is the time during which one first has the cognitive capacity to realize how problematic the self can be. The adolescent, unlike the child, is able to *not* take the self for granted.

There is some indirect support for the notion that identity crisis is connected with a developmental advance in cognitive capacities. Leadbeater and Dionne (1981) found a greater use of formal operations (an advanced stage of cognitive development in Piaget's scheme), in solving problems that dealt with identity issues, among subjects with achievement and moratorium identity status than among those with foreclosure and diffusion (i.e., no identity crisis) status. Another study found greater cognitive sophistication ("integrative complexity") among subjects with identity crises than among those who had never had identity crises (Slugowski, Marcia, & Koopman, 1984).

The second possibility has to do with the situational demand for choices. During the teen years one's behaviors rule out certain possibilities for one's future—for example, one cannot become a physician without taking an organic chemistry course during college. A young child can oscillate freely between simultaneous ambitions—to be a cowboy, a garbage collector, a locomotive engineer, a computer programmer, a teacher—but the adolescent often must face the incompatibility of various future identities. In short, the adolescent has to give up some of his or her options for future identities—has to abandon some potentialities. That hurts. Why are adolescents sometimes reluctant to commit themselves? A major part of this reluctance could be that such commitments entail letting go of other possibilities. Any career path one chooses will tend to seem limited, finite, even drab, when compared to the broad range of options and possibilities that the uncommitted adolescent has.

FEMALE ADOLESCENTS. Most of the research discussed so far has dealt with males because most research on adolescent identity crises has emphasized males. One of the few to have seriously studied both female and male adolescents is Orlofsky (e.g., Ginsburg & Orlofsky, 1981; Orlofsky, 1978). He and his colleagues have observed that female adolescent identity crises show much more conflict than do those of males. This raises a very interesting possibility—perhaps female adolescents are prone to identity conflicts rather than deficits.

If this observation is correct, it would be consistent with some other observations about feminine development. Observers as different as Peter Blos (1962) and Nancy Friday (1978) have remarked that females are much less likely than males to go through a drastic, I-don't-care-if-I-never-speak-to-you-again break with the parents during adolescence. Females may be unlikely to reject and repudiate the parental influence to the extent that many adolescent males will. This has two related consequences. First, no identity deficit is created, so the female may not have a deficit crisis. Second, the female adolescent may continue to feel committed to the values and aspirations taught by her parents. There are then two possible courses of development. One is to remain foreclosed on identity issues. The other is to have an identity conflict. The idea that identity foreclosures may be more normal and healthy for the female than for the male is supported by several studies—female foreclosures do not show the same problems or shortcomings that male foreclosures do (Damon, 1983; Waterman, 1982).

The identity conflict may develop during adolescence, as the young woman chooses life-styles or career options and then discovers them to be in conflict with the deeply felt values or goals she has retained from her upbringing. For example, she may commit herself to a professional career but experience a crisis when she discovers career demands will make motherhood impractical. When choosing the career, she may have assumed motherhood could be worked in somehow, or she may not have realized that her socialization had instilled a deeply rooted desire to be a mother.

These suggestions are highly speculative, but they do seem to fit what little evidence is available. It is perhaps no coincidence that, unlike the male-oriented studies of motivation crises, the sections on legitimation crises *do* contain a number of studies focusing on identity conflicts in females.

MID-LIFE CRISES. The so-called mid-life crisis also seems to fall into the category of identity deficit. Levinson and his colleagues (1978) describe the male mid-life crisis as a failure of the values and goals that have sustained the man for the past two decades of his life—roughly from age twenty to age forty. This failure and resultant identity deficit can be brought about in two ways.

Both paths to mid-life crisis concern what Levinson calls "the Dream." The young man embarks on his career with a certain image of the type of successful person he hopes to become—a company vice-president, a Nobel Prize winning scientist, a great novelist, or whatever. During his thirties, in particular, the man devotes himself wholeheartedly to "climbing the ladder" toward realization of this Dream. Around age forty, however, a critical event may happen that renders the Dream inadequate as the overriding motivation for the rest of his life and for his identity.

One such event is a major development that shows the forty-year-old that he will never reach this Dream. As an example, Levinson and his colleagues cite the pyramid structure of business management. If, in a given company, there is one vice-president for every twenty managers, then nineteen of those managers will be unable to fulfill their Dream of becoming vice-president. Levinson suggests that this typically becomes clear around age forty. An organizational shake-up may result in a lateral move instead of a promotion or may assign the man a boss younger than he is. One or another such sign conveys to the man that he is no longer on the inside track to the top. Although he will still get salary raises and even perhaps some minor promotions, he will not fulfill his Dream.

The other possible cause of the mid-life crisis is what happens to the "lucky" few who do fulfill their Dream or some facsimile of it. This is perhaps one of the great cruel ironies of life—you experience letdown, disappointment, and crisis whether you reach your goals or not. Consider the case of the man who at age forty does get the promotion to vice-president that he has coveted for so long. Levinson and his colleagues say that most men's Dreams contain a certain fairy-tale quality, the belief that one will live happily ever after if one can only achieve such-and-such. Well, one reaches that goal, and there are some weeks of congratulation and fulfillment. But there is no "happily ever after." Relationships with spouse and family are as problematic as ever; the increased salary is soon overtaken by increased expenditures; the ulcers or overweight do not vanish; and the car or plumbing still refuses to work properly. One thing has changed, though. The man can no longer convince himself that all his problems will vanish once he reaches his goal. He has reached it, or enough of it, to know better.

Either way, then, the mid-life male finds himself unable to continue structuring his life around this Dream. That deficit constitutes the mid-life crisis.

Causes of identity conflict. The identity deficit seems to occur because the person does not have enough commitments (to values and goals) to enable him to make choices and plans. The identity conflict, on the other hand, occurs when the person has too many conflicting commitments; he is unable to make choices and plans. In both cases, the impending necessity of making choices presumably contributes to the beginning of the crisis.

A good illustration of the emergence of identity-conflict crises is provided by Roeske and Lake's (1977) study of female medical students. These women were firmly committed to becoming physicians, and the sex role of being a woman was also a major component of their identities. Early in medical school, however, they recognized that the two components made conflicting demands about how they should behave. For many of them, being a woman meant having babies, being noncompetitive and nonaggressive, and so forth. These seemed incompatible with pursuing their careers in medicine.

Another obvious example of identity conflict is provided by immigrants who expect to retain allegiance to their native culture while participating in their adopted culture (e.g., Goldstein, 1979; Mostwin, 1976). It is not normally possible to comply with the customs, practices, styles, and norms of two different cultures at once. Interestingly, some evidence points to the fact that the identity conflict can be deferred by a generation. If the immigrant retains primary allegiance (in feeling and behavior) to the native culture, the immigrant's children may be the ones to experience the identity crisis (see Sommers, 1969). They are brought up by their parents according to the values and patterns of the old culture, but their socialization by schools and other sources conforms to the new culture. The lessons of the parental family generally comprise the most deeply felt beliefs, but these persons ultimately have to leave the family and make lives for themselves in the new culture.

Because adolescence is such a pivotal point in terms of career, marriage, and so forth, the identity conflict can occur there just as the identity deficit does. (It has already been suggested that this may be especially likely among females.) People who might otherwise get through adolescence with foreclosed identities might thus end up by having a crisis because of conflicting imperatives. During adolescence, the identity conflict may typically involve a young person who knows what he or she wants but finds that desire incompatible with other deeply felt motivations. An illustration of this is provided by Greenspan's (1972) study of youth on an Israeli kibbutz. These people grew up in a small, intensely loyal community. They were taught the importance of abiding loyalty to the kibbutz, and most did indeed want to remain there for their entire lives. However, they were also taught the importance of education and of cultivating oneself so as to be best able to serve others. But the small kibbutz did not offer training for occupations in law, medicine, or other such careers (even beyond the training, the opportunities to practice such careers were very limited). Young people who wanted to pursue such careers—a pursuit consistent with the community's esteem for learning and education—were thus faced with the difficult choice of abandoning those ambitions or leaving the kibbutz. Either choice betrayed one of their basic values. For promising and intelligent young pupils, at least, adolescence was a time of difficult identity conflict between incompatible value commitments.

Still, it is probably more common for the identity conflict than the identity deficit to appear at times other than adolescence and mid-life, because a situation can arise at any time that makes you choose between conflicting prescriptions of different identity components. Two cases of postadolescent identity conflict are reported by Beit-Hallahmi (1977). The subjects of these were torn between internalized parental expectations and personally acquired ambitions. The first case was a twenty-eight-year-old male graduate student who wanted to be a professor of physics. His father considered academic pursuits as useless and pressured him into becoming a businessman. The son had internalized these expectations to the point of enrolling in a business administration program. The second case was more complex. A twenty-four-year-old female wanted to be just like her mother and yet be different and independent. Her mother was a professional woman who had raised a family and now, single again, frankly described her sexual relationships to her daughter. The daughter internalized these values to the point of enrolling in professional school, carrying on an "extremely promiscuous" life style, and hoping vaguely to marry and raise children too. Yet she felt a miserable failure in comparison to her mother, and she wanted to get involved in politics and do other things that had no relation to her mother's life.

The essential prerequisite for an identity conflict is a strong personal and emotional commitment to two distinct identity components that become incompatible. There seem to be two ways in which the crisis could arise. In the first, the two components have always been compatible but suddenly make conflicting recommendations for action. This probably happens because a new situation is encountered that brings out the contradictory demands of the two components. The conflict between career and motherhood is a good illustration. The woman may have held both ambitions for a long time before they actually began to conflict. In the second, circumstances or choices dictate the acquisition of a new identity component that is soon found to be in conflict with long-standing components. The case of the immigrant illustrates that process. The first model might be regarded as an emergence of latent conflict, whereas the second is an adjustment problem following change or transition of identity.

The causal role of circumstances seems much more central for conflict than for deficit crises. Few people have sets of identity components that are always in conflict. The conflict arises because the person gets into a situation in which the different components prescribe different, incompatible behaviors. Neither the situation nor the commitments alone are enough to bring about an identity conflict.

Subjective Experience of Identity Crises

What does it feel like to have an identity crisis? Typically, it is unpleasant, of course. It may also feel as if you are looking for something—the popularity of "quest" metaphors (searching one's soul, finding oneself) in describing identity crises suggests as much. What is sought is presumably a satisfactory way in which to make the choices that confront one. As long as a person has a reliable way of making those choices, he or she is unlikely to have an identity crisis. One of the themes of this book is that identity has become regarded as the receptacle for these "metacriteria" used in making choices. Hence people feel they can search within themselves to find the resolution of these difficult issues during crises of self-definition.

Subjective experience of identity deficit. Subjects having an identity deficit are characterized by a lack of identity commitments coupled with an ongoing struggle to make some. The struggle is what differentiates them from people who lack commitments but don't care ("identity diffusion" status; Marcia, 1966), and those alienated few who have chosen to live without commitments (Orlofsky, Marcia, & Lesser, 1973).

The subjective experience of an identity deficit undoubtedly varies from day to day and from person to person. But there are some general patterns noted by various observers. Although each pattern may be common among people with this type of identity crisis, not everyone with an identity-deficit crisis will have all of them.

The recurrent themes mentioned by those who have studied identity deficits include the following: vacillating commitment and confusion about values (Newman & Newman, 1978); periodic feelings of vagueness (Marcia, 1966), feelings of emptiness (Rubins, 1968; Schafer, 1973), or "generalized malaise" (Bickford, 1971); preoccupation with great, seemingly unresolvable questions (Marcia, 1966), often with the result of an apparent detachment from or loss of interest in the mundane issues and concerns of everyday life (Bickford, 1971); anxiety (Marcia, 1967); self-consciousness, including rumination about the meanings and implications of one's actions, leading to an "overexamined life" (Keniston, 1965); feelings of confusion, bewilderment, and occasional discouragement (Bickford, 1971; Marcia, 1967; Schenkel & Marcia, 1972). There is also some suggestion of a tendency in these people to be dissatisfied and hostile toward authority (Bourne, 1978; Marcia, 1966, 1967; Marcia & Friedman, 1970; Podd, Marcia, & Rubin, 1970; Schafer, 1973; Schenkel & Marcia, 1972). Contempt and hostility toward the parents may well be one form that this anti-authoritarianism can take (Rubins, 1968).

This is quite a diverse set of feelings. One way to make sense of them is to suggest that there is a basic underlying emotional conflict. Emotionally, the person is torn between a *desire for commitment* and the *reluctance to give up any options*. Making a commitment means giving up certain possibilities in order to pursue others. You cannot really develop any of your potential beyond a certain preliminary stage without making a commitment. But by committing yourself you renounce other potentialities, a painful act. (The most common metaphor, "making sacrifices," expresses the painfulness of commitment.) Adolescence may be the first point at which most people have to face that pain, also known as ontological guilt.

Thinking of the identity deficit as centered around that basic emotional conflict furnishes a way of looking at two of the other identity statuses (other than moratoriums) as outcomes of that conflict. If the desire for commitment triumphs, identity is "achieved." If the reluctance to forfeit any of one's possibilities triumphs, identity "diffusion" results.

The subjective states listed above can be linked to this basic ambivalence. On the one hand, the desire for commitment can explain several of the subjective states: the vacillating feelings of commitment, the emptiness, the preoccupation with ultimate questions, and the self-consciousness. On the other hand, the reluctance to forfeit any options could be the basis for the confusion about values, the vagueness, and also the self-consciousness. The anxiety, too, may be linked to the reluctance to let go of any of one's possibilities—the "ontological guilt" over failing to fulfill some of your potentiality is a form of existential anxiety. This suggestion is supported by evidence that anxiety is high both among moratorium-status subjects and among identity-diffusion subjects (Marcia & Friedman, 1970; Schenkel & Marcia, 1972). It was suggested in the previous paragraph that identity diffusion occurs when the moratorium's reluctance to give up any options predominates. This reluctance correlates with anxiety in that both occur predominantly in the same two identity statuses (moratorium and diffusion).

To round out the explanation of the various subjective states associated with identity deficit, it is useful to recall that the two basic desires are in conflict; some subjective signs of conflict would be expected. The tension arising from this conflict could explain the confusion and bewilderment, the discouragement, the anxiety, and the "generalized malaise."

As for the anti-authoritarianism, it may be due to the fact that identity deficits are often begun by a repudiation of the values and goals one has learned from one's parents. It is widely believed that attitudes toward authority are first shaped by attitudes toward parents, and the two attitudes continue to be related. The adolescent's attempt to break free of the parents is therefore probably accompanied by some antagonism toward authority figures in general. Two observations are consistent with this interpretation. The first is that adolescents with foreclosure-status identity have the highest levels of authoritarianism (Marcia, 1966, 1967). These are typically the people who never repudiate their parents' values and aspirations. The fact that they tend to be pro-authority lends credence to the idea that the anti-authoritarianism of moratorium-status subjects is linked to attitudes toward parents. The second observation is that the anti-authoritarianism is not mentioned in Levinson's account of the mid-life crisis, which is also an identity deficit but does not begin in any obvious way as a repudiation of the parents.

Apart from the anti-authoritarianism, the subjective experience of the mid-life crisis resembles that of the adolescent identity deficit. Levinson et al. (1978) refer to "emotional turmoil, despair, the sense of not knowing where to turn or of being stagnant and unable to move at all" and to a "need to explore, to see what is possible" (p. 199). In their discussion and examples one can see all the subjective features listed for the adolescent crisis (again, with the exception of the anti-authoritarianism).

There may be another difference between the adolescent and mid-life identity deficits, though. The underlying reluctance to make any commitments that marks the adolescent crisis does not seem to appear in the same literal form in the mid-life crisis. However, the reluctance to forfeit part of one's potential *is* clearly a feature of the mid-life crisis, so the underlying emotional ambivalence may be the same. In the mid-life adult (unlike the adolescent), the concern over the loss of potentialities derives in part from an awareness of mortality, a sense that time is running out. Levinson et al. quote the novelist James Baldwin on the painful recognition that "between what one wishes to become and what one has become there is a momentous gap, which will now never be closed." The tension between fear of unfulfilled potential and desire for stable commitments is thus common to the identity deficits of mid-life as well as adolescence.

Subjective experience of identity conflict. During an identity-conflict crisis, you feel that you are in an impossible situation. The situation, of course, is not entirely to blame; what makes it impossible is personal commitments. These commitments cannot be reconciled in the situation at hand. The person feels it impossible to act without betraying oneself and one's loyalty to some other persons, to an ideology, or to an institution. If such action is necessary, the person may acutely sense this betrayal and may feel guilt over being a "traitor."

A study of Israeli Arabs by Peres and Yuval-Davis (1969) sheds some light on what an acute identity conflict must feel like.

Israelis and Arabs have been in conflict for a long time; it is not easy to be both an Israeli and Arab. Indeed, the researchers found that these persons felt it difficult to maintain their basic "dignity and integrity" through this conflict. An interesting consequence of the identity conflict was that the individual tended to feel that both the conflicting components of identity were threatened; Israeli Arabs often felt they were neither real Israelis nor real Arabs.

The onset of the Six-Day War between Israelis and Arabs intensified the identity conflict for Israeli Arabs for obvious reasons—the war increased the likelihood of having to choose between the two identity components and thus betray one of them. Peres and Yuval-Davis reported that many Israeli Arabs had a definite feeling of impending doom when that war started. War does portend doom for many, so there was an objectively valid reason for that feeling. But it is quite plausible that part of the feeling of impending doom derived from the perceived necessity of betraying part of one's identity by taking sides.

Another observation of Peres and Yuval-Davis suggests that an identity conflict of this type can result in exaggerated passivity or even emotional paralysis. They noted that many Israeli Arabs seemed to want to postpone taking sides as long as possible. When someone (e.g., the local authorities) tried to coerce them into some action which implied taking sides, the Israeli Arabs would respond with hostile resentment—but not with overt revolt. This is consistent with the picture of an identity conflict as feeling that an impossible choice is required. The person prefers not to act, for any action is unacceptable to one component of the identity. The person resents being forced to act and will not even act out that resentment and resist the force; even doing that would constitute taking sides.

Behavior in Identity Crises

Researchers have not shown a great deal of interest in the behaviors associated with identity crises, perhaps because it is not what an identity crisis makes you do that is important about the crisis (unless perhaps you do something drastic such as killing yourself or vanishing). Even such extreme behaviors are rare and are probably caused by a combination of factors of which the identity crisis may be only one.

Behavior during identity deficit. Erikson has generally emphasized the exploratory nature of behavior during the adolescent identity crisis. The adolescent "tries out" different ideologies, interpersonal styles, and career options. Erikson's insight enabled psychologists to make sense out of the seemingly chaotic and contradictory behavior of adolescents.

Erikson, indeed, says that the "psychosocial moratorium" of adolescence is valuable because it enables the young person to experiment without first making long-term self-defining commitments. Some evidence exists that he is correct about this—identity crises occur in part when there is such an opportunity for nonbinding experimentation. Morash (1980) found that working-class youth were much less likely to have identity crises than were middle-class youth, and she attributes this difference primarily to the lack of such an opportunity in the lives of the working-class adolescents. In particular, she noted that they often begin working right out of high school and thus skip a college education. College affords an excellent opportunity for a moratorium because one lives apart from direct parental or institutional control, because one has few long-term obligations, and because one is confronted with a series of novel ideas and persons. The chance to explore alternative ideologies and relationships is thus maximized. In bypassing college, working-class youths get settled into stable and committed patterns earlier than do middle-class youths.

Active experimentation is not the only form an adolescent identity deficit may take. Instead, the person may shrink from making choices, adopt an avoidant stance, and ruminate alone. Orlofsky, Marcia, and Lesser (1973) say that during identity crises some adolescents are "active, engaging, and creative" while others are "paralyzed by an inner turmoil of indecisiveness" (p. 211). Some try everything, others nothing. It is difficult to escape the impression, though, that the former (trying everything) is the more adaptive approach. If a case of "paralyzed indecisiveness" becomes chronic, such as prolonging adolescence toward age thirty, it becomes appropriately described as identity diffusion.

The experimentation with new activities can be seen in some instances of the mid-life (identity-deficit) crisis as well. This experimentation will sometimes seem especially dramatic in the mid-life crisis. This is probably accentuated by the contrast with the stable, committed, orderly ("dull") pattern of life typical of persons in their thirties (Levinson et al., 1978). Levinson records various examples of change of career and marital breakup that derive from the mid-life identity deficit. He and his colleagues point to the experimental, exploratory character of such behavior at mid-life, including "false starts" (p. 199) similar to those of the adolescents.

One final feature of the behavior patterns of persons with identity deficits has emerged from laboratory studies of behavior. Subjects classified as having moratorium-status identity (i.e., identity crisis in progress) seem unusally susceptible to influence. These subjects are more likely than others to go along with the group, to express an opinion that seemed obviously false but agreed with what everyone else was saying (Toder & Marcia, 1973). (Everyone else had been contacted by the experimenter in advance and had been told when to express certain false judgments to see whether the actual subject would concur or not.)

Conceptually similar results were reported by Podd, Marcia, and Rubin (1970). These authors used a "prisoner's dilemma" game, a test of whether a pair of subjects will cooperate with each other for mutual advantage, or will try to take advantage of each other. One subject in each pair was contacted by the experimenter in advance and told to follow a prearranged pattern of cooperative (or exploitative) moves. The researchers found that "moratorium-status" subjects were the most likely to follow the other player's lead and match their responses to their partner's responses. (There was one exception. If the partner was portrayed as an authority figure, moratorium subjects tended not to cooperate, probably just another sign of their anti-authoritarianism.)

Neither of these experiments can be regarded as definitive. But they do suggest that the absence of commitment, combined with the struggle for identity, leaves one susceptible to external influence as long as this influence does not manifest itself in an overtly authoritative fashion. This may explain why cults are most successful at recruiting adolescents. The initial approach of cult recruiters is generally carefully designed not to be authoritative—the cult members may even emphasize their opposition to "Establishment" authorities. The young person may then find that the cult community and ideology contain seeming solutions to his or her identity deficit.

Behavior during identity conflict. People having identity conflicts are not noted for any particular type of behavior. Studies of conflict-type crises are noticeably lacking in behavioral indications. This should not be surprising, since the hallmark of the identity conflict is the subjective experience of being torn between conflicting commitments. Such a problem should not induce any particular behavior. The identity conflict differs from the identity deficit in that the conflict presents no vacuum to fill; there is no need for exploration, experimentation, or new information. The dramatic behavior patterns of the identity deficit, such as finding a new hobby, new lover, new job, or new ideology, have no value in solving an identity conflict. And new commitments could only make the problem worse by increasing the likelihood of conflicting loyalties and obligations!

The only type of information-seeking behavior that might be expected from persons with identity conflicts is their trying to get advice or guidance about how the conflicting commitments can be reconciled. The person might seek out persons affiliated with neither side of the conflict or persons associated with both sides. One illustration of the latter was noted by Roeske and Lake (1977) among the female medical students they studied. The younger women students displayed a strong desire for contact and study with a female physician, which suggests that they wanted exposure to a role model who had presumably successfully managed to integrate being a physician and being a woman. The desire to work with a female physician decreased greatly as the female students progressed through medical school. Unlike the first- and second-year students, the advanced students did not have a special desire to work with a woman. The identity crisis had probably been somewhat resolved by the time the woman was farther along in medical school. The desire for such a helpful role model was strongest among the young students, who presumably had not yet resolved the identity conflict.

Other than seeking help in resolving conflict, persons suffering from identity-conflict crises may exhibit behaviors designed to avoid or escape the problem. This could be especially true if no chance for compromise is apparent—if the conflict persists as impossible. The avoidant passivity of the Israeli Arabs (Peres & Yuval-Davis, 1969) is an example of this. An extreme form of attempted escape would be suicide. It is plausible that suicide may be one behavior associated with identity conflict, although there are no systematic data on this. Suicide might appear as a way of escaping the intolerable conflict while being "fair" to both commitments. With suicide, one does not abandon one commitment for the sake of the other; rather, one abandons both equally.

It is thus plausible that the greatest danger in the identity conflict is the possibility of suicide, compared with the danger in identity deficit of being caught up in some religious cult or political terrorist group. If so, whenever adolescents begin career decisions and commitments early (before college), there will be a shift from deficit to conflict crises during adolescence, resulting in an increase in teenage suicide rates but a decrease in political activism and membership in cults and communes.

Resolution of Identity Crises

Resolution of identity deficit. The identity deficit is a lack of commitment that is resolved when the commitments are made. Based on Erikson's work, Marcia (1966) conceptualized the identity crisis of adolescence as the process of adopting an ideology (religious and political beliefs) and choosing a career. Unfortunately, research so far has shed little light on the process by which these commitments are made.

The process of resolving an identity-deficit crisis can be broken down into a two-step process. The first step involves resolving issues of value. The second addresses the practical, instrumental issue of how to put these values and subsequent goals into practice. The typical adolescent identity crisis may begin with a struggle with basic values and beliefs. Once some closure is attained on those, the adolescent can turn to the problem of forming a life plan that is consistent with such values.

The first step could be bypassed if the person has foreclosed values. For example, an adolescent might never question her (value) basic desire to help others but might still undergo the (instrumental) phase of an identity crisis in trying to decide whether to help others as a physician, teacher, politician, or nurse. (Whether that choice alone may qualify as a full-fledged identity crisis is a thorny issue of definition.)

Resolving the value stage of an identity deficit is probably more difficult than resolving the instrumental stage. To do it properly, the adolescent must question and doubt each possible value and belief in order to ascertain which ones hold up. A lot of "soul-searching" is necessary for such a process. Most adolescents may do a less than thorough job of this, but even so it has to be a long and difficult process.

The process of questioning and doubting one's values (and the alternatives) can help explain one apparent contradiction. Evidence has already been cited that adolescents having identity crises are both anti-authoritarian and vulnerable to influence. It seems difficult to reconcile being open to influence with being resistant to authority. But the key is that authority tends to expect dutiful, unquestioning compliance (reminiscent of the parent who justifies commands with "Because I said so, that's why!"). Because the moratorium-status individual is prone to question everything, he will want to make up his own mind about whether to do such-and-such, rather than simply acting out of faith or obedience toward the authority figure. On the other hand, the identity deficit means that in a certain sense there *is* indeed an inner vacuum. If the moratorium-status person finds a given value acceptable, he can accept it and start acting on it much more quickly than someone who has no such deficit. These persons can thus adapt to influence more easily than can others.

Just *how* the adolescent decides which values are correct and acceptable is unclear. The adolescent's project is actually impossible, for it is impossible to generate or select a system of values without taking anything on faith or for granted. This is the case with religious beliefs. There is no absolute way of deciding whether a God or an afterlife exists. Both theism and atheism require leaps of faith. The adolescent searches for a foundation or basis for making such decisions. The seemingly endless adolescent debates over what seem to be trivial or minor points can be understood as part of the quest for such firm ground. For example, if the adolescent can decide that one of the miracles attributed to Jesus in the Bible really happened, then it would seemingly follow that Jesus did indeed have divine powers; therefore, there must be a God, and so forth. On the other hand, if the adolescent can decide that one of those miracles was misreported, a trick, or otherwise non-divine, then that suggests that the Bible cannot be trusted, and so forth. The point is that the adolescent typically may not realize that to form a system of values and beliefs one must uncritically accept something. He thinks there must be some unassailable truths, and if he can find them, the rest will follow.

Somehow, then, the adolescent accepts certain beliefs, values, or presuppositions as correct—with the result that their implications seem justified. The adolescent could simply have certain ideas that are above questioning. For example, one might not question the value of love, the desirability of happiness, or the ineluctable necessity of earning a good salary. The person's other values can then be tested for compatibility with these basic, unassailable convictions. Another way some basic beliefs might escape critical evaluation is by consensual acceptance by the peer group, or advocacy by some admired role model. Once someone or some group has gained the adolescent's trust and respect, the adolescent may be ready for uncritical acceptance of beliefs and values from that person or group. With the peer group it is probably necessary that it have consensus about some belief or value in order for it to be accepted uncritically. Mindless conformity to a group is sharply reduced if the rest of the group is not unanimous—if one person disagrees with the group, others become more willing to do so (Asch, 1955).

A third likely source of basic beliefs and values is the mass media. It is difficult to believe that television and movies have no effect on identity crises, although data are not available. The influence of television and movies is decidedly non-authoritarian (many youth films are clearly rebellious or iconoclastic), which means that their influence is not likely to generate resistance among adolescents with identity deficits.

Once a set of basic values and beliefs is accumulated, the first stage of resolving the identity deficit can be completed by making one's system (of values and beliefs) complete and consistent. This does not necessarily get done to perfection. A workable approximation probably suffices in most cases—that is, obvious contradictions are settled but latent or potential ones may be ignored, which may give rise to identity conflicts later on.

Resolving the value issues enables the person to form an abstract goal, a vague concept of a desired future self. The person can then move to the second stage of resolving the identity deficit. In the second stage, that abstract goal or vaguely envisioned future self must become a specific, viable ambition; the person then initiates activities designed to fulfill that goal. The basic and abstract values resulting from the first stage must be translated into specific behavioral patterns.

Translating the abstract goals into specific ambitions is presumably a process of collecting various options and then eliminating those that fail to satisfy the requirements of the abstract goals and values. It is in this second stage, for example, that the adolescent might seek out and benefit from vocational counseling, which would have been relatively useless during the first stage. Finally, the person settles on a particular option or pattern and begins to work toward it. This constitutes the commitment, and the identity crisis is ended.

Some observations are consistent with the two-stage model of resolving an adolescent identity crisis. Authors have noted that identity-related psychotherapy with adolescents can evolve from a ruminating, present (and past) oriented stage to a stage that is focused on the future (Engle, 1960; Kahn, 1969). The appearance of the second stage is regarded as a good sign of progress—it seems to suggest that one stage (the more difficult one) of the crisis has been resolved.

It is not clear whether mid-life (or other) identity deficits are resolved by this same two-stage process or not. Only when more research on those crises has accumulated will it be possible to tell.

One final point. It is not safe or necessary to assume that all identity deficits are resolved. Some identity crises may simply end without being resolved. Kahn (1969) mentions the traditional folk belief that adolescents just "grow out of" their problems. Circumstances may sometimes dictate that the person adopt a certain style or pattern of life, such that there is no room and no need for further self-questioning. Morash's (1980) finding that identity crises are relatively rare among working-class youth who skip college does support the view that circumstances can prevent the use of crisis to achieve identity. If a person in the midst of an identity crisis were abruptly thrust into bankruptcy, prison, or combat, it is conceivable that the signs of identity crisis would vanish. Such situational exigencies may put an end to an identity crisis without resolving it.

Even without special circumstances, adolescents may just tire of the identity struggle and may abandon it. There seem to be two main outcomes of this "giving up." One is to stay in a chronic state of identity diffusion—perpetually uncommitted, perpetually adolescent. This state could deteriorate into a more serious form of psychopathology.

The other is to return to the values and aspirations one had before the identity crisis began—usually the ones the person learned from parents and other agents of socialization. (In most such cases a few modifications are to be expected. The person probably got *something* out of the identity crisis.) Such returning would account for the puzzling research finding that persons who are classified as having moratorium-status identity—having an identity crisis in progress—are sometimes later classified as foreclosures, which means they never had an identity crisis (Waterman, 1982). Strictly speaking, this is impossible. If you have an identity crisis, you cannot later have an identity status that is defined by never having had an identity crisis. But if people leave the identity crisis by returning to their pre-crisis values and attitudes, there may be no sign that an interviewer would notice of the past identity crisis. The interviewer would just perceive that the person was committed to the same values learned as a child from the parents.

Returning to one's original values and goals is not necessarily an abandonment of the identity crisis struggle. It could be a legitimate resolution of the struggle, in which the person seriously makes a new commitment to old values. As an early prototype of this, Greven's (1977) portrayal of the "sins of youth" in evangelical Puritans comes to mind. Many of these male Puritans rebelled against their straitlaced and sober models during adolescence, but following a religious conversion experience they typically went back to being proper and pious.

Blos's (1962) classic book on adolescence contains an interesting and relevant suggestion. In his view the adolescent's concern with ideological questions (religion, philosophy, the meaning of life, ultimate values) is caused by a basic unconscious disturbance. The adolescent male is trying to break free of the oedipal emotional attachment to his parents. He rejects their values and their influence on him because these rejections help him to overcome his desire to love them, which would entail going back to being a child whose world was completely managed by the parents. In Blos's view, this powerful emotional bond is finally and more or less thoroughly broken during adolescence (more so among males than females). This development is signified by the formation of intimate relationships with same-age peers of the opposite sex. Once the emotional attachment to the parents is broken, there is no longer such a great need to reject the parents' values, goals, and ideals. At the end of adolescence, the male therefore begins to return to these and to adopt and integrate them into his adult personality.

Blos thus gives a model to explain why the end of an identity crisis might contain a partial or nearly total return to parental values and attitudes. This is an intriguing suggestion, which doubtless has some validity. However, it suggests that the achievement of heterosexual intimacy is a prerequisite for the achievement of identity. This is contrary to the views of Erikson (1968) and the research findings of Orlofsky, Marcia, and Lesser (1973), all of which indicate that the development of intimacy in males comes after the achievement of identity. Blos's suggestions must be modified to account for this before his model can be taken as a general pattern.

Resolution of identity conflict. There seem to be two types of processes that would resolve identity conflict. One involves choice, the other does not.

In some cases, *the situation* decides that one of the conflicting components of identity becomes the victor. The individual has little or no choice. Immigrants provide a clear illustration of this type of enforced resolution. The immigrant must abide by the laws and obligations of the adopted country even if he or she retains strong emotional ties to the former nationality. And even if the immigrants do cling to some of the social and cultural practices of the old country, their children will gradually have to embrace the practices of the new country. Sommers (1969) provides a detailed case study of a young American male brought up by immigrant Japanese parents in a strictly Japanese fashion. He felt guilt and conflict over deviating from the Japanese practices but found it necessary to do so to live as an American citizen.

In such cases the individual does not resolve the identity conflict by making a choice. The choice is enforced by the situation, and the individual must learn to accept it, and betray the one commitment. The resolution of the crisis involves coming to terms with the guilt and the grief over this betrayal. Some kind of partial compromise may be found that will enable the person to integrate some features of the rejected identity component into the final identity. For example, Sommers's (1969) patient adopted the American identity but undertook some scholarly work on Japan; his Japanese background still had some place in his American life and identity.

When circumstances do not enforce the decision about which of the conflicting components is to be betrayed, the individual must make a choice, must decide which commitment to betray. In such cases the person probably looks for a single criterion by which to evaluate the conflicting components. In practice, unfortunately, such criteria are rather rare. What single, unimpeachable criterion can decide between the conflicting demands of career and family, or between two religious faiths? There may be lots of criteria but there is rarely just one. A multiplicity of conflicting criteria does not help—the person then needs a metacriterion to decide which of the criteria should be most important.

Compromises may be quite appealing if they can be found. For example, Roeske and Lake's (1977) female medical students typically decided not to forego motherhood altogether but to postpone it until after completing their residencies. At that point, presumably, their physician identities could in turn be relegated to secondary importance for a few years while they had their babies.

Compartmentalization is another kind of compromise. In compartmentalization, one confines the potentially conflicting components to separate spheres of one's life so that they do not actually conflict. For example, Peres and Yuval-Davis (1969) note that some of their sample of Israeli Arabs managed to act like Israelis in public life but like Arabs in private life. Compartmentalization is not a resolution of identity conflict but is a strategy for preventing it. The fact that the conflict exists is proof that the two components have not been kept in separate spheres. Once the choice is made about which of the conflicting components to betray, however, compartmentalization can soften the blow, and some domain may be reserved for the defeated component.

Value of identity crisis. One peculiar feature of identity crises is the contradiction in the way they are generally regarded, by laymen as well as experts. On the one hand, an identity crisis is a "problem," an illness, a form of psychopathology. It is listed in the *Diagnostic and Statistical Manual of Mental Disorders, Volume 3,* by the American Psychiatric Association. On the other hand, many people seem to regard an identity crisis as a valuable and desirable experience.

The experience of an identity-deficit crisis does seem to have value in that the subsequent (achieved) identity is superior to one not forged in crisis. Erikson (1968) felt that adolescent identity crises were essential to proper growth and development. Blos (1962) observed that such a crisis strengthens the ego. Levinson and his colleagues (1978) suggest that the mid-life crisis is desirable, too; people who do not have one, at least unconsciously, "will pay the price in a later developmental crisis or in a progressive withering of the self and a life structure minimally connected to the self."

Some research evidence is consistent with the idea that identity crises are good for you (see Bernard, 1981, and Bourne, 1978, for reviews). People who experience identity crises—especially those who have had them and have successfully resolved them—tend to be superior to others on various dimensions, including academic achievement (Cross & Allen, 1970), achievement motivation (Orlofsky, 1977), the ability to adapt and perform under stress (Marcia, 1967), and interpersonal intimacy (Orlofsky et al., 1973; Marcia, 1976). Of course, questions of interpretation arise regarding this research. For example, it is not clear that having an identity crisis causes you to get better grades afterward—perhaps you were more intelligent than others in the first place, and being intelligent predisposed you to have an identity crisis. At present, however, the evidence is more consistent with the notion that identity-deficit crises are good (rather than bad) for you.

A major qualification on the apparent value of adolescent and mid-life identity crises is the fact that most work suggesting such value is based on studies of males only. Whether such crises have a similar value for females is not known. On one dimension at least, the male pattern does not hold for females—the development of intimacy is not better among women who have had adolescent identity crises than among women with foreclosed identities (Marcia & Scheidel, 1983). Even this finding is complicated by the possibility that females tend not to have deficit crises during adolescence. I suggested earlier (based on Orlofsky's work) that when females do have adolescent crises these may tend to be conflict rather than deficit crises. At present, it seems that identity deficits have value for males, but their value for females can be neither asserted nor denied.

Whether identity *conflicts* have any value is unclear. There is far less reason to suppose they should, than there is for identity deficits. What is the value in being forced to betray a commitment?

Relationship to model of identity. Before ending this discussion of identity crisis, the material covered needs to be considered in relation to my model of identity. The identity conflict appears to be a crisis of the *components* of identity; the identity deficit seems to be focused on the three *functional aspects* of identity.

The identity conflict is basically a conflict between two components of identity. The person finds it necessary to act so as to betray one component. Presumably the individual would be happy to keep the identity as it is if circumstances did not pressure him or her to betray one commitment (and thus forsake one identity component). The behavior itself does not cause the crisis; rather, the implication of that behavior—specifically, the implication that one has to give up the betrayed component of identity—causes it.

The functional aspects of identity are involved in the identity conflict in a secondary or ancillary fashion by means of the components. For example, the value aspect of identity may become involved when the individual seeks a "higher" priority or value to decide between the conflicting obligations of the two components. The interpersonal aspect of identity may become involved when betraying an identity component entails disrupting some personal relationships. For example, to choose family obligations over career opportunities may cause one's colleagues and superiors at work to feel one has let them down.

In the identity deficit, the problem is focused on the functional aspects of identity. The components are secondary, partly because the components do not yet exist. An identity deficit is not a lack of a specific, known component but is rather an inadequacy in one's identity for dealing with the basic issues of identity—one's values and priorities, one's guiding image of personal potential, and one's interpersonal self.

The central importance of the three functional aspects of identity can readily be seen in the adolescent deficit crisis. The (especially male) adolescent rejects some parental and socialized *values* and therefore seeks replacements. The struggle to form new types of *relationships* is associated with adolescence by nearly every observer. The cultivation of a clear image of *personal potential* is also a central issue in the adolescent identity deficit. The quest for values, after all, is not just an intellectual exercise. Rather, to resolve the identity deficit one must appraise one's capacities and form a realistic goal of specific, viable, future fulfillment within the context of those general, basic values.

Moreover, the interpersonal aspect of identity is centrally and decisively involved in the process of identity crisis. Erikson (1968) portrayed the adolescent moratorium as a process of experimentation, and he noted that one way the adolescent judged the outcome of a given "experiment" was by how others reacted; the adolescent tries out various modes of behaving to see how others respond.

The male mid-life identity crisis also seems centrally concerned with the three functional aspects of identity. First, according to Levinson et al., the crisis is often provoked by an acute sense of nonfulfillment. Failure to achieve one's Dream, or disappointment upon reaching it, sets off the crisis and necessitates a reassessment of one's potential. The heightened awareness of mortality, the sense that time is running out, is also disturbing precisely because it denotes a limit on one's potential. The "Dream," a guiding concept of one's personal potential for fulfillment, is radically reevaluated and is usually modified at mid-life.

Second, one's general values and priorities undergo reevaluation and change. Levinson et al. note that mid-life men sometimes feel that their lives up to this point of crisis have been wasted, misguided by fallacious or unrealistic values and priorities. Modifying or replacing one's Dream also obviously calls the value aspect of identity into play. Interestingly, Levinson and his colleagues found confirmation of Jung's hypothesis that the priorities among one's basic values become rearranged at mid-life. Values that the man has espoused but neglected will often be felt and reasserted. For example, men who have been single-mindedly focused on their careers may begin to devote themselves to their families.

Third, the interpersonal aspect of identity is also subjected to reassessment and change during mid-life crisis. There are basic relationship changes, such as divorce. There are new interpersonal patterns that the mid-life male may adopt. One example in particular discussed by Levinson et al. is the relationship as mentor to one or more younger adults. Finally, the process of "turning inward" described be Levinson et al. implies that one's approach to interpersonal relationships is altered fundamentally.

Thus, identity conflicts concern identity components, but identity deficits concern identity's functional aspects. What does that imply? Again, it reflects the basic difference between the two crisis types. The identity conflict is the imminent loss of an identity component and is caused by the need to betray its commitments. The identity deficit is an inability to deal with life in certain very important respects. Put another way, it is an inability to deal with the basic issues identity addresses—what values and priorities to espouse, how to relate to other people, and what personal potential to strive to fulfill.

Summary

This chapter distinguishes between two kinds of identity crises: identity deficit and identity conflict. A model for each is offered, including cause, subjective experience, behavior, and resolution.

What I call *identity deficits* are most common during adolescence and mid-life. In identity deficit, the person lacks guiding commitments in life but struggles to make some. For males at least (unfortunately, there is a paucity of studies about women), the adolescent identity deficit seems to derive from an ambivalence in the relationship toward the parents. It is brought on by the need to make the choices regarding adult life, and by developmental gains in cognitive abilities. The mid-life identity deficit (also mainly studied among males) is the result of one of two major disillusionments in one's career. Either one recognizes that one will never reach one's "Dream" ambition, or one does reach it and finds it less fulfilling and less satisfying than one had expected.

The subjective experience of an identity deficit involves a wide range of emotional turmoil and activity. Research suggests that its subjective side includes confusion, vacillating commitment, feelings of vagueness and emptiness, hostility toward authority, preoccupation with ultimate and unresolvable issues, self-consciousness, bewilderment, and anxiety. Underneath all these feelings may lie a basic ambivalence—the desire to make commitments versus the desire not to give up any options or potentialities.

Behavior during identity deficit may range from active, kaleido-scopic experimentation to detached, ruminative solitude. People experiencing identity deficits are vulnerable to many sources of influence but tend to resist and oppose authority figures.

The resolution of identity deficits proceeds in two steps. The first involves establishing some basic, general values. The second in-volves working out activities and commitments that incorporate these general values.

Identity conflict, in contrast to identity deficit, is not associated with any particular stage in life. It arises from an interaction between personal commitments and circumstances. Circumstances force one to make a choice that will involve betraying one or another commitment.

The subjective experience of an identity conflict is of being in an impossible situation, or of being torn between two deeply felt values. One feels that one will be a traitor if one acts, so one is inclined not to act. No behavior is associated with identity con-flicts, except possibly that of seeking advice and comfort from others who have made similar difficult choices.

Identity conflicts are sometimes resolved by circumstances: The person has no choice but to accept the betrayal or loss of one identity component. In other cases, the person makes the choice between the conflicting components. Often the person will seek to maintain the betrayed component in some minor fashion via com-promise and compartmentalization.

There is some evidence that going through an identity deficit can be good for you, at least if you successfully resolve the crisis. This may not apply to females. But potential value of identity conflicts is not clear.

Finally, identity deficits are focused on the three functional as-pects of identity; identity conflicts are focused on the components of identity.

10

Brainwashing: Identity Renovation

How can identity be undermined, changed, or destroyed in the individual? In this chapter, brainwashing techniques will be examined as methods of forcibly altering identity.

Good research on brainwashing is rare. Obviously, there are no experimental studies. First-person accounts of cult indoctrinations are vivid but not entirely reliable. The authors usually have axes to grind, and they may suspect that sensationalism broadens popular appeal. My discussion is restricted to the observations of some researchers who studied brainwashing during and after the Korean War. Their observations and conclusions were published in 1957 by the Group for the Advancement of Psychiatry. These authors—Lifton, Schein, West, Hinkle, and Wedge—focused on the techniques used by the Chinese to influence American prisoners of war and to influence other Chinese.

"Brainwashing" is an American term, with its odd physical metaphor and unsavory connotations. Oriental terms for these techniques would be accurately translated as thought reform, ideological reform, or ideological remolding (Lifton, 1957). These latter terms make clear the purpose: to change the person's basic values, beliefs, goals, and *Weltanschauung* ("world view"). It is not just a matter of cleansing impurities, as the term "brainwashing" seems to imply. Old ideas are to be replaced by specific, new ideas.

It should be emphasized that the Chinese did not begin with a firm psychological theory of how best to accomplish brainwashing. Instead, they developed their techniques by trial and error, settling on whatever worked best. The fact that a particular technique was used is a testimony to its effectiveness, not to its resemblance to a prevailing theory in Chinese psychology of the early 1950s.

In considering the techniques used on captured American soldiers, one must keep in mind that they were only partially successful. In fact, they were rather dismal failures in terms of actually converting Americans to accept Chinese Communist ideology, although there was significant compliance and collaboration, along with confusion, doubt, and anxiety. While few American soldiers were converted, many were brought to an intermediate stage by these techniques.

The techniques seem to fall into five rough categories, which were usually used jointly. The first category involved breaking up the group solidarity among the prisoners (Schein, 1957). The structures of military authority were undermined. Officers were kept away from enlisted men, or group leaders were designated arbitrarily among the prisoners. The prisoners were taught not to respect their officers—instead, they were encouraged to blame their superiors for their current predicament. Group meetings among prisoners, including religious services, were strictly prohibited. Resources such as food were inadequate, forcing the prisoners to compete against each other. This encouraged the prisoners to view each other as enemies, instead of focusing on the Chinese as the enemy. (The Chinese blamed the lack of supplies on the American bombings, thus again deflecting frustration and blame away from themselves and onto the Americans.) The prisoners were encouraged to feel abandoned, alone, helpless.

Distrust of fellow prisoners was further promoted by creating the impression that there were informers and collaborators. If necessary, this was accomplished by bestowing special favors arbitrarily on certain prisoners. Even if these men had not collaborated or informed, others began to suspect that they had. When a prisoner's life revolves around competing for an inadequate supply of food and he suddenly sees another prisoner being given an extra helping by the guards, he is unlikely to think this is being done arbitrarily or at random. It is interesting to note that the same technique for disrupting group solidarity was reinvented by the college students who took part in the famous prison-simulation study done by Zimbardo and his colleagues at Stanford in the early 1970s.

In addition, isolation was used to cut the individual off from his group of peers. Solitary confinement has always been a powerful intervention for bringing prisoners into line. The Korean War was no exception.

The second category of techniques involved an assault on the physical being of the captive. Chronically inadequate food and rest rendered the person weak and exhausted (Schein, 1957). Physical humiliations and degradations, beginning with the impossibility of maintaining personal hygiene, undermined the prisoner's basic sense of dignity and physical self-respect (West, 1957). In some cases, beatings and torture were used to sap the prisoner's strength to resist, but these were rather uncommon, perhaps because they were not generally effective. The point was to generate chronic fatigue and generalized suffering, not to inflict pain as a means of coercion. Indeed, physical brutality might *increase* resistance (especially perhaps among other prisoners) and thus could be counterproductive.

The third category of techniques (also emphasized by Schein) involved developing a positive relationship between the prisoner and his specific Chinese interrogator. While the prisoner's old relationships were disrupted and undermined, a new one was cultivated. The prisoner's utter dependency on the Chinese was repeatedly pointed out to him. ("We can make you feel better. Your life is in our hands.") West (1957) adds that small, unexpected acts of kindness by the interrogator tended to cause the prisoner to feel gratitude and obligation. The interrogator would present himself to the prisoner as a teacher, liberator, even as benefactor. If torture was used, it was not performed by this interrogator.

The fourth category involved control over information. Americans are accustomed to freedom of the press and full-disclosure practices; it is difficult for us to appreciate the power that is wielded when the information available in someone's world is completely controlled. This control extended from inundating the prisoner with an endless stream of Communist propaganda, to the complete suppression of alternative viewpoints and information, to misinformation about important news. (War news, for example, was made to look as if the Americans were losing badly.) Confessions and testimonials from other prisoners were publicized, which disrupted group solidarity all the more.

The fifth and final category of techniques emphasized getting the prisoner to react and respond. Any collaboration with the Chinese was promptly rewarded with food or privileges. Out of misery or boredom, a prisoner would sometimes give them information he knew they already had or that was obsolete. The prisoner might feel he was doing nobody any harm (because the Chinese already knew what he told them), but was only helping himself. The Chinese, though, always rewarded such actions. The point was to encourage collaboration in general (Schein, 1957).

When the prisoner resisted, he was threatened with various punishments. Demands were repeated again and again. The demands always required the prisoner to take an active part. A curious variation on this (reported by West) was the practice of getting the prisoner to "torture himself" such as by having him stand up for hours during interrogation. The prisoner suffered, but not in any way he could blame on the interrogator.

One last technique involved asking the prisoner endless and detailed questions about his past life, including much that had nothing to do with war or politics, in the attempt to find some action the prisoner regretted or remembered with guilt. Once found, this was brought up again and again as the interrogator tried to amplify and generalize the prisoner's feelings of guilt (West, 1957; also Hinkle, 1957).

Before discussing the implications for identity, a second set of techniques, those used by the Chinese Communists to reform their own citizens, deserves mention. These techniques were, in general, far more successful than the brainwashing used on captive American soldiers.

They were commonly used at special "reform schools" or certain institutes in China (Lifton, 1957). Persons judged to need such reform were sent there at specific times. The individual was put in with a group of strangers who had been sent there for the same purpose. This tended to foster a feeling of group solidarity and of working toward common goals—that is, reform. There was thus considerable social support for change because everyone was trying to achieve this. At least, everyone said he wanted to reform, in public. In private—but there was no privacy. Everyone thus acted and lived as if resolved to change.

The group then began its task. Considerable time and effort were devoted to criticism. First criticism of others, and then, increasingly, self-criticism. All aspects of the person's character and behavior were subjected to criticism, and the intensity of this gradually and steadily increased. It was considered poor form to defend yourself when criticized. Instead, you were supposed to accept the criticism gratefully and gracefully, and then expand on it. This began the confessional habit. Students began to compete at self-criticism—the one who confessed the most, denounced himself most ferociously, would paradoxically have the highest prestige (Lifton, 1957).

The students were encouraged to criticize each other, even to criticize the self-criticisms. The teachers would, of course, also take part in this. For example, a lengthy self-indictment might be criticized for lacking "depth of feeling" even though the content was acceptable (Lifton, 1957, p. 239). Those who did not show suitable progress were singled out for criticism, which included special attacks in front of the entire school. Threats and warnings were also used as motivation. The process was extremely stressful. The persons undergoing it experienced considerable pain, conflict, and anguish. Psychosomatic side effects tended to appear during this process (Lifton, 1957).

The course drew to a close with the writing of a "final confession." The person had to write a detailed, critical history of himself and his thinking, beginning two generations back! Successive drafts were, of course, criticized by teachers and by fellow students (to whom they were read aloud). A final draft was turned in. This was often *rejected*—the individual then had to revise it again. This procedure tended to make the person eager to have his denunciation of himself, of his whole life and recent ancestry (especially his father), judged acceptable. Consider his situation: He has thoroughly denounced and repudiated his old identity but is not yet accepted in his new identity. He must begin to *want* this acceptance more than anything. Not surprisingly, when finally approved the person felt a tremendous relief. The confession was kept on file as part of the person's permanent record (Lifton, 1957).

Several other features of this program (again, as described by Lifton) need to be mentioned. First, as noted above, there was no privacy. Everything you said or did could be reported to others, especially to the faculty. Given the ethic of mutual criticism, such reporting must have been almost inevitable.

Persons were led to feel guilt over their past, sinful behaviors and identities, and to feel shame over any current failures to live up to group standards. Confession served the dual function of atonement for the guilt and as a means of achieving prestige in the group, thereby ending shame.

Information control was thorough. All the students were to use only the new (Communist) terms and ideology to explain everything. In short, people learned to think and talk in certain terms and only in those terms.

Finally, a new identity was readily available to each student as a "zealous participant in the new regime" (Lifton, 1957, p. 248). The guilt and shame were attached to the old identity, which the person was permitted to abandon and replace.

Similarities

To discuss the implications of brainwashing for identity change, it is first useful to list the similarities between the two sets of techniques described here. Recent accounts of cult indoctrination (e.g., Kennedy & Kennedy, 1982) also contain all five of the features listed below as common to both sets of brainwashing procedures, so perhaps they do indeed constitute an essential core of brainwashing technique. Cutting the person off from all previous interpersonal ties seems fundamental in both accounts of brainwashing. Old relationships create and constitute social support for the identity to be discarded. The importance of the interpersonal aspect of identity for generating stability and sameness over time is apparently very strong.

A second common feature is the attempt to build a new relationship, or many such relationships, based on the intended new identity. Again, the interpersonal aspect of identity is implicated in identity change.

The emphasis on the guilt, decadence, or depravity of the old self is a feature that probably contributes to making the person want to change. The person is made to feel that he or she has been bad. Once this is accepted, there is a desire to change, and the brainwashers can exploit this desire. With cult indoctrination, it is possible that this feature may be unnecessary if the subjects are adolescents in the midst of an identity-deficit crisis; these persons are already motivated to find a new identity.

The fourth feature also underscores the importance of making the person want to change. This is the attempt to get the person to participate *actively* in the process of change. It seems that identity is not susceptible to real change while it submits passively to influence; rather, the person must take an active part.

Finally, both sets of techniques emphasized information control. The subject is gradually forced to talk and think in terms of the desired ideology. Presumably, by using its vocabulary, one begins to use and then to accept its values. Changing the values aspect of identity is, of course, an ultimate goal of brainwashing.

Differences

In considering the differences between the two sets of techniques, it is important to remember that the second set (used in the Chinese thought-reform schools which Chinese citizens attended) was far more effective than the first set in bringing about drastic and thorough identity change. Therefore, where the two sets of techniques differ, it seems reasonable to assume that the second set has the characteristics most conducive to effective brainwashing.

One key difference is that a viable, desirable new identity was readily available to the Chinese subjects (Lifton's "zealous participant in the new regime") but not to the American captives. What could the captives do—become Chinese? Chances for acceptance, even if they could learn the language and customs, were slim. And returning to America as a committed Communist and as a collaborator with the enemy was also not practical or appealing. The third aspect of identity—sense of personal potentiality—was thus not used by the unsuccessful brainwashing regimen but was used by the effective one. This was not mere coincidence; it may have been *the* decisive factor. Without providing a specific image of personal potential, you cannot effectively get a person to adopt a new identity.

Several differences between the two sets of techniques are differences in the *extent* to which something was done. The social support for change to the new identity was considerably greater in the second set of techniques. With the American prisoners, only one relationship, the one with the interrogator, supported the intended new identity, but in the reform institutes numerous relationships supported that change. The effectiveness with which the person was cut off from relationships that evoked the old identity was also probably much greater in the reform institutes than in the POW camps because in the camps the individual would have opportunities for contact with other American prisoners. The degree of success in converting the interpersonal sphere to the new identity was thus correlated with the success of the brainwashing techniques.

The individual's felt need to change and his active participation in the change were similarly greater in the second set of techniques. The students at the reform institutes were eager to change (or else!), and they took an extremely active part in criticizing and denouncing their previous identities. Criticizing oneself feels quite different from being criticized by other persons. I suggested that active participation seems important for identity change. The differences between the two sets of techniques on this dimension supports my suggestion that active participation is crucial.

The extensive confession and self-criticism were central features of the reform-institute procedure. Undoubtedly, one reason for its power was its effectiveness in motivating the person to want to change. By dwelling at length on the guilt and wickedness of the previous identity, one made it very difficult for oneself ever to return to that identity. The interpersonal aspect helped too; by the end of the term one had denounced one's past identity to many other people. (One had also written that denunciation, in detail, for one's permanent file.)

There may well be more to the power of the confession than increasing motivation, though. The act of confession has numerous subtle but potent effects, as Foucault (1980) has hinted in his discussion of the history of sexuality. Confession takes something private or secret and makes it public; by making it public, it can be disavowed and removed from the self. I do not propose to offer a psychological model for how this effect works, but identity change may be facilitated by the public articulation of the identity that is to be rejected.

A last difference between the two sets of techniques is the greater reliance in the first set on physical manipulation such as deprivation of food, rest, and personal hygiene. The fact that these were relatively absent from the more effective regimen suggests that they are not essential or fundamentally important for brainwashing. This implies again that the body's contribution to identity, and to the continuity of identity over time, is limited.

Conclusions

This discussion of brainwashing as identity change thus implicates each of the three major functional aspects of identity, as well as the need for active participation and the desire for change in the person involved.

The interpersonal aspect of identity seems to be involved in a fundamental way in many of the specific techniques. This could be because interpersonal matters are the easiest for brainwashers to manipulate. Still, their extensive use testifies to the importance of the interpersonal aspect of identity for making the self stable across time. In ordinary life we think of others in terms of stable traits, although we perceive our own behavior as changing as a result of situational factors (Jones & Nisbett, 1971). The public self or reputation may thus be comprised of stable traits more than is the private self-concept. Remove the public self by isolating the person from all who have known him, and the private self becomes surprisingly malleable.

To change the structure of values and priorities, a second functional aspect of identity, is probably the central goal of brainwashing. To some extent, the tampering with the interpersonal aspect is a means toward changing the values and priorities. Values are much less accessible to direct tampering than is the interpersonal environment. The main environmental manipulation aimed directly at the value aspect of identity is information control. By controlling what the person sees and hears, the brainwashers hope to influence what he thinks. Again, this is a powerful technique, but it is probably, by itself, not enough to be effective. The history of research on attitude change in social psychology is relevant here. At first researchers studied persuasion techniques, which regarded the subject as basically the passive recipient of information. Beginning late in the 1950s, however, they began to discover that attitude change was produced much more effectively and powerfully by inducing the subject to take an active stance, such as by asking him to make a speech in favor of the desired attitude, a speech which was often contrary to what the subject initially believed. For about fifteen years, this phenomenon (cognitive dissonance; see Festinger & Carlsmith, 1959, for seminal experiment) was probably the most studied topic in social psychology. The point here is that opinions and values are most effectively altered by getting the person to make public affirmations and statements of the desired opinion. His private opinions will gradually come into line with his public pronouncements. The brainwashers seem to have realized this.

The importance of furnishing the individual with a concept of personal potentiality to go with the identity he is supposed to have at the end of brainwashing has already been noted. You cannot just instill a radically changed set of opinions in someone, turn him loose, and expect him to keep the new beliefs. He must come to see his own life as having value that is conferred by particular goals, purposes, and aspirations consistent with the new set of beliefs. The potentiality aspect of identity must thus be rebuilt for brainwashing to be effective.

There is a connection between religion and brainwashing, which probably derives from this third functional aspect of identity. Religions, almost by definition, contain some notion of human perfectability, some ideal to which the believer should aspire, whether this be salvation, enlightenment, or virtue. Communist brainwashers cannot permit their subjects to persist in their religious practices because these will sustain the person's old concept of personal potentiality, whereas the brainwashers want to give the person a new identity. It is likely that religious cults offer their initiates an altered or expanded concept of what their lives are good for (i.e., to serve the cult).

Finally, active participation seems essential for identity change, as was suggested in connection with value change. Perhaps a thoroughly passive and uncooperative person cannot be brainwashed. Not all people who were brainwashed were willing participants in the process. They probably did not realize the effects their own behavior would have on them. Telling the captors some military information that the captors already possessed may seem like an innocuous way to get oneself a blanket for a cold night, but doing that probably increased the likelihood that one would tell them something else, something more important. Social psychology has demonstrated again and again that people are affected by their own behavior in ways they did not intend and do not realize.

The relevant point for identity change is clear. One's identity cannot be fundamentally altered by a process in which one remains passive. One has to participate actively in the process of changing one's identity, although active participation does not necessarily mean informed participation. People may often fail to realize how their own actions can further the process of identity change. Successful brainwashing often means getting people to participate actively in changing their identities, without letting them fully realize that that is what they are doing.

Summary

Brainwashing is an intervention aimed at changing someone's identity into a new one, especially where the person's basic values are involved.

Discussions of two sets of brainwashing procedures yield several similarities. Both sets involved cutting the person off from prior interpersonal relationships that were based on the old identity, and attempting to set up one or more new relationships based on the new identity the brainwashers wished to instill. Both sets tried to associate guilt and depravity with the old identity and to make the person confess and recognize this guilt and depravity. Both sets sought complete control over the information available to the person, presumably in order to force the person to talk and think in the brainwashers' terms. Finally, both sets tried to get the person to participate actively in the process of change.

Several differences between the two sets of techniques were apparent. These are of interest because one set of techniques was in fact quite a bit more successful than the other, so some of these differences in technique presumably account for that differential success. A key difference was that the more successful procedure was able to offer a viable, desirable new identity to the persons it tried to brainwash. The social support for change, the thoroughness with which the person's interpersonal relationships were based on the new identity instead of the old, and the person's degree of active participation in the change were all greater in the more successful brainwashing regimen. The more successful also used personal confession and self-criticism by the person undergoing the treatment more than did the other, less successful set of techniques. The less successful technique used more physical manipulations (e.g., exhaustion, hunger, torture) than did the more successful, which suggests that physical manipulation is not as effective in successful brainwashing.

Brainwashing thus involves all three aspects of identity. The interpersonal aspect is altered by cutting the person off from old relationships; new ones are established instead. The values aspect is approached directly through information control; indirectly, of course, all the brainwashing techniques are designed to change the person's values. Finally, the potentiality aspect is altered by offering the person a new life's meaning and purpose within the context of the new values. In addition, it seems important that the person participate actively in the process of change if brainwashing is to be successful.

11

The Nature of Identity:
Outer Context and Inner Self

In the beginning of this book, I observed that social scientists used the term "identity" in different ways, with different meanings. Now, at the book's end, I return to that observation. The contrast between psychological and sociological approaches clarifies two ways of understanding identity and its problems.

Psychologists tend to think in terms of individuals and inner processes. To a psychologist, identity seems to be something that exists within the individual as a part of personality or a set of cognitions. The broader society is regarded rather vaguely as the agent that puts things into the individual; identity may or may not have a lot to do with social institutions. (When I mentioned my work on identity to a psychologist colleague, he thought I would conclude my work by discovering that identity is part of the brain!)

In contrast, sociologists tend to think in terms of society and its institutions. In this view identity is a set of roles and statuses, arranged according to how they are defined by society. Occupation, socioeconomic status, marital status, gender, race, educational level—these are the main parts of identity in the sociological sense. The actual physical self of the person, with his or her individual set of memories and motivations, can seem almost irrelevant.

Each approach, by itself—the psychologist's and the sociologist's—neglects some identity issues. If identity exists mainly within the individual mind, why are identities so dependent on society? And if identity is mainly a set of social roles, what is identity crisis apart from role conflict? An adequate view of identity must synthesize both parts, the inner self and the outer context.

The inner and outer features of identity do not necessarily have a stable, constant relation, however. Their relative emphasis and importance may fluctuate. In a famous article, Turner (1976) argued that twentieth century Western society has seen a shift in emphasis from the institutional components of identity to identity as a set of inner motives and impulses. Institutional transitions in identity, such as the actual ceremonies of a wedding or graduation, are not as intense emotionally as they were a century ago. Personal desires and needs, however, have become more important as the focus for defining the self.

To conclude this book, I review the causes of the modern conditions of identity twice—once from the perspective of the social context of identity, and once in terms of the inner self. Both are necessary in order to grasp the nature and problem of identity in modern Western life.

What must a context for identity do? There are two answers. First, it must provide individuals with identity components that satisfy the two defining criteria. Changing social conditions have made it more difficult to meet identity's defining criteria with the major components society offers. Destabilization and trivialization have undermined the extent to which social identity is continuous across time and is different in important ways from the identities of others.

The second answer concerns the three functional aspects of identity. Here it might be better to think of these aspects as *answering questions* than as *serving functions*. The three questions, in general form, would be: How shall I relate to others? What shall I strive to become? How will I make the basic decisions needed to guide my life? Identity in this sense can be understood as a theory about the self (cf. Schlenker & Leary, 1982; also Epstein, 1973). Theories do not exist by themselves. They only exist within a paradigm, a context of concepts, evidence, and other theories. Two such contexts may be cited for identity—religion and society. These are not separate, and in fact they may overlap substantially. Before assessing the modern status of identity in relation to its context, it is necessary to clarify how religion and society work as contexts for identity.

Religion

Religion can be a very effective context for identity. A religion, almost by definition, contains some explicit concept of human potentiality such as salvation or enlightenment. The potentiality aspect of identity is thus well-defined by religious faith. Personal potentiality only became a problem in Western society when people were no longer satisfied with the Christian concept of fulfillment in heaven.

Religions are also generally accompanied by moral systems. These support identity by establishing basic values of right and wrong, good and bad, and by regulating interpersonal conduct. The interpersonal and values aspects of identity are well-grounded within the context of a religion.

An established religion tends to acquire a moral system even if that system was not part of the prophetic vision of the religion's founder, almost as if there is some inherent affinity between religion and morality. Some thinkers have suggested that this is because of an analytic, conceptual relationship between religion and morality (e.g., Kant, 1793; Spinoza, 1670). But another type of relationship is possible. If people want religion to serve as the context for identity, religion may need to be supplemented by morality for the sake of the interpersonal aspect and values aspect of identity. The affinity between religion and morality may derive from the psychological needs of the believers, that is, from what they expect religion to do for them.

Religion, then, puts all three functional aspects into clear questions with definite answers. Personal choice is not needed to develop a concept of potentiality or a set of moral values; the religion provides them. Indeed, when the society consensually accepts the religion, such questions cease as questions of identity at all and become instead matters of objective reality.

Some empirical evidence for the link between religion and identity has been offered. Perhaps the most important evidence was the suggestion that the religious conversion experiences of eighteenth and nineteenth century adolescents were the true predecessors of the modern identity crisis. But why should there be a relationship between religion and identity crisis?

As argued earlier, there are two kinds of identity crises. Identity deficit, in which the person lacks sufficient commitments to make choices and lead a purposeful, directed life, is a lack of metacriteria needed as the basis for making decisions. The individual has multiple possibilities but seeks a metacriterion to determine which possibilities to commit to and which to reject.

It is unlikely that someone with strong religious convictions could have an identity-deficit crisis. Religious and moral values furnish a powerful and reasonably consistent set of metacriteria by which to sort one's options. A two-stage model of the process of identity deficit was proposed. Religion and morality take care of the first (basic values) stage rather well, which leaves the less problematic second (practical implementation) stage. If a religious person were to experience an identity-deficit crisis, it would almost certainly begin as a failure of religious faith. As long as the religious belief is secure, there seems little possibility of this type of identity crisis.

It should be noted that in the Middle Ages religious duty extended even to choice of occupation. One's duty was to perform well at the station assigned (presumably) by God. Even in the nineteenth century, choice of occupation was still to some extent conceptualized in religious terms as one's "calling" to a certain job. In fact, modern German retains the term "calling" (Beruf) as the most common word for occupation, although modern usage probably does not retain the term's spiritual connotation. People gradually began to make occupational decisions on the basis of secular criteria. As they did, it became possible to have an identity deficit, in the sense of a lack of metacriteria by which to make those choices. But as long as they kept their religious and moral beliefs, the first (basic values) stage of such a crisis was minimized, and the problem would be mainly one of implementation.

The other type of identity crisis is identity conflict. To be sure, the difficulty of acting despite conflicting imperatives is ancient. It may not always have signified identity crisis, however. Consider the Arthurian conflict between the knight's love for a woman and his oath of loyalty to her husband. The oath signified identity; the love probably did not. Being the woman's adulterous lover was probably not an identity that attracted the knight. His desire for her may have been physical and emotional, but it probably had nothing to do with self-definition. His religious and moral values thus prevented him from committing himself to a certain kind of identity. The conflict became one between identity and something else—the latter being a class of motivations with which the person would not identify himself even if he acted on them. In the Christian context, these motivations were called "temptations."

Defining some human motivations as temptations had several effects that helped minimize identity conflict. First, the motivations were externalized—it is not that you choose to desire this woman but rather that she tempts you. Second, even if you succumb to this temptation and act on it (presumably by having intercourse with the temptress), you did not commit yourself to really being that sort of person. Rather, you had erred only temporarily. The church could then provide appropriate penance through which the act's implications could be nullified. Third, therefore, acting upon such motivations did not emerge as a continuous pattern, even if done repeatedly, because each act was repented and repudiated. By treating each such act as an exception, the religion prevented the motivations from achieving continuity—thereby preventing them from constituting identity by virtue of the defining criterion of continuity. (In the most general sense, one was a sinner, but so was everyone else. Being a sinner did not differentiate; it did not fulfill the second defining criterion of identity.)

Identity conflict is not completely absent among people with strong religious faith. Identity crises among religious people are likely to center around religious doubt or loss of faith. As long as the faith is secure, however, the religion and its morality do provide a context that minimizes such conflict.

Religion and morality thus form a context that can effectively furnish metacriteria. Moreover, the context is coherent—in logical terms, it is a fairly complete and consistent system. Within such a context, identity is firmly grounded. Its three aspects are fairly well-defined, thus not problematic. Self-definition does not have to follow the most problematic Type V process, and identity crises are prevented or minimized.

Society

Society is not necessarily effective as a context for identity. How society works as a context for identity can be understood by considering identity's three functional aspects. Society's relationship to the interpersonal aspect of identity is obvious, for social life consists of interpersonal relationships and roles. Each person's identity exists amid the contextual network of other persons and their roles.

The potentiality aspect of identity is likewise defined by society. Society sets the range of meanings and purposes to which people can devote their lives. Occasionally, a culture evolves an ideal of fulfillment apart from social life, such as that of the mystic hermit or the reclusive transcendentalist. For the most part, however, ideas of fulfillment and success are defined and validated by society. A society thus teaches its citizens to have certain ambitions and goals, and individual persons form their concepts of personal potentiality out of these.

Finally, values are acquired during the process by which society teaches its members how to think and act (e.g., child-rearing patterns, schools, initiations). Again, society specifies the general set of values, and the individual forms his or her own identity from the large set provided by society.

As contexts for identity, societies vary along one main dimension—how directive or restrictive they are in defining identity. At one extreme, a society can be rigid and inflexible. Each person's identity tends to be fixed firmly by the society, and the individual has little freedom to choose or to change it. Obviously, in such a society self-definition tends to emphasize the simple types of processes (I to III). Identity is generally not problematic. There is little individual freedom. Each person has to want to be whatever society says because there is little possibility of altering this. If society can give people identities they are happy with, this type of system can work quite well. On the other hand, if society cannot induce people to be satisfied with the identities it assigns to them, then the lack of freedom is experienced as oppressive. Individuals may struggle to change society, or they may seek escape into alcoholic oblivion or private pleasures.

At the other extreme, a society can be loose, tolerant, and flexible. Society gives each individual a large range of possibilities for identity, and the individual can or must shape identity by acts of personal choice and commitment. Self-definition tends to emphasize the complex and problematic types of processes (III to V). Individuals thus have substantial freedom, but identity is quite problematic. The individual needs personal metacriteria for sorting out the numerous options that society provides.

The relationship of the individual to society is not problematic if society is fairly restrictive and if two beliefs are accepted. The first belief equates the person with his or her position in society. The individual does not realistically wish or hope to have another position in society or indeed to live apart from it. The second belief holds that each person will achieve fulfillment by doing the tasks and roles assigned by society. With this belief, one *trusts* society to make one's choices for one and to reward one for complying. (Obviously, the trust may be in the religious system rather than in society per se.)

Medieval Christian society held both of these beliefs. The individual was equated with his or her position in society (cf. MacIntyre, 1981; Nisbet, 1973). Moreover, one believed that God specified and legitimated the social order; it was therefore trustworthy. If one did one's duty, one could expect to be rewarded in heaven.

These two basic beliefs were undermined and destroyed at the end of the Middle Ages. Social mobility detached the individual from the rank and station to which he or she was born. The person could no longer be equated with his or her place in society, for the place could be changed. Moreover, the growing belief that inner selves were different from overt behavior also detached the individual from the position in society. People came to believe in an inner self separate from the social self. Social mobility and belief in internality thus undermined the belief that the person was equated with social position.

The second belief, that fulfillment would follow if one did one's duty as society bid, was also undermined. As the population ceased to live by Christian faith and imagery, the divine legitimacy of the social order was questioned. There was no longer a good reason for believing that reward and fulfillment would result from doing society's bidding. Moreover, society gradually stopped giving such definite messages about how to live and what to do. Liberal reforms gave rise to an increasing array of options for the individual.

Once the individual's relationship with society had become problematic, the problem evolved through four stages. Believing that society was to blame for preventing fulfillment, people first struggled to win freedom within society. Specifically, they wanted freedom to seek fulfillment in the individual ways they thought best. Society did in general give people more freedom; but as it became more flexible it offered less and less directed guidance about how to live, thus requiring people to make more of their own decisions. Fulfillment did not ensue.

Next, individuals sought fulfillment in private, away from society. The transcendentalists attempted this but hardly had a fair chance, because while they were trying to turn away from social life, other forces were making that impossible. Social evolution was linking people closer and closer, via such agencies as communications media and economic interdependence. Thoreau's approach to fulfillment is simply not feasible for twentieth century Americans.

The third stage in this progression was alienation. Upon recognizing that there was no escape from society, people discovered themselves to be society's helpless victims. They complained bitterly about society and about their dependency on it.

The fourth and current stage is the "accommodation" stage. Individuals began to accept the fact that society neither permitted escape nor promised fulfillment. They began to seek ways of achieving fulfillment as individuals in the midst of society.

Individual development. The infant is born into a mini-society, namely, the family. This little society provides the child with identity. The child's relation to that society is at first not problematic for the same reasons that the medieval adult's relationship to society was not problematic. That is, the society is narrow, inflexible, and well-defined, and the child holds the two basic attitudes that make the individual's relationship to society unproblematic. First, the child is equated with its place in the family. The infant's and small child's role in the family is not open to much redefinition, at least not from the child's perspective. The very young child has no private self or life apart from its role in the family. And if the child has an interesting experience during the parents' absence, the child will probably tell them about it as soon as they return. Second, the child believes fulfillment to be contingent on performing its role in the family. The child trusts the family to love and care for it as long as the child does what it is supposed to do (cf. Erikson, 1950, on "basic trust").

As the child grows, these two basic attitudes are undermined, and the child's relationship with the family gradually becomes problematic. First, the child slowly ceases to equate itself with its role in the family as its social world expands through school, peer interactions, sports, and so forth. The family may remain the most important society for the child, but it is not the only one, and therefore the child can conceptualize itself apart from the family. The second attitude is the belief that one will be fulfilled simply by doing what one's parents tell one to do. This attitude tends to die a complex and multifaceted death. By adolescence, the boy or girl is generally convinced of the necessity of becoming emotionally detached from the parents and seeking fulfillment elsewhere.

The child's relationship to the family does not necessarily go through the same four stages (after becoming problematic) that the individual's relation to society evolved through historically. The main difference lies in the fact that the family can be escaped more effectively than can society at large, so the basic cause of the third and fourth stages is absent. Moreover, society has ceased to give persons clear messages about what is expected of them, but parents often do have clear expectations for their children, and the children know them. These expectations should not be underestimated, for they form a basic set of metacriteria that can be used to begin to shape one's life. Even if the individual undergoes a major identity-deficit crisis, he or she will not reject all the values and attitudes internalized from the parents. The system of metacriteria may undergo some overhaul, but it is not completely replaced.

The modern adult, then, has an array of options as to possible identities as far as society is concerned. The individual therefore needs metacriteria to sort out the options and to make choices. Where do these metacriteria come from? The main sources appear to be the remnants of parental and familial expectations, and whatever else the person might have managed to pull together during his or her adolescent identity-deficit crisis. Sources for the latter presumably include peers, experiences in college, and possibly art or entertainment. Mentors other than parents may also influence the formation of values.

Current Status

Many people know that identity is a problem today, but the precise nature of the problem is difficult to articulate. Statements like "I don't know who I am" or "I need to find myself" are metaphors for a very elusive phenomenon. Perhaps identity problems are so difficult to articulate with any precision because of the vagueness and inadequacy of a context. It is difficult to formulate questions without a coherent, understandable context.

Religion can be an effective context for identity, but modern attitudes have relegated religion to a rather minor role. Society can also be an effective context for identity, but it works most efficiently if the society is rigid. Our society has evolved into one that is flexible and loose. This has many advantages but makes it inefficient as a context for identity. Without religion, however, it is the best one we have.

There may be psychological consequences from relying predominantly on society rather than religion to serve as identity's context. Concern with the self is linked to social validation and recognition instead of to spiritual ends. For this reason, perhaps, people are more and more concerned with impressing peers and neighbors. If identity is interpreted solely within the context of society,[1] these impressions and evaluations ultimately form a powerful judgment on our worth as people.

It has been suggested in this chapter that our culture produces identity problems because it is a poor context for identity. It has largely abandoned one context, religion, and made the other, society as a whole, complicated and problematic. Individuals may perhaps evade identity problems if they do not share the general condition of the society in this respect. Two ways to do this have been suggested. Persons with strong religious faith may avoid identity crises. And persons who internalize and accept their parents' expectations for them may avoid identity crises. In fact, that is the typical pattern among people with "identity foreclosure"—they remain with the values and goals their parents taught them and are therefore able to avoid identity crises. I am not advocating that our society promote identity foreclosure or religious faith. My point is that a single person who manages to maintain a firm, stable, and well-defined context for his theory about himself will be able to

---

1. On the other hand, concern with pleasing and impressing others has undoubtedly existed in most if not all cultures and eras, so it would be difficult to prove an increase or change in that motivation even if it has happened.

avoid identity problems. Identity problems arise when that context become unclear, incoherent, incomplete, contradictory, or otherwise ineffective.

The Inner Self

The modern understanding of identity has come to rely heavily on the odd spatial metaphor of the "inner" self, which is often regarded not as a metaphor but as a literal fact. Again, there is a distinction between the concept and the phenomena. All of us experience thoughts, wishes, and emotions—the phenomena. None of us has seen an inner self—the concept. We tend to take the existence of thoughts and feelings as evidence of the inner self, but other concepts are possible. Upon reflection, the "inner" self is actually a less than satisfactory metaphor because traits and emotions are not "in" the self the way cookies are "in" a jar. Moreover, the belief in inner selves has generated a fair amount of conceptual mischief within the general population. People believe that their inner selves contain undiscovered treasures waiting for self-actualization, contain the solutions to their problems and decisions, and so forth. How did this happen? How did our culture's way of understanding identity develop this concept of the inner self?

It seems likely that our belief in an inner self can be traced to the medieval Christian concept of soul. The earliest notions of soul did not distinguish it very carefully from the body, but that distinction *was* accepted by the Middle Ages. By the early Middle Ages, people believed that an invisible, nonphysical entity was an important part of each person's existence.

By the late Middle Ages, the concept of soul had evolved into a rather good forerunner of the concept of inner self. Early medievals probably did not believe one person's soul was much different from another's. The late medievals, however, believed that each soul was judged individually upon death. For this, each soul had to be different, at least insofar as it contained some record of the moral quality of the person's actions. By the end of the Middle Ages, the concept of human being thus included a vitally important nonphysical entity that was continuous over time and different from others, and that changed with the person's actions and experiences. That description of the medieval concept of soul could apply equally well to the modern concept of inner self.

The next big step toward the modern inner self occurred during the sixteenth century. The popular discovery of that period was that visible phenomena often disguised or concealed underlying realities that were quite different from the visible phenomena. Applied to human beings, this discovery meant that people's appearance and behavior were often misleading. People pretended to have motives, intentions, and social rank other than what they really had.

The spatial metaphor was adapted or adopted to express this difference between the true motive and the dissembled motive. The true motive was "inside," the overt one "outside." Thus, the concept of inner self encompassed motives, intentions, and true social rank.

Social rank was an important identity component during the early modern period. I have argued that personality later replaced social rank as identity's most important component. A conceptual connection between personality and social rank already existed by the early modern period. Evaluative traits, including moral traits, were thought to derive from physical, family heritage ("blood"). People believed that the aristocracy were innately better people than were the common people, with superior moral and personal traits. It was accepted that the aristocrats were more honorable, courageous, and so forth, than were the commoners. By implication, a commoner pretending to be an aristocrat did not "really" have those traits, regardless of how he or she acted.

In what sense do personality traits exist? They are patterns in behavior—regular, consistent, and in some sense intentional. The personality trait is thus something about the behavior. If someone consistently behaves in an honest or talkative fashion, it makes no sense to say that that person does not really have the trait of honesty or talkativeness. But that is exactly what the aristocrats wanted to do—to separate the trait from the behavior. A commoner could not really be courageous, no matter how he behaved, because courage was reserved for the aristocracy. Conversely, many aristocrats were in actual behavior consistently idle, lecherous, drunken, petty, vindictive, frivolous, and so forth, but class prejudice insisted that the noble traits of the upper class were really there. They were supposedly just not readily visible at the moment.

The inner self was thus a very convenient heuristic because it enabled society to sustain its beliefs about traits and social class despite the evidence that contradicted those beliefs. The point is that conceptions about social rank probably helped introduce personality into the inner, invisible self.

I reiterate that I am discussing general trends among common, widespread beliefs. A few medievals may have endowed the immortal soul with personality traits, but most did not. Similarly, when I say that the Puritans discovered self-deception, I do not mean that no one had ever recognized self-deception before. Undoubtedly some wise and observant ancients knew of self-deception. The Puritans, however, made self-deception a common and familiar concept that was everyone's concern.

Of course, the Puritans were primarily concerned with their immortal souls. In today's society only a very small and rather noninfluential part of the population worries about immortal souls as much as the Puritans did. But even though we no longer have the Puritan attitudes and concerns, they left some lasting influences on the way we think about inner selves.

First, the Puritans regarded the soul as fixed and unchangeable in its essential properties. The condition of the soul was thus something you could learn or discover but could not create or modify. Self-knowledge came to be conceptualized in metaphoric terms of search and discovery—searching for something that is already there, has always been there. Today we still think that way about inner selves.[2] Even great single acts of achievement are greeted with "I didn't know you had it in you." We think of finding and

---

2. The concept of authenticity is an exception because it suggests a concept of self-knowledge in terms of process instead of in terms of discovering a static entity. The general population, however, probably does not think in terms of authenticity.

exploring our inner selves as if it were a forest. There is some paradox here because we associated thoughts and feelings with the inner self, but we know they are transient. To resolve this, perhaps, we are inclined to regard the transient states as indicative or expressive of underlying, stable factors.

The second contribution of Puritanism was the awareness of self-deception. As a consequence of that awareness, self-knowledge became suspect and presumably difficult. In the modern concept of the inner self, one's desires and intentions do exist, but they are hidden even from oneself. It is necessary to exert oneself to discover one's own desires and intentions! And even with exertion one might not succeed. The twentieth century developed an entire science and therapy—psychoanalysis—aimed at studying and revealing the hidden continents of the inner self. Psychoanalysis, and the cultural attitude it embodies, regards overt behavior with suspicion, as a "tip of the iceberg." Thoughts, feelings, and acts are mere symptoms of the stable reality hidden within the self.

Thus the construct of an inner self already has the makings of a major entity. It is unknowably large, stable and continuous over time, unique to the individual, vitally important, difficult to know, and more real than one's everyday behavior and experience. But there's more.

In the medieval Christian system, the fulfillment of human life was salvation in heaven. Fulfillment therefore depended on the soul because the condition of the soul determined whether one went to heaven, and if so, it was the soul that went. I have discussed the Romantic era as the approximate period during which our culture rejected the Christian model of fulfillment and began to seek alternatives such as passion and artistic creation. Perhaps because people were accustomed to associating the nonphysical soul with fulfillment, they came to associate the nonphysical inner self with fulfillment.

How artists create has long escaped popular understanding. The classical mentality conceptualized an external source—the muse—who gave inspiration to the artist. By the Romantic era, however, artistic creation was believed to come from hidden sources within the artist. The public developed a special interest in artists, in part because their inner selves were thought to be especially fascinating due to the creative process (Altick, 1965). The concept of the inner self is appealing as an explanation of artistic creativity because it pictures the self as containing hidden treasures. Yet, paradoxically, it takes the creation out of creativity. Creating art becomes a matter of revealing the hidden contents of the inner self, which have been there forever (more or less), rather than creating something truly new.

The notion of fulfillment through passionate love brought emotion into the inner self. This was perhaps not a major innovation in the concept of inner self, for that concept already included secret desires and motives. Still, locating fulfillment in the inner self further elevated the inner self's importance.

By the Victorian era the inner self was thus commonly understood to contain goals and ambitions, virtue or vice, personality traits, the wellsprings of creation, and feelings, and it was presumed to be the key to a fulfilled life. That encompasses quite a lot—no wonder the transcendentalists thought the single person had sufficient inner resources to lead a fulfilled life with minimal or nominal involvement in society. Nor is it surprising that the Victorians came to fear involuntary disclosure of the contents of the inner self (Sennett, 1974). If you could not be certain yourself of what secret, inner passions you had, your reputation could be ruined if someone else could discern them just by looking at you.

The last thing to be added to the inner self was metacriteria. Or perhaps I should say "putative metacriteria," because it is not clear whether they really exist or not. People assume that the inner self contains the keys to making difficult choices. The popular belief holds that identity crises are resolved by searching within oneself, implying that the solutions to one's problems have existed all along, hidden in the inner self.

Again, I am arguing that the inner self does not have an objective existence. It is merely a construct—an entity consisting of meaning, like justice or credit. We use this construct to explain and discuss certain phenomena. Our culture has come, however, to regard this metaphoric construct as something that exists literally. The concept has also evolved into an elaborate and complex one. In its complexity, however, there is ample opportunity for mixtures of the real and the unreal, of the experienced and the inferred. The concept of inner self refers to a large assortment of phenomena. Some of them really exist, such as thoughts and feelings, or secret intentions that someone pretends not to have. Others may not exist; these sometimes include latent works of art, personality traits contrary to our behavior, marvelous capacities awaiting self-actualization, and correct solutions to all our identity problems. The difficulty lies in the fact that there is no reliable way to know whether the phenomenon is real or not given our use of the concept of inner self. Our culture has its images of the inner search, and it has members who deny the possibility or validity of inner search. It has no image for a type of inner search that is sometimes effective and sometimes a fool's errand.

How were metacriteria included within the inner self? When identity was firmly grounded in religion and morality, metacriteria were derived from that context. Telling one lie defined you as a liar, an identity component whose continuity extended forward and backward in time from the event. Virtues also entailed identity because they signified continuity across time. Identity was thus conceptualized in a way that involved moral metacriteria. The liar, in other words, was a person whose identity was presumed to include the metacriterion that made him choose to act in a dishonest fashion. The honest man had an identity with a metacriterion that was expressed in choosing honesty. With the decline of religion and morality as a context for identity, and with the modern proliferation of possibilities and options, there arose a considerably increased need for self-defining choices. Self-definition has come to involve increasingly active participation by the individual, both in choice and achievement. Metacriteria are needed to choose spouses, cars, occupations, hobbies, furniture, family size, and so on. The inner self proved once again to be a convenient heuristic. It treated all such acts as identity-related because the acts presumably expressed permanent attitudes of the inner self. Moreover, uncertainty about such decisions could be understood in terms of the hiddenness of the contents of the inner self. One says, "I don't know what I want to be" instead of "I have no preference for any occupation." Saying "I don't know what I want" implies that the desire exists, waiting to be known. One thus describes one's uncertainty in terms of one's ignorance of one's inner self, the contents of which are nonetheless presumed to exist.

In short, our culture presents individuals with many choices for which there is no reliable or correct way of choosing. Some people choose one thing and others another, probably often under the influence of immediate circumstances and subtle situational influences. But our culture prefers to see such different choices as reflecting differences among the inner selves of the individuals. Choices that define identity are therefore regarded as expressing hidden somethings from within the inner self or, to use my term, metacriteria.

Our modern concept of the inner self has shaped and biased the way we think of identity and of identity problems. The inner self, according to this modern concept, is stable and continuous across time. It is large, unique, and complex. Because of the alleged difficulty of knowing the contents of the inner self, the modern inner self is believed to have its particular characteristics even if it does not seem that way at a particular moment. We assume that the inner self contains one's true interpersonal style, including personality traits, motives, and intentions. We trust that the inner self contains the ingredients for our fulfillment. We trust that it contains the solutions to the dilemmas of choice and decision by which we define identity. That explains why, when faced with a major choice and no good reason to go either way, or faced with a lack of fulfillment that is sensed as pervasive discontent with one's life and lot, or faced with a basic uncertainty about how to treat other people in one's personal relationships, modern individuals can say "I don't know who I am." And that is also why they think of resolving those dilemmas as acts of finding rather than of creating.

Summary

Two different approaches can be taken to understand identity: from its outer contexts, such as religion and society, or in terms of the inner self.

Religion and morality can be an effective contextual paradigm for identity because they provide firm, presumably trustworthy answers to life's problems and decisions; there is thus no need for personal metacriteria. Identity is clearly defined within the context of religion and morality, so it tends not to be problematic. Identity crises are minimized or avoided. Faced with some difficult decisions, nonreligious persons might have an identity crisis as they seek metacriteria by which to make the decisions. Religious people may typically get the needed metacriteria for making those same decisions from their religion and morality.

Some societies are rather rigid and restrictive. They define identity in a firm and clear-cut fashion, giving individuals little opportunity to choose or change their identities. Other societies are tolerant, loose, and flexible, requiring the individual to carry much of the responsibility for self-definition. In both cases society forms a context for identity, but in the latter case the individual must establish personal metacriteria for making many decisions; this can make identity problematic.

In our culture the individual's relation to society has become problematic. Our society is of the loose and flexible type, requiring that the individuals define themselves. The individual is understood as separate from his or her place in society, and people do not trust society to provide them with fulfillment in exchange for doing their assigned tasks and duties.

Families furnish people with some metacriteria—expectations about who to be and specific images of success or failure. But in many respects the individual's relationship with the family can be problematic, too, because it is possible to define oneself and seek fulfillment apart from the family. The modern individual approaches adulthood with a chaos of options and furnished with remnants of parental influences and expectations as metacriteria.

Society—both the general society at large and the specific family and social world of the individual—thus forms a rather incomplete context for identity today.

The concept of the inner self has expanded over the recent centuries. The inner self is considered large, stable and continuous, unique, vitally important, real, and difficult to know. It is presumed to contain thoughts, feelings, intentions, personality traits, latent capacities, sources of creativity, ingredients of fulfillment, and solutions to the dilemmas of identity. The contents of the inner self thus refer to some real phenomena and some that do not, in any sense, exist.

A final reason for the problematic nature of identity can thus be suggested. Identity is a theory of self associated with an inadequate contextual framework and with a concept that injudiciously blends reality and unreality.

Bibliography

Adorno, T. (1951). *Minima moralia* (tr. E. Jephcott). Frankfurt, West Germany: SuhrKamp.

Altick, R. (1965). *Lives and letters: A history of literary biography in England and America.* New York: Knopf.

Anderson, Q. (1971). *The imperial self.* New York: Knopf.

Arendt, H. (1951). *The origins of totalitarianism.* New York: Harcourt Brace Jovanovich.

Ariès, P. (1962). *Centuries of childhood: A social history of family life* (tr. R. Baldick). New York: Random House.

Ariès, P. (1981). *The hour of our death* (tr. H. Weaver). New York: Knopf.

Asch, S. (1955). Opinions and social pressure. *Scientific American,* Nov. 1955, pp. 31–35.

Auerbach, E. (1946/1974). *Mimesis: The representation of reality in Western literature* (tr. W. Trask). Princeton, NJ: Princeton University Press.

Babbage, C. (1963/1832). *On the economy of machinery and manufactures.* London: C. Knight & Co.

Baumeister, R. F. (1982). A self-presentational view of social phenomena. *Psychological Bulletin, 91,* 3–26.

Baumeister, R. F., & Placidi, K. S. (1983). A social history and analysis of the LSD controversy. *Journal of Humanistic Psychology, 23,* (4), 25–58.

Baumeister, R. F., Shapiro, J., & Tice, D. M. (1985). Two kinds of identity crisis. *Journal of Personality.*

Baumeister, R. F., & Tice, D. M. (1985). How adolescence became the struggle for self: A historical transformation of psychological development. In J. Suls and A. G. Greenwald (eds.), *Psychological perspectives on the self,* vol. 3, Hillsdale, NJ: Erlbaum.

Becker, E. (1973). *The denial of death.* New York: MacMillan.

Beit-Hallahmi, H. S. (1977). Identity integration, self-image crisis and "super-ego victory" in postadolescent university students. *Adolescence, 12,* 57–64.

Bem, D. (1965). An experimental analysis of self-persuasion. *Journal of Experimental Social Psychology, 1,* 199–218.

Bercovitch, S. (1975). *The Puritan origins of the American self.* New Haven, Conn.: Yale University Press.

Bernard, H. S. (1981). Identity formation during late adolescence: A review of some empirical findings. *Adolescence, 16,* 349–357.

Bickford, J. (1971). The search for identity. *School Counselor, 19,* 191–194.

Blofeld, J. (1970). *The Tantric mysticism of Tibet.* New York: Dutton.

Blos, P. (1962). *On adolescence.* New York: Free Press.

Bourne, E. (1978). The state of research on ego identity: A review and appraisal. Part II. *Journal of Youth and Adolescence, 7,* 371–392.

Braverman, H. (1974). *Labor and monopoly capital: The degradation of work in the twentieth century.* New York: Monthly Review Press.

Brim, O. G. (1976). Life-span development of the theory of oneself: Implications for child development. In H. Reese (ed.), *Advances in child development and behavior,* Vol. 2, 241–251. New York: Academic Press.

Brittan, A. (1977). *The private world.* London: Routledge & Kegan Paul.

Broad, C. D. (1925). *The mind and its place in nature.* New York: Harcourt, Brace & Co.

Bronfenbrenner, U. (1963). *Two worlds of childhood: U.S. and U.S.S.R.* New York: Simon & Schuster.

Bronfenbrenner, U. (1974). The origins of alienation. *Scientific American, 231* (2), 53–61.

Broughton, J. (1978). Development of concepts of self, mind, reality, and knowledge. *New Directions for Child Development, 1,* 75–100.

Burgess, E. W., & Locke, H. J. (1945). *The family: From institution to companionship.* New York: American Book Co.

Burke, P. (1978). *Popular culture in early modern Europe.* New York: Harper.

Camus, A. (1954/1942). *The stranger.* New York: Vintage.

Castaneda, C. (1972). *Journey to Ixtlan.* New York: Simon & Schuster.

Cohen, S. (1967). *The beyond within.* New York: Atheneum.

Cox, H. (1977). *Turning East.* New York: Simon & Schuster.

Cross, H., & Allen, J. (1970). Ego identity status adjustment and academic achievement. *Journal of Consulting and Clinical Psychology, 34,* 288.

Damon, W. (1983). *Social and personality development.* New York: Norton.

Damon, W., & Hart, D. (1982). The development of self-understanding from infancy through adolescence. *Child Development, 53,* 841–864.

Deci, E. L. (1971). Effects of externally mediated rewards on intrinsic motivation. *Journal of Personality and Social Psychology, 18,* 105–115.

Dellquest, A. (1938). *These names of ours.* New York: Crowell.

Demos, J., & Demos, V. (1969). Adolescence in historical perspective. *Journal of Marriage and the Family, 31,* 632–638.

de Rougemont, D. (1956). *Love in the Western world* (2nd ed.); (tr. M. Belgion). New York: Pantheon.

DesCartes, R. (1901). *The method, meditations and philosophy of DesCartes.* J. Veitch, editor & translator. New York: Aladdin.

Dilthey, W. (1976). *Selected writings.* H. P. Rickman, editor & translator. Cambridge, England: Cambridge University Press.

Ditzion, S. (1969). *Marriage, morals, and sex in America.* New York: Norton.

Elder, G. H. (1974). *Children of the great depression.* Chicago, IL: University of Chicago Press.

Elkind, D. (1978). Understanding the young adolescent. *Adolescence, 13,* 127–134.

Elkind, D., & Bowen, R. (1979). Imaginary audience behavior in children and adolescents. *Developmental Psychology, 15,* 38–44.

Engle, M. (1960). Shifting levels of communication in the treatment of adolescent character disorders. *Archives of General Psychiatry, 2,* 104–109.

Epstein, S. (1973). The self-concept revisited: Or a theory of a theory. *American Psychologist, 28,* 404–416.

Erikson, E. H. (1950). *Childhood and society.* New York: Norton.

Erikson, E. H. (1956). The problem of ego identity. *Journal of the American Psychoanalytic Association, 4,* 56–121.

Erikson, E. H. (1968). *Identity: Youth and crisis.* New York: Norton.

Fagan, J. F. (1972). Infants' recognition memory to faces. *Journal of Experimental Child Psychology, 14,* 453–476.

Falk, A. (1976). Identity and name changes. *Psychoanalytic Review, 62* 647–657.

Fass, P. (1977). *The damned and the beautiful: American youth in the 1920s.* Oxford: Oxford University Press.

Festinger, L., & Carlsmith, J. M. (1959). Cognitive consequences of forced compliance. *Journal of Abnormal and Social Psychology, 58,* 203–210.

Fiedler, L. A. (1982/1966). *Love and death in the American novel.* New York: Scarborough.

Foucault, M. (1980). *The history of sexuality.* New York: Random House.

Freud, S. (1959/1905). Fragment of an analysis of a case of hysteria. In A. Strachey & J. Strachey (tr.), *Collected papers* (Vol. 3). New York: Basic Books.

Friday, N. (1977). *My mother, my self: The daughter's search for identity.* New York: Dell.

Friedan, B. (1963/1974). *The feminine mystique.* New York: Dell.

Friedenberg, E. Z. (1959). *The vanishing adolescent.* Boston: Beacon Press.

Fromkin, H. (1970). Effects of experimentally aroused feelings of undistinctiveness upon valuation of scarce and novel experiences. *Journal of Personality and Social Psychology, 16,* 521–529.

Fromm, E. (1969/1941). *Escape from freedom.* New York: Holt, Rinehart and Winston.

Garvey, C. (1977). *Play.* Cambridge, MA: Harvard University Press.

Gillis, J. R. (1974). Youth and history: Tradition and change in European age relations, 1770–present. New York: Academic Press.

Ginsburg, S. D., & Orlofsky, J. L. (1981). Ego identity status, ego development and locus of control in college women. *Journal of Youth and Adolescence, 10,* 297–307.

Glass, D., Singer, J., & Friedman, L. (1969). Psychic cost of adaptation to an environmental stressor. *Journal of Personality and Social Psychology, 12,* 200–210.

Goffman, E. (1959). *The presentation of self in everyday life.* Garden City, NY: Doubleday.

Goldstein, E. (1979). Psychological adaptations of Soviet immigrants. *American Journal of Psychoanalysis, 39,* 257–263.

Gordon, C. (1968). Self-conceptions: Configurations of content. In C. Gordon & K. J. Gergen (eds.), *The self in social interactions,* 115–136. New York: Wiley.

Greenspan, S. I. (1972). Leaving the kibbutz: An identity crisis. *Psychiatry, 35,* 291–303.

Greven, P. (1977). *The Protestant temperament.* New York: Knopf.

Grinspoon, P., & Bakalar, J. (1979). *Psychedelic drugs reconsidered.* New York: Basic Books.

Grof, S. (1975). *Realms of the human unconscious: Observations from LSD research.* New York: Viking.

Group for the Advancement of Psychiatry. (1957). *Methods of forceful indoctrination: Observations and interviews.* New York.

Habermas, J. (1973). *Legitimation crisis.* Boston, MA: Beacon Press.

Hanning, R. W. (1977). *The individual in twelfth-century romance.* New Haven, CT: Yale University Press.

Harris, M. (1981). *America now: The anthropology of a changing culture.* New York: Simon & Schuster.

Heidegger, M. (1927). *Sein und Zeit.* Tuebingen, West Germany: Niemeyer.

Heilbroner, R. L. (1980). *An inquiry into the human prospect.* New York: Norton.

Henry, J. (1963). *Culture against man.* New York: Random House.

Hinkle, L. (1957). See Group for the Advancement of Psychiatry.

Hofmann, A. (1983). *LSD: My problem child.* Los Angeles, CA: Tarcher.

Hogan, R. (1982). A socioanalytic theory of personality. In M. Page (ed.), *Nebraska Symposium on Motivation,* 55–89. Lincoln, NE: University of Nebraska Press.

Houghton, W. E. (1957). *The Victorian frame of mind: 1830–1870.* New Haven, Conn.: Yale University Press.

Howe, D. W. (1976). Victorian culture in America. In D. Howe (ed.), *Victorian America*. Philadelphia, PA: University of Pennsylvania Press.

Howe, I. (1969/1959). Mass society and post-modern fiction. Reprinted in M. Klein (ed.), *The American novel since World War II*. New York: Fawcett.

Huizinga, J. (1954/1924). *The waning of the Middle Ages*. Garden City, New York: Doubleday.

Hull, J. G. (1981). A self-awareness model of the causes and effects of alcohol consumption. *Journal of Abnormal Psychology, 90*, 586–600.

Hull, J. G., Levenson, R. W., Young, R. D., & Sher, K. J. (1983). Self-awareness-reducing effects of alcohol consumption. *Journal of Personality and Social Psychology, 44*, 461–473.

Hume, D. *A treatise of human nature*. Originally published in 1738.

Hunt, D. (1970). *Parents and children in history*. New York: Harper.

Jones, E. E., & Berglas, S. C. (1978). Control of attributions about the self through self-handicapping strategies: The appeal of alcohol and the role of underachievement. *Personality and Social Psychology Bulletin, 4*, 200–206.

Jones, E. E., & Nisbett, $. (1971). The actor and the observer: Divergent perceptions of the causes of behavior. Morristown, NJ: General Learning Press.

Jordan, D. (1971). Parental antecedents and personality characteristics of ego identity statuses. Unpublished doctoral dissertation, State University of New York at Buffalo.

Jung, C. G. (1971/1928). The spiritual problem of modern man. Reprinted in J. Campbell (ed.), *The portable Jung*. New York: Viking.

Kagan, J. (1981). *The second year: The emergence of self-awareness*. Cambridge, MA: Harvard University Press.

Kahn, M. P. (1969). The adolescent struggle with identity as a force in psychotherapy. *Adolescence, 3*, 395–424.

Kant, I. (1956/1787). *Kritik der reinen Vernunft (Critique of pure reason)*. Frankfurt, West Germany: Felix Meiner Verlag.

Kant, I. (1956/1793). *Die Religion innerhalb der Grenzen der blossen Vernunft (Religion within the boundaries of pure reason)*. Hamburg, West Germany: Felix Meiner Verlag.

Katz, M.B., & Davey, I. E. (1978). Youth and early industrialization in a Canadian city. In J. Demos & S. S. Boocock (eds.), *Turning points: Historical and sociological essays on the family*. Chicago: University of Chicago Press.

Keller, A., Ford, L.H., & Meacham, J. A. (1978). Dimensions of self-concept in preschool children. *Developmental Psychology, 14*, 483–489.

Keniston, K. (1965). *The uncommitted: Alienated youth in American society*. New York: Harcourt, Brace & World.

Keniston, K. (1968). *Young radicals*. New York: Harcourt, Brace & World.

Kennedy, K., & Kennedy, T. (1982). The devil's work. *Penthouse, 13* (7), 52–61, 192–198.

Kett, J. F. (1977). *Rites of passage: Adolescence in America 1790 to the present.* New York: Basic Books.

Kiell, N. (1959). *The adolescent through fiction: A psychological approach.* New York: International Universities Press.

Klavetter, R., & Mogar, R. (1967). Peak experiences: Investigation of their relationship to psychedelic therapy. *Journal of Humanistic Psychology, 7,* 171–177.

Klein, M. (1964). *After alienation: American novels in mid-century.* Freeport, NY: Books for Libraries Press.

Landmann, M. (1971). *Das Ende des Individuaums.* Stuttgart, West Germany: Klett.

Langbaum, R. (1979). *The mysteries of identity: A theme in modern literature.* New York: Oxford University Press.

Lange, K. (1960). Illusion in play and art. In M. Rader (ed.), *A modern book of esthetics,* 5–15. New York: Holt, Rinehart and Winston.

Larkin, R. W. (1979). *Suburban youth in cultural crisis.* New York: Oxford University Press.

Lasch, C. (1978). *The culture of narcissism.* New York: Norton.

Leadbeater, B. J., & Dionne, J. P. (1981). The adolescent's use of formal operational thinking in solving problems related to identity resolution. *Adolescence, 16,* 111–121.

Lepper, M. R., Greene, D., & Nisbett, R. E. (1973). Undermining children's intrinsic interest with extrinsic rewards: A test of the overjustification hypothesis. *Journal of Personality and Social Psychology, 28,* 129–137.

Levi, D. L., Stierlin, H., & Savard, R. J. (1972). Fathers and sons: The interlocking crises of integrity and identity. *Psychiatry, 35,* 48–56.

Levine, L. E. (1983). Mine: Self-definition in 2-year-old boys. *Developmental Psychology, 19,* 544–549.

Levinson, D. J., Darrow, C. N., Klein, E. B., Levinson, M. H., & McKee, B. (1978). *The seasons of a man's life.* New York: Ballantine.

Lewis, M., & Brooks-Gunn, J. (1979). *Social cognition and the acquisition of self.* New York: Plenum.

Lifton, R. J. (1957). See Group for the Advancement of Psychiatry.

Livesly, W. J., & Bromley, D. B. (1973). *Person perception in childhood and adolescence.* New York: Wiley.

MacIntrye, A. (1981). *After virtue.* Notre Dame, IN: University of Notre Dame Press.

Mahler, M. S., Pine, F., & Bergman, A. (1975). *The psychological birth of the human infant: Symbiosis and individuation.* New York: Basic Books.

Mann, J., Berkowitz, L., Sidman, J., Starr, S., & West, S. (1974). Satiation of the transient stimulating effect of erotic films. *Journal of Personality and Social Psychology, 30,* 729–735.

Marcia, J. E. (1966). Development and validation of ego-identity status. *Journal of Personality and Social Psychology, 3,* 551–558.

Marcia, J. E. (1967). Ego identity status: Relationship to change in self-esteem "general maladjustment" and authoritarianism. *Journal of Personality, 35,* 118–133.

Marcia, J. E. (1976). Studies in ego identity. Unpublished manuscript. Simon Fraser University.

Marcia, J. E., & Friedman, M. L. (1970). Ego identity status in college women. *Journal of Personality, 38,* 249–263.

Marcia, J. E., & Scheidel, D. G. (1983). Ego identity, intimacy, sex role orientation, and gender. Presented at the annual meeting of the Eastern Psychological Association, Philadelphia, PA.

Margolis, M. L. (1984). *Mothers and such.* Berkeley, CA: University of California Press.

Maslow, A. H. (1968). *Toward a psychology of being.* New York: Van Nostrand.

May, R. (1953). *Man's search for himself.* New York: Dell.

Meehl, P. (1956). Wanted—a good cookbook. *American Psychologist, 11,* 263–272.

Meyer, D. H. (1976). American intellectuals and the Victorian crisis of faith. In D. Howe (ed.), *Victorian America,* 59–80. Philadelphia, PA: University of Pennsylvania Press.

Mitford, J. (1978). *The American way of death.* New York: Simon & Schuster.

Modell, J. Furstenberg, F., & Strong, D. (1978). The timing of marriage in the transition to adulthood: Continuity and change, 1860–1975. In J. Demos & S. S. Boocock (eds.), *Turning points: Historical and sociological essays on the family.* Chicago, IL: University of Chicago Press.

Mogar, R. (1965). Current status and future trends in psychedelic (LSD) research. *Journal of Humanistic Psychology, 5,* 147–166.

Mohr, D. M. (1978). Development of attributes of personal identity. *Developmental Psychology, 14,* 427–428.

Montemayor, R., & Eisen, M. (1977). The development of self-conceptions from childhood to adolescence. *Developmental Psychology, 13,* 314–319.

Morash, M. A. (1980). Working class membership and the adolescent identity crisis. *Adolescence, 15,* 313–320.

Morris, C. (1972). *The discovery of the individual: 1050–1200.* New York: Harper & Row.

Mostwin, D. (1976). Uprootment and anxiety. *International Journal of Mental Health, 5,* 103–116.

Newman, B. M., & Newman, P. R. (1973). The concept of identity: Research and theory. *Adolescence, 13,* 157–166.

Nietzsche, F. (1964/1887). *Zur Genealogie der Moral (Toward a Geneology of Morals).* Stuttgart, West Germany: Alfred Kroener Verlag.

Nisbet, R. (1973). *The social philosophers: Community and conflict in Western thought.* New York: Crowell.

Nisbett, R. E., & Wilson, T. D. (1977). Telling more than we can know: Verbal reports on mental processes. *Psychological Review, 84,* 231–259.

O'Neill, W. L. (1971). *Coming apart: An informal history of America in the 1960s.* New York: Quadrangle Books.

Orlofsky, J. L. (1977). Identity formation, *n* achievement and fear of success in college men and women. *Journal of Youth and Adolescence, 7,* 49–62.

Orlofsky, J. L., Marcia, J. E., & Lesser, I. M. (1973). Ego identity status and the intimacy versus isolation crisis of young adulthood. *Journal of Personality and Social Psychology, 27,* 211–219.

Orwell, G. (1949). *Nineteen eighty-four, a novel.* New York: Harcourt, Brace.

Peres & Yuval-Davis. (1969). Some observations on the national identity of the Israeli Arab. *Human Relations, 22,* 219–233.

Podd, M. H., Marcia, J. E., & Rubin, B. M. (1970). The effects of ego identity and partner perception on a prisoner's dilemma game. *Journal of Social Psychology, 82,* 117–126.

Potter, D. M. (1954). *People of plenty.* Chicago: University of Chicago Press.

Pütz, M. (1979). *The story of identity: American fiction of the sixties.* Stuttgart, West Germany: Metzler.

Riesman, D. (1950). *The lonely crowd.* New Haven, CT: Yale University Press.

Roeske, N. A., & Lake, K. (1977). Role models for women medical students. *Journal of Medical Education, 52,* 459–466.

Rogers, C. (1961). *On becoming a person.* Boston, MA: Houghton Mifflin.

Rosenberg, M. (1979). *Conceiving the self.* New York: Basic Books.

Rosenthal, P. (1984). *Words and values.* New York: Oxford University Press.

Ross, L. (1977). The intuitive psychologist and his shortcomings: Distortions in the attribution process. In L. Berkowitz (ed.), *Advances in experimental social psychology,* vol. 10. New York: Academic Press.

Roth, P. (1969/1961). Writing American fiction. Reprinted in M. Klein (ed.), *The American novel since World War II.* New York: Fawcett.

Rubins, J. L. (1968). The problem of the acute identity crisis in adolescence. *American Journal of Psychoanalysis, 28,* 37–44.

Ruble, D. (1983). The development of social comparison processes and their role in achievement-related self-socialization. In E. T. Higgins, D. Ruble, & W. Hartup, (eds.), *Social cognition and social behavior: Developmental perspectives.* New York: Cambridge University Press.

Schafer, R. (1973). Concepts of self and identity and the experience of separation-individuation in adolescence. *Psychoanalytic Quarterly, 42,* 42–59.

Schein, E. H. (1957). See Group for the Advancement of Psychiatry.

Schenkel, S., & Marcia, J. E. (1972). Attitudes toward premartial intercourse in determining ego identity status in college women. *Journal of Personality, 40,* 472–482.

Schlenker, B. (1980). *Impression management: The self-concept, social identity, and interpersonal relations.* Monterey, CA: Brooks/Cole.

Schlenker, B. R., & Leary, M. R. (1982). Social anxiety and self-presentation: A conceptualization and model. *Psychological Bulletin, 92,* 641–669.

Secord, P. F., & Peevers, B. (1974). The development and attribution of person concepts. In T. Mischel (eds.), *Understanding other persons.* Oxford, England: Blackwell.

Seeman, M. (1959). On the meaning of alienation. *American Sociological Review, 24,* 782–791.

Sennett, R. (1974). *The fall of public man.* New York: Random House.

Shoemaker, S. (1963). *Self-knowledge and self-identity.* Ithaca, NY: Cornell University Press.

Simmel, G. (1950). *The sociology of Georg Simmel* (K. Wulff, tr. & ed.). Glencoe, IL: Free Press.

Simmons, R., Rosenberg, F., & Rosenberg, M. (1973). Disturbances in the self-image at adolescence. *American Sociological Review, 38,* 553–568.

Slugowski, B. R., Marcia, J. E., & Koopman, R. F. (in press). Cognitive and social interactional characteristics of ego identity statuses in college males. *Journal of Personality and Social Psychology.*

Smith-Rosenberg, L. (1978). Sex as symbols in Victorian purity: An ethnohistorical analysis of Jacksonian America. In J. Demos & S. S. Boocock (eds.), *Turning points.* Chicago, IL: University of Chicago Press.

Sommers, V. S. (1969). Resolution of an identity conflict in a Japanese-American patient. *American Journal of Psychotherapy, 23,* 119–134.

Spinoza, B. (1955/1670). *Theologich—politischer traktat (Theological—political tractatus).* Hamburg, West Germany: Felix Meiner Verlag.

Stone, L. (1977). *The family, sex and marriage in England 1500–1800.* New York: Harper & Row.

Sullivan, H. S. (1953). *The interpersonal theory of psychiatry.* New York: Norton.

Sypher, W. (1962). *Loss of self in modern literature and art.* New York: Random House.

Thernstrom, S. (1973). *The other Bostonians.* Cambridge, MA: Harvard University Press.

Thompson, T. (1979). *The '60s report.* New York: Rawson, Wade.

Tice, D. M., Buder, J., & Baumeister, R. F. (1983). Development of self-consciousness: At what age does audience pressure harm performance? Unpublished manuscript, Case Western Reserve University, Cleveland, OH.

Timerman, J. (1981). *Prisoner without a name, cell without a number.* New York: Random House.

Toder, N. L., & Marcia, J. E. (1973). Ego identity status and response to conformity pressure in college women. *Journal of Personality and Social Psychology, 26,* 287–294.

Toffler, A. (1970). *Future shock.* New York: Random House.

Trilling, L. (1950). *The opposing self.* New York: Viking.

Trilling, L. (1955). *Freud and the crisis of our culture.* Boston: Beacon Press.

Trilling, L. (1971). *Sincerity and authenticity.* Cambridge, MA: Harvard University Press.

Tuchman, B. W. (1967). *The proud tower.* New York: Bantam.

Tuchman, B. W. (1978). *A distant mirror.* New York: Ballantine.

Turner, R. H. (1976). The real self: From institution to impulse. *American Journal of Sociology, 81,* 989–1016.

Veblen, T. (1953/1899). *The theory of the leisure class.* New York: Mentor.

Veroff, J., Douvan, E., & Kulka, R. (1981). *The inner American: A self-portrait from 1957 to 1976.* New York: Basic Books.

Waterman, A. S. (1982). Identity development from adolescence to adulthood: An extension of theory and a review of research. *Developmental Psychology, 18,* 341–358.

Weaklund, J. (1969). Hippies: What the scene means. In R. H. Blum & Associates. *Society and drugs,* 342–372. San Francisco, CA: Jossey-Bass.

Wedge, B. (1957). See Group for the Advancement of Psychiatry.

Weintraub, K. J. (1978). *The value of the individual: Self and circumstance in autobiography.* Chicago: University of Chicago Press.

West, L. J. (1957). See Group for the Advancement of Psychiatry.

Wheelis, A. (1958). *The quest of identity.* New York: Norton.

Whyte, L. L. (1960). *The unconscious before Freud.* New York: Basic Books.

Withycombe, E. G. (1947). *Oxford dictionary of English Christian names.* New York: Oxford University Press.

Index

155.2   Baumeister, Roy   3822
Bau   Identity
                               19.95

	DATE DUE		
	JUN 27 2003		
	DEC 09 2003		

LIBRARY
MONROE BUSINESS INSTITUTE

434 MAIN STREET
NEW ROCHELLE, NY 10801